FOUR FEET UNDER

Tamsen Courtenay

Unbound

This edition first published in 2018

Unbound

6th Floor Mutual House, 70 Conduit Street, London W1S 2GF

www.unbound.com

Text design by Patty Rennie

A CIP record for this book is available from the British Library

ISBN 978-1-78352-572-0 (trade hbk)
ISBN 978-1-78352-570-6 (ebook)
ISBN 978-1-78352-571-3 (limited edition)

Printed and bound in Great Britain by Clays Ltd, Elcograf S.p.A.

3 5 7 9 8 6 4 2

A Note on the Author

TAMSEN COURTENAY worked as an investigative journalist for the BBC's *Panorama* and Channel 4's *Dispatches*. She lives in central Italy, and wrote a blog called *Land of the Forgotten Earthquakes* about the seismic destruction of the region.

For my mum, Gill 'Dill' Courtenay

Dear Reader,

The book you are holding came about in a rather different way to most others. It was funded directly by readers through a new website: Unbound. Unbound is the creation of three writers. We started the company because we believed there had to be a better deal for both writers and readers. On the Unbound website, authors share the ideas for the books they want to write directly with readers. If enough of you support the book by pledging for it in advance, we produce a beautifully bound special subscribers' edition and distribute a regular edition and ebook wherever books are sold, in shops and online.

This new way of publishing is actually a very old idea (Samuel Johnson funded his dictionary this way). We're just using the internet to build each writer a network of patrons. At the back of this book, you'll find the names of all the people who made it happen.

Publishing in this way means readers are no longer just passive consumers of the books they buy, and authors are free to write the books they really want. They get a much fairer return too – half the profits their books generate, rather than a tiny percentage of the cover price.

If you're not yet a subscriber, we hope that you'll want to join our publishing revolution and have your name listed in one of our books in the future. To get you started, here is a £5 discount on your first pledge. Just visit unbound.com, make your pledge and type UNDER5 in the promo code box when you check out.

Thank you for your support,

Dan, Justin and John
Founders, Unbound

Contents

Where there is ruin, there is hope for treasure

RUMI

A Note on Style
and a Word of Warning

I decided to use three different ways to reproduce the conversations that I recorded out on the street.

Sometimes I have simply typed up the words that were spoken in response to my questions or comments and haven't included my words or contributions. I used this method where people were particularly chatty or they told their stories in a way that needed less in the way of questions and comments from me.

Other conversations are more conventionally reproduced as questions and answers. I did this when there was more banter between the two of us or when people responded more readily to questions.

There are also eight much briefer accounts of encounters with some people. I felt that each of these people contributed something interesting to an understanding of homelessness, although they may have actually said very little indeed. In these cases I found it simpler to use a mix of their words and my observations. The ellipses reflect pauses as a person speaks.

And that word of warning?

These stories and interviews are transcribed verbatim, so there are masses of spicy expletives. Quite a few are mine, I have to confess – swearing is my default setting when I'm shocked, amused or angry. So, you might want to keep teeny little hands away from these pages. Some of the stories are about prostitution, underage sex, drug use and other complex issues that kids might not be ready for.

Snakes and Ladders

One grim autumn I spent many weeks watching a strange game of Snakes and Ladders being acted out on the streets of one of Europe's great capital cities. For the players, it was often a discouraging game and it was very difficult to get ahead – and when they did, it was just a matter of luck. A throw of the dice, really.

Under glitzy lights, in smart shop doorways, urine-stained tunnels and dirty alleyways, I met the people who just kept landing on the 'go back three spaces' square and then slipping down the snake. Again.

Even with a lot of mental agility it's almost impossible to imagine how people who are homeless actually manage to live their lives and get through each long day.

Like me, you probably have an address. Electricity bills, birthday presents, and friends arrive at that address. You can tell a cab driver exactly where you live and he'll take you there. An address means you belong. Not having one creates a whole world of pain and sorrow – a world that I was about to enter and explore.

Try closing your eyes for a moment and picture yourself with flu and no one there holding your hand or with food poisoning, needing to be very close to a loo. Now imagine these things again, but this time you've got no roof over your head, no walls and no privacy. You're out there in the open. You've lost your kettle, every stick of furniture, and just about everything you ever cared about.

Now it's just you and the rubble of your life. The entire neighbourhood walks past you every day. You, on the absolute worst day of your life. And so it goes on, day in and day out.

Between us, the homeless and I tried to make sense of their lives – lives lived four feet below the rest of us, on the pavement – where they laugh, think, worry and sometimes die, and keep only what they can carry. Living alone, they're always on the move, rootless – and wherever they are, they're rarely welcome. Through tragedy, misfortune and occasionally bad decisions, they've ended up with no home to call their own.

This book turned out to be both a celebration *and* a lamentation – for all those who do not have an address, who are hidden in plain sight on the streets of London.

Accidental Heroes

In my previous job as an investigative journalist I often dealt with those whose life experiences were far removed from most people's. These lives were generally secret or hidden away from the rest of us, involving things like domestic violence, miscarriages of justice, deaths in prison and so on.

What particularly struck me about the homeless was that their lives are indeed secret but they are *not* hidden: quite the reverse – they are there, in ever-growing numbers, for everyone to see. They are in every city in every country.

I started out with just one assumption – that virtually no one would actively choose to be displaced, dispossessed and destitute. But if they *hadn't* chosen it, how did they end up living in a shop doorway at the bottom of my road? And if they *had* chosen it, what was so horrific about their life before, that it made this the better option?

I wanted to know what happens to the minds and bodies of those who are reviled, rejected and have absolutely nowhere left to hide.

I asked countless questions of London's homeless which they answered with candour and grace. What was their childhood like? How do they manage to stay alive? What do they think about when they fall asleep at night? (In fact, I learned that many of them *don't* fall asleep at night – they're too scared.) Where are their families? Where are they when I can't see them? What do they *do* all day?

Along the way I amassed all kinds of new insights, revised my entire understanding of cardboard, got battered by a drunk wielding a chunk of wood, and laughed like a drain. This mini-odyssey was spent mostly on damp pavements, with chewing gum stuck to my frozen backside, aching joints, a permanent cold (later to become bronchitis), blistered feet and coffee stains down my front where passers-by had knocked into me as I sat. I loved every minute of it.

It's a weird dynamic when you know absolutely nothing about a person and yet within two hours they've told you that they've been raped, that they're scared of spiders and they miss their mum. To hear their terrible jokes and to feel the hurt and anger in their voices as they talk about their dreams and dreads is deeply intimate. The people in this book entrusted me with a great deal and I gave them little in return. They earned my respect, admiration and, sometimes, affection. With scant reason to, they welcomed me into their lives.

And so it was that over time they became my heroes. Accidental heroes, but heroes all the same. Not because they are homeless but because they are brave. Bravery isn't doing something that *doesn't* frighten you – it is doing something even though it *does*. There is no courage without fear, and the people I met had both.

Thirty people talked very openly and straightforwardly for this collection of stories. People like Benji (a chef-cum-builder), Edward (a marine biologist), Jade (a child prostitute), Kenny and Jane (an elderly couple), Brad and Patrick (businessmen), Jasmine (a transexual) and Scott (a coach driver). There are also soldiers, young adults (who've never had the chance to become anything at all) and many others. Aside from Brad, Patrick and Jasmine, everyone gave me their real names, let me photograph their magnificent faces and capture sometimes shocking and intimate images connected with their lives – images of their drugs, injuries, artwork, possessions and pets.

As a group, 'the homeless' turned out to be no more (or less) homogeneous than the people who live on your street or work in your office. Some are witty and some aren't. Some are generous and some are downright stingy. Some are very bright, and some less so. But the one thing that binds them together, to the exclusion of all the rest of us, is that not one of them has a home.

I'm not an expert on homelessness – or anything else much, for that matter. This is not a piece of research; it's a storybook. I just wanted to find out, by asking the people who know, how it feels to be homeless.

Like a child listening to fairy tales, I sat for hours on cold, wet pavements or in dingy cafes, enthralled by life stories that opened up other worlds to me. Eventually, I came to believe that we've been peddled an ugly and dishonest version of the homeless, as latter-day goblins whose plight is their fault, their choice.

In these pages my heroes are stripped bare, pared down to the bone, all vestiges of pretension gone. Sharing their company was entertaining, harrowing and everything in between. Even when they'd had a miserable start in life or unforeseen disasters had befallen them later, they remained self-deprecating and breathtakingly non-judgemental of others.

I didn't have to go very far to find these home-grown exiles. I didn't need foreign currency, a phrase book (although there were times when one might have been handy) or a passport. My travelcard was enough. They aren't on distant shores, they're at the bottom of my road in central London.

The Birth of the Book

Sometimes my job in television just wore me down, depressed me even. So one day I skived off work and went shopping in Covent Garden to cheer myself up. By the end of an afternoon's shopping I felt guilty about quite how many times I'd whipped out my credit card, so I found an outdoor cafe, ordered a coffee and began rationalising my spending spree. A man came over and hovered at my table. He looked like a pile of dirty tea-towels balanced on two toothpicks. I felt pity for him and offered him a cigarette, a coffee and a sit-down. He accepted, but only on the condition that he perform a magic trick – his way of thanking me. With half a pack of filthy playing cards he executed a totally useless 'illusion', making us both laugh at his ineptitude. He coughed almost continuously, the sound like a series of explosions in a mine-shaft, and I really thought he should go to hospital. St Thomas' was just across the river, and I offered to pay for a taxi. He told me buses and taxis wouldn't let him on or in, so I suggested walking there together.

And this, I suppose, is where the seed for the book was sown. Pulling off one of his oversized shoes and peeling down a stained sock, he showed me his foot. It was rotten – just a mass of weeping, stinking infection, crusted with blood and pus. Every step that man took must have been an agony. I can't remember his face or his name but I will never forget his foot. I wondered how he had come to this sorry pass. And then I went home with my new clothes.

Then, shortly before Christmas, my mum died, in appalling circumstances. I couldn't face the seasonal excesses so decided to escape by working the night shift at a shelter for homeless men, covering the festive fortnight. It turned out to be not only a great salve for my grief, this pageant of merriment and sorrow, but it also left me with sense of affection for the downtrodden.

There I met Mark, a lorry driver who'd suffered a head injury in a driving accident, developed epilepsy, lost his wife and job and now lived in a car park. His violent fits often dislocated his shoulder so I'd have to call the paramedics who'd come out and put it back where it belonged. Afterwards, exhausted, he'd lay with his head in my lap making witty but scandalous suggestions about things we might do in the utility room. One night I was on toilet-duty, having a crafty fag just outside the urinals when a young lad came racing towards me, doing up his flies and excitedly telling me he was *sure* the old man having a pee next to him had been his trial barrister in court a couple of years earlier. He couldn't believe it. Then there was computer-room duty. The managers of the shelter had drummed it into me that no one, absolutely no one, was to look at porn sites. Which were, of course, the *only* sites people did want to look at. These guys probably couldn't remember the last time they'd had sex, and I didn't want to be mean and censorious, so we came to an agreement. I had two rules. Rule One was that any living thing on the site had to have no more than two legs and be legally able to vote. Rule Two was that *both* of the men's hands had to be on the desk, where I could see them, at *all* times.

And there were sorrowful moments, too. Dormitory duty meant spending the night in a room with thirty camp beds, lit only by soft lava lamps (many homeless seem to be afraid of the dark), listening to the sounds of snoring and the muffled sobs of grown men crying. I began to wonder what stories, dreams or horrors had propelled these people to this desperate point.

One year later I moved to Italy. Other things consumed me – work, family, setting up a home in a new place – and while I sometimes thought about the people I'd met that Christmas, my life was elsewhere now. And then something happened that prompted me to buy a ticket, pack my camera and get on a plane back to London five years after working in the shelter.

My stepfather, Tony – a cruel, tyrannical man that none of my mum's family would miss – died. We'd never understood why my mum had stayed with him until we read her diaries, months after her death. We discovered a secret world of emotional blackmail and abuse. But they had been together for thirty-odd years, so we reluctantly decided to go to his funeral. I urgently needed to renew my passport, so I made two frantic trips to the embassy in Rome. On the second trip I had a couple of hours to kill and decided to wander around the city centre. I was turning into possibly the most uber-chic street in Rome – Via Condotti, near the Spanish Steps – when I virtually tripped over a teeny, ancient-looking woman called Maria.

She was homeless, crumpled up on the pavement beneath the heaving mass of the larvae-like rich, in this pedestrianised area full of shops like Prada, Ferragamo and Jimmy Choo. Shops that never have price tags and are staffed by terrifying harpies who, on the rare occasions I've ever gone in, manage to make me feel like the janitor turning up late for work. I no more belonged in Via Condotti than Maria did, so I sat with her for about twenty minutes, talking. She had lost her home and her husband in a fire.

Maria would become a symbol of what was about to happen to my brother, Brooke, and me as well as the catalyst for this book being written.

Maria in Rome

The very day we arrived in England for Tony's funeral, we learned that he had betrayed our mum by changing his will – while she lay dying at home – to favour his two children, Sam and Chasca, from a previous marriage. And so, with a stroke of his pen, Tony had split my family apart, and we would never see our family home again. We felt utterly betrayed by our step-siblings. In the end, none of our mum's family went to the funeral. The day we discovered Tony's treachery, we had been at the family home and I had taken some photographs of it, as mementos, it turned out. That same evening, back in our hotel, crying as I scrolled through the images on my camera, I saw the photograph I had taken of Maria, just days before. Losing my *sense* of home and family was incredibly distressing, so what must it be like to have lost the real thing?

I returned to Italy with my husband. I had retrained as an English teacher and buried myself in my work.

One night months later, I lay in bed thinking about mum, my head a jumble of all these things that had happened. Suddenly, everything seemed clear. I resolved to go to England and make a book about homeless people. The next morning I got up early and booked the flight for two days' time. At breakfast, I sat my husband down and told him my plan. I was expecting him – with some justification – to say, 'What? Are you mad? You can't just clear off. What about your job, your income? What about *me*?' Instead he just said, 'Yes, you need to do this.' So I did.

I phoned my stepdaughter, Alice, and alerted her to my plan or 'harebrained scheme', as she called it and my imminent arrival at Stansted. She was, typically, totally unfazed and said she'd get the spare room ready. I ordered a cheap little digital recorder online from Argos to be delivered to London and started packing. I phoned all my students to explain I wouldn't be teaching them, all the time thinking, *what on earth have I just done?*

Turns out it was one of the best decisions I ever made.

Day One and No Proper Plan

The truth is I never had a proper plan.

What I did have was a tote bag with my posh Nikon camera and my not-so-posh Argos digital voice recorder, along with wet wipes, loads of fags and my notebook and pen. And chewing gum. I didn't want to breathe faggy breath on people who already had enough problems.

I had promised myself I would never look at a homeless person and think, 'Oh, you look a bit scary/dodgy/dangerous, I think I'll just skip you.' I'd talk to anyone who'd talk to me. But first I wanted to get the lie of the land at dawn, when most homeless people's day begins.

I set off from Highbury at about 3:30 a.m. and started walking towards the West End. I was excited, walking through familiar streets that now, in the darkness and near silence, felt alien – bereft of movement and life. I walked through Islington, King's Cross and Euston, then turned towards Soho, Covent Garden and the Strand.

In the coming weeks I rarely deviated from this route, this territory, although sometimes when I felt too exhausted to walk to the West End I went instead to Camden, which was closer to home. I looked at a map of London the other day and saw that the little areas that became my stomping ground all fitted into a space smaller than Hyde Park. I found that depressing. I stopped counting the sleeping homeless, that first morning, when I reached about 150. There were more than twenty people sleeping in Charing Cross tube station alone when I got there at about 5:30 a.m. What I was seeing didn't quite seem to tally with what the official figures I had read seemed to be suggesting. Virtually every doorway had at least one body in it, people asleep, bathed in melancholy drizzle, looking like corpses wrapped in shrouds. The scene was spectral.

On the Strand, a little later, I saw the first stirrings of the people I'd come all this way to meet. I could hear the sounds of nylon sleeping bags rustling and their inhabitants muttering amiably to one another as befuddled people of all ages crawled out of them and from under musty blankets. They had made it through another night.

It was a dispiriting sight, these worn-out people hastily cramming everything they owned back into plastic bags and then trying to stand on aching, cramped legs before disappearing off-stage. I would see this change of set so many times – the new scene would soon be full of different people with important things to do, interesting places to go, and little idea of who had lain at their feet just hours before. The elegant Strand would look very different in a few short hours as busy working folk and excited tourists reclaimed this famous London street.

I went into the twenty-four-hour McDonald's and bought four coffees: one for me – I was desperate for a hot drink by this time – and three for some bleary-eyed lads who were waking up just outside. As I handed them the drinks, one of the cups fell to the ground. I turned to go back into Mackie's (as it seems to be known to many of London's homeless) to get a replacement, but two security guards barred my way. A fast food joint with security on the door? At *dawn*? They said I couldn't buy coffees to give to the homeless as it 'only encourages them'. It was my first experience of the prejudice the homeless endure from the moment they open their eyes. My manners and temper deserted me and a huge slanging match ensued as I hurled (eloquent) abuse at the men with earpieces. By 6:30 a.m. I was officially banned from the premises. Annoying, as I would have liked to use their loo, but it did earn me brownie points with the homeless outside, who'd been watching the show. 'Go at it, girl.'

The dawn chorus was not birdsong. Delivery lorries were starting to unload: van doors slamming, those big metal delivery trolleys clattering up and down the pavement just inches from people's sleeping faces and screeching brakes as yet more vehicles turned up. Drivers and workers were shouting at each other, oblivious to the homeless at their feet. So many frail little bodies sitting up, bewildered by all the noise and activity. It was their alarm call. Their warning to move on. Their time was up.

14

I ambled about for the next hour or so, shocked at how many elderly people I saw, and I chatted here and there with folk as they folded up their blankets and put away their sleeping bags, newspaper and cardboard.

Somewhere along the way I'd lost my lighter. I saw a figure sitting smoking in the doorway of a bank and went over to cadge a light. His name was Alan and he was waiting – as were most of the others up and down the Strand – for the charity food run to appear at 7:30 so they could get a cup of tea and a sandwich. He suggested we move next door and sit outside Ryman – who leave their shop lights on overnight – so we could feel a little of the fluorescent cheer spilling out onto the pavement. As Alan loomed up out of his darkened doorway, I realised he was holding a bottle of wine and was, in fact, totally pissed. He staggered around and made sterling, but ultimately futile, efforts to grab my arse.

I politely laughed it off and we made it to Ryman, where I sat down, the better to see the food van when it arrived. Alan was weaving around on unsteady legs trying to focus his watery eyes on the spot where he wanted to sit, but he couldn't judge the distance correctly and just carried on weaving. It was like watching a grown man walk on a bouncy castle. I didn't look my best after very little sleep and was backlit by unflattering shop lights, but was nevertheless shocked when Alan craned his neck, looked at me and said, 'Ah! For fuck's sake! I thought you was *young*!' Drunk and enraged at my deception, he lunged towards me. Being sober, I eluded him, shot this picture and beat a hasty retreat, thinking – uncharitably – 'You are SO not going to be in my book, you rude git.'

Alan

By mid-morning my failure to plan was becoming painfully evident, on two fronts.

Firstly, my jeans were soaked through on the bum, from sitting on wet pavements (and that was *with* cardboard underneath) and my circulation had stopped circulating somewhere around my knees after sitting cross-legged in jeans that were too tight for the job at hand. The tote bag was hopeless. Every time I stood up, it swung forward off my shoulder and everything fell out. It was embarrassing and I looked chaotic. My feet were blistered and bleeding so I was hobbling. I felt like I'd circumnavigated the globe in a pair of stilettos.

So, feeling chilled, damp and inadequate, I made an unscheduled emergency stop at Primark. I bought dreary grey and black leggings (soft and would dry overnight on the radiator, I thought, sagely) and a rucksack (ditched the tote bag in the changing room) plus a hideous pair of trainers and a little umbrella. I then went next door to the KFC and changed in the loo. I went in looking pretty ghastly and came out looking worse.

Now I had to lug around the carrier bags full of the clothes and boots I'd been wearing plus the clothes I'd just bought. Frankly, I looked exactly like the people I was all set to meet. Bedraggled, with two Primark carrier bags. Fitting in didn't take long at all.

I trudged off to a cafe on the Charing Cross Road to sit down and consider my next move, once I'd addressed the second flaw in my 'non-plan'.

My idea of approaching every homeless person I saw (unless they were sleeping) was, I had thought, brilliant and somehow 'honest'. However, while it worked very well at dawn, when they were all lying in doorways, patently homeless, sometimes even with a helpful little cardboard sign declaring the fact, it was a different matter entirely when they were just sitting down on the pavement or walking around in the crowds that had, by now, started to appear.

The homeless spend almost as much time schlepping around with their belongings as they do hunkered down on the street. My original strategy had been to approach people who I thought might be homeless and ask them for directions to any nearby hostel, where, I told them, I wanted to interview homeless people for a book. A clever ploy that usually worked a treat, with the person saying, 'Oh, I'm homeless, I'll talk to you.'

Less successful was when I got over-confident in my spotting abilities and abandoned my opening speech, opting to go straight for the kill. There were several scruffy young men, minding their own business, who I walked straight up to and said, eagerly, 'Hi! I'm Tam . . . are you homeless, and can I talk to you?' Not cool. They were usually Australian tourists or cycle couriers having a break and a smoke. Middle-aged women sporting bad haircuts, dull clothes and big bags also caused me one or two false starts.

Wheelie baskets turned out to be too cross-cultural to be of use as an indicator of anything at all. I'd have to revert to the original, 'I wonder if you could help me? I think there's a hostel for the homeless nearby . . .'

With that all sorted in my mind I decided to go home (I *had* been up since just after two o'clock in the morning). I'd got a sense of things, talked to a few people and felt somehow justified in starting again the next day. The truth was, I was fed up carting around the bloody carrier bags, and it had started to rain so even when I managed to light a cigarette, a fat raindrop would extinguish it so it became impossible to smoke, carry everything *and* walk. The brolly was just one more thing to hang on to. Getting my camera in and out of the new rucksack was beginning to irritate me in the stop–start rain. It was all getting a bit much. Plainly, I was going to have to toughen up, and quickly.

I wasn't to know then, but it would be much longer than I expected before I reached the sanctuary of home.

Melissa

'People think I'm a scrounger but I won't take benefits'

Crossing Trafalgar Square towards Charing Cross tube station on my way home, I saw Melissa.

She was standing outside St Martin-in-the-Fields church, a slight fig-ure in a huge black biker jacket. I wouldn't have known she was living on the street but for the fact that she was talking to some homeless guys I'd met earlier that morning. I stopped to watch her for a moment. She had an economy of movement, a delicacy that made me think she could have been a dancer. I went up to her, abandoning all ideas of a warm bed, and she agreed to talk to me about her life.

In spite of the rain and the wind pinching our faces, Melissa did not want to go *into* a cafe. So we huddled together around a wobbly little metal table under a brazier outside a coffee bar on Garrick Street, drinking hot chocolates. I thought she wanted to be outside so she could have a cig-arette, but in fact she was a non-smoker. She was just shy and said didn't want to be stared at by the people inside because it made her feel uncom-fortable.

When I met Melissa she was twenty-one years old, and had been on the street for a year and a half. She had made a little family with two other young men (one was Darryl, whose story is next) and they took great care of each other. She kept her tiny nail-bitten hands mostly inside the sleeves of her over-sized jacket, and with her soft, matter-of-fact voice took me through her life. It was a sad story but her voice didn't betray any self-pity. She was the first person I'd had a proper, lengthy conversation with and as I listened I realised that most of Melissa's world had just crumbled away, leaving her with nothing but her dreams of working in the theatre.

But Melissa tells her story better than ever I could.

Melissa

I should have come down here with a better plan, like got a job here, and *then* moved down. I have been homeless before – the odd few days or the odd week. When I was younger I often stormed out of the house but I always came back a few days later. This is the longest long term I've done.

Occasionally, I have to go off for a walk on my own – I tend to wander off and just think about life and look at the city. I like having that hour on my own, looking like a tourist. I leave my bags with my street friends because if you've got no bags, people don't look at you. It's when you carry everything around that people know you're homeless.

When I came to London, I wanted to work in the West End, in the theatres – backstage, front of house, anything. I used to work at Pontins as a Bluecoat and I love entertaining! I wanted to get into acting school. They do a summer school, where you're taught by West End stars how to sing and dance, but it's only eighteen to twenty-one and I just missed this year, the age thing. A charity is helping me, they do courses as well, so I signed up for them when they start in January.

That first night on the street was scary. Scary. I didn't sleep properly. Every noise, every person that went past, I shot awake. I kept a little pair of nail scissors, just in case, for self-defence.

I had a good childhood. It was just me, my dad and my brother. Dad always, like, took us to football matches and when I got into trouble at school, he was always there to sort it out, and if I got bullied my brother was there. Sunday was a family day out, for roast dinner, or we'd all chip in and do it together. It used to be good.

And then . . . I fell out with my dad when I was fifteen. I said a few things that I didn't mean. After that, I lived with my brother, in Wales, but he went off to join the army – he always wanted to do it – so then I had no one else. I was at school then, and I thought that I could keep the house on my own, but the council said, because of my age, I wouldn't be able to. So I had to leave.

I miss things. Coming downstairs and play-fighting with my brother – more than anything. There's not that much of an age gap between us, so we got on like a house on fire . . . we never argued. He had a girlfriend but he always found the time at the weekend for me and him. It was always like, Friday and Saturday nights, a takeaway and one night was gaming night and one was film night . . . he did it so no one would get jealous! Keep everybody happy! Now I don't make plans. Just take every day as it comes.

I've not seen my mum since I was ten months old. She didn't want us. She had other kids before she met my dad, and they were her main priority . . . so she just left me and my brother with my dad. I tried to find my mum. When I was 16. I knew her name, date of birth, and what she looked like 'cos I had pictures. I went to places I knew, from the pictures that we'd seen – I went to Birmingham, Scotland . . . just . . . I couldn't find her. Everyone was saying they'd not seen her for years and . . . I just wanted to ask her why she left us and let her know my brother was all right, you know? I looked for her for about three years and then I gave up and came down here last March, so about eight months ago.

I chose to sleep outside the *Phantom* theatre [Her Majesty's Theatre, Haymarket] 'cos it was the only place that I knew in London . . . as soon as I got off the coach at Victoria, I knew where it was from the times when I'd been down in the holidays . . . I knew exactly where to go because my dad took me there for my fifth birthday. I love *Phantom of the Opera* – it's my favourite! And, now, every time I get £28, I go and watch it. I know every word, every person . . . my favourite Phantom was Ramin Karimloo.

Every time I go in, the staff tell me how many tickets I've got left till it's a thousand times! And I've got, like, eight tickets left. I was twenty-one this May, and they let me go backstage and sit and have a meal with them. They had three jobs going last year but because of my housing situation – and you are a 'public face' – they said I need somewhere where I can get a decent night's sleep and freshen up in the morning, and as soon as I get that sorted, I can go in and give them my CV.

Back at school, I was like a tomboy. I've always got in trouble with the police because I got in with the wrong crowd. I got taken home by the police *every* Saturday night.

Now I hang around with the *right* people, like Chuckie [Darryl's nickname] and that. The drinkers are the *wrong ones* and the ones that start trouble for no reason.

The first group of people I got in with down here, they were all alcoholics. I wasn't an alcoholic, but I was drinking a lot – about five bottles of vodka a day between all of us. I ended up in hospital three times, because of it, and they were putting tablets in my drink as well, Vetranquil [an animal tranquilliser] 'cos they thought it was funny. I remember blacking out and waking up in hospital. There were a few people in the area who didn't drink, and knew me, and they looked after me and waited outside the hospital. I was in overnight, the first time, 'cos I had to have a CPR done. I died for seven-point-five seconds. They said it was because my body wasn't used to it, 'cos I'd never done it before. I never drank . . . well, I drank at Christmas times . . . and I'd never taken anything, tablet-wise, apart from paracetamol.

Now I'm just trying to keep out of the way, because I've got forty-nine cautions [an official warning from the police, but doesn't result in being charged]. I got arrested last year, for theft – an iPad – I thought, 'That's going to make me more money to survive,' but I couldn't sell it because it had a passcode. It was reported stolen and the police caught up with me. I chose to do a face-to-face apology and the person said they would drop the charges because I was homeless – and there were reasons why I needed it, to get the money and survive and . . .

One of the police officers that arrested me sat in the cell and said, 'You're a kid . . . I don't want to have to ring the MOD [the Ministry of Defence, who are responsible for the army] and tell them that you've been sent down because then your brother's going to worry, he's not going to do his job – he's going to end up dead' – 'cos he wouldn't have been focusing on the job . . . and that's when I thought they would tell him, so I said, 'I want my brother home.' I decided then, 'That's it. Finished. I'm not doing this any more.' I've not been in trouble since.

There's a police officer who goes down the tube station in the morning and he whistles – he lets you know that it's him – he lets you do whatever down there as long as you're not smoking or being aggressive. He whistles if the sergeants or the inspectors are coming down so you know to pack up and move! And then he comes down an hour later with cheeseburgers, coffees, milk . . . yeah, he's all right. Because they're the ones that if you get into trouble, you know you can go to.

I use the day centre for a shower every morning – change my socks, put my clothes in the wash . . . but we're not allowed in at the weekend. Some of the Prets [Pret A Manger] have got the big toilets and they let us go in and do it there because they've got the sinks and everything . . . and we get free coffee off them as well.

We go in the day centre for our hot meals probably twice a week, depending . . . but for a decent breakfast, dinner, pudding, it's about £4 each. Mostly it's biscuits, crisps . . . some hot meals. Other than that you get food drops, food runs, soup runs.

Friday and Saturday nights and Thursdays we all sit together and do a bit of begging. If it's busy it can be good, like if it's a payday weekend. A good week is £300 and a bad one is, like, £20 [referring to what her little group can earn collectively]. I either put the money in my jacket or my friend puts it in his suitcase. Each one of us has a certain amount on us, so if one of us gets robbed there's still money to split between us. And they always say to me, 'You sleep in the middle,' so no one's going to sneak up on me. We just pool it all and then buy food, tobacco . . . it's like a little kitty.

I don't take drugs. I've *tried* it the once, when I came down . . . 'cos I'll try anything . . . if I don't like it, I won't do it. It was horrible. It feels like your stomach is coming up. Some people can handle it. They relax and concentrate more . . . and then you get the people who pass out or they get nasty.

I've seen the way that alcohol takes people. Like after Christmas, you go in the day centre and it's a long list of people who've died from alcohol or drugs. They do a service every Christmas and they read all the names out – last year it was more than seventy.

I get worried and depressed, I do. Sometimes. When I hear something on the news about the army, you know, my brother . . . and well, with my mum leaving me . . . not my brother . . . he'll always . . . I've got a picture of him in my bag, in the day centre, and it's me and him and he's got, on the back, 'A brother's love is forever.'

I cry every day about the soldiers that get killed. When he comes back he'll see how much I've changed, how I've grown up more. And I am learning. Before, if I needed something done, I'd ask him to do it, whereas now, I have to figure it out myself. Like, I've learned how to sew while I've been down here, 'cos I ripped my old sleeping bag and I had to sew it back up again. I've become more independent. It's like if I wanted to live with him again, when he comes back for good, I won't need him as much as . . . I'd *need* him for certain stuff – I can't cook, that's one thing I can't do – but the other stuff . . . I'd clean, I'd do that roommate, flat-sharer kind of stuff instead of the annoying little sister that had everything done for her.

A bracelet in honour of her brother
and a tattoo in honour of her dog

I do miss my dad. I know he lives in London. I just don't know where. I know where he works but I don't want to, like, just turn up at his work because of the things that I said to him, when we had the last argument, heat of the moment things, but I could tell they hurt him. I wouldn't want to turn up and him not want to know . . . I just don't want to call him. Just yet.

I would rather get myself settled and say, 'I am in London but I have this, this and this and I got it from *nothing*.' I feel like I've let my dad down . . . like a lot. Because of the way he brought us up. Like we got educated, you don't back down, you follow your ambitions . . . and I haven't done *any* of that. He's got a good job, my brother, and I have *nothing*. So I want to get a job, get somewhere to live, and then I can say, 'It's been ten years – I was down, on the streets, but this is what I've got now . . . and I did it all on my own.'

People think I'm a scrounger but I won't take benefits . . . I used to. I used to do the speedway bike racing, at weekends, and I came off my bike and popped my kneecap so I had to get time off work from Pontins and 'sign on the sick' and then I signed off and went back to work.

Here, you need to sign on to get a hostel, but I don't want to do it, because it's easy money, I think. I want to say that I worked for it . . . that I spent seven or eight hours earning a tenner begging 'cos then it shows . . . it's like working, in a way . . . even though it's begging . . . but with the Job Centre, it's like a cash machine – money – sorted. Even when I was off ill, I never spent it, I just put it upstairs in my little tin and then used it for Christmas.

I tried selling the *Big Issue* but then you get the people who walk by and go, 'Oh, you're not really homeless.' The public . . . they make me sad . . . as soon as one person is kind of like, 'Oh, you're a druggie', or they say you're not what you are . . . it kind of like puts a dampener on the whole day.

I just own a blanket, no, two blankets. My valuable stuff, I keep in my locker at the day centre – the picture of my brother – and because my dad's a Catholic, the little Catholic cross that he got us as kids, with our names on it – one name going down and the other name going across. And then my dad's old boxing ring, I've got that. I got my passport last year, and then someone nicked it so I had to beg £82 for a new one, but I keep that in my pocket all the time now.

I would like a stable future. A job, somewhere to live. I'd still have the same friends that I've got now, I'd still come and hang around with the same people . . . but then, like, have something that I *know* I can keep. Permanent, rather than temporary. And hopefully, get my dad back . . . I've given up on finding my mum, though . . . like, I'm twenty-one . . . and in my eyes she should be the one who's looking for me. Even the homeless lot, the ones we all hang around with, we all say we *are* family – even if we don't like someone, you're always there for the person. It's like we're all in the same boat.

I don't want a family. I'd rather have a house full of dogs or a kennel rather than kids and settle down. I love dogs. I used to have a dog on the street . . . but . . . I had the decency to give her up 'cos she was only a puppy and I couldn't like . . . it was hard. [Sob in her throat and then a long silence.] She was a ten-month-old husky. But I found one of my old school friends and they were moving to a farm and they send me pictures every so often [some homeless people have email and Facebook accounts, which they can access in certain McDonald's and internet cafes]. She was huge! She used to snuggle up in my sleeping bag but then I was finding it hard, 'cos I couldn't even feed myself.

My friends, with my dog, have said that as soon as I get a place I can have my dog back. So that's why I mainly want to get a place – so I can get my dog back.

Morphing After Melissa

After we left the cafe, I took the picture of Melissa outside her old bedding-down spot by the theatre and we parted. She went off to find Chuckie and I decided to walk home. I didn't have the energy to deal with all my bags and kit on the tube, at what was now rush hour. I felt shabby, couldn't face all the pushing and shoving and preferred the idea of getting home without sitting opposite someone who might be scrutinising me because I looked so unkempt. So I hauled myself back to Highbury on foot.

By the time I got to the Angel, my calves were aching and I was borderline frantic to get under a hot shower. Just another two miles to salvation, during which I gave myself a stern lecture. I told myself I'd adjust to the insanely early starts and get used to the damp, the rain, the chill and the walking (*so* much walking). I would have to do something about the quantity of coffee I was consuming as it was making me feel nauseous (I never did manage this). I'd also need to reorganise and reduce the contents of my rucksack so it didn't feel like I was carrying a Mini Cooper around on my back. And I'd wear thicker socks. And pack Nurofen for the constant headache I'd developed. That should do it.

I'd barely got the key out of the front door before I was standing under pounding hot water. Glorious. I was clean. I got out and put on what Alice refers to as my 'pachyderm pants' but which I prefer to think of as stylish palazzo pants. I just wanted to feel soft and comfortable to neutralise the effect of the brutal pavements I'd walked and sat on for God knows how many hours. I did get comfortable – so much so that, for the rest of my trip, I never got properly dressed again. It became a routine: on the street I wore my grim and dirty tat and at home I wore my clean and cheerful tat. I was officially and permanently scruffy. Alice raised an eyebrow.

It had taken just one day, but already I'd I felt something of how being 'on the streets' just knocks the stuffing out of you. It's relentless – the noise, the discomfort, the commotion – and barely a moment of peace to be found. I had managed a single day, had come home to a goose-down duvet and hot water and I didn't have the energy to even get dressed properly.

Darryl 'Chuckie' Borden

'You could say, I'll give you six months' rent to live in the Savoy Hotel or I'll give you a dog – I'd take the dog, all day long – because a dog will always be there for you, no matter what'

Melissa had said her friend Chuckie would be happy to talk to me. When I'd asked her how I would find him, she told me he was mostly out on the Strand and I'd spot him easily enough – he had bright red hair and would be drawing something colourful in his sketch pad. The day I found him, he was doing exactly that.

His real name was Darryl John Junior Borden and his charm and warmth were irresistible. I would bump into him a lot over the coming weeks and I never tired of his company. Sometimes, if I was feeling low, I would go and look for him – a little guy, cross-legged on the pavement and hunched over a work in progress, perched on his suitcase, his nose virtually touching the paper.

Chuckie was twenty-one years old, a waspish creature with flaming hair. He grew up in care and had been on the streets since his sixteenth birthday, when the system bade him farewell.

He bewitched me.

Darryl 'Chuckie' Borden

Do you want to tell me what the events were in your life, that made this come to pass?

The care system basically washed their hands of me as soon as I turned sixteen.

What happened on that day, the day you left?

Basically, they gave me a grant of £2,000 – a 'leaving after care grant' – and they said, 'Get a place, do what you want with it.' What would you do if you were sixteen years old and you got given £2,000 cash? Yeah, I put it straight down the toilet, literally. And I've got mental illness. Apparently, I'm a paranoid schizophrenic and I've got ADHD.

[And here we began a Monty Python-esque dialogue. I'd developed a head cold and couldn't hear very well. That, combined with screeching bus brakes and the generally appalling noise at ground level, rendered me virtually deaf. So, at first (and at second, actually) I couldn't understand Chuckie when he said 'paranoid schizophrenic'. All I could hear was a word that sounded like 'parrot'. Like a deaf granny I just kept saying, 'What? A parrot? What do you mean, "parrot"?' Chuckie, heroically I felt, kept his temper, until, at last . . .]

Oh! *Paranoid!* **. . . You don't look remotely paranoid, or schizophrenic, you look quite chilled.**

[He showed me his rolled-up legal high, also called Spice: a dry brown powdery substance bought in little plastic tobacco-like pouches from certain newsagents. It's smoked in a joint and has mind-altering effects.]

34

It's the reason that I smoke legal highs.

Ah, self-medicating. So, sixteen years old, two grand, on the street – what happened?

I smoked it all. Cannabis. I'd been smoking cannabis since I was nine years old.

What?

Gave up on 23 December last year and I've not touched it since.

So, it's just the legal highs, now?

Yeah.

But who gave it to you, when you were *nine*?

I was hanging around with the wrong people at a very young age.

At *nine*?

Yeah – when you're nine years old and you see older boys, what do you think? I was this kid and thinking, 'Oh, if I don't, he's going to beat me up or something,' so I did. And that was it.

Did you leave care with a bag?

Yeah, basically, I had a big gym bag, just clothes really, and spray paint.

What was the spray paint for?

That's how I started all this drawing and that.

What, graffiti and murals and whatever?

Yeah, but I'd get in trouble! I started off with drawing pictures and people would buy them off me.

When you came out of care, did you have any family that you could pick up a phone to? Or a door that you could knock on?

No. I've got sisters, but they don't want to know me.

Why?

Because I've got a very nasty temper.

But you look so sweet and nice.

But you know what they say – the nice ones are usually the worst! And I'm ginger! Fiery temper!

Yeah, well, just don't kick off while we're talking, I haven't got the bloody energy. How did it feel, when you were first on the street?

Oh, it wasn't that bad. When I was in care, I got moved around a lot, I mean, the longest foster place I was in was six months, so I got used to moving around a lot and me being on the street, homeless, now, it's just, 'Right, I'll sleep here one night and then the next week I'll be down there and next week, down there', know what I mean? If you don't move around, that's how you cause trouble . . . look, I'm wearing girls' trainers right now because someone stole my shoes.

Show me your girl trainers!

They were a fourteen-year-old's PE shoes.

So you wear those because somebody stole yours?

Yeah. Also someone stole my glasses – *off my face* – while I was asleep. At the London Coliseum, that's where I slept then. I thought – it's ridiculous – you can take my bag, you can even try and touch me up but now I can't *see*, I'm blind, yeah? You taking my 'eyes' is like me taking your arms and legs.

Because you need your 'eyes' for this art?

Yeah.

How *do* you manage, then?

My nose is on the paper. Look! I've got paint on my nose!

Before I turned on the recorder, you told me you had a detached retina – what the fuck was *that* about?

Basically, it was just something that happened when I was a kid – it started off as a lazy eye and then deteriorated.

So, you're blind in one eye, you've got a detached retina but still you produce this art, with no glasses?

Yes.

Do you feel proud of yourself, for that?

Depends if I can get some money out of it or not!

You should feel proud of yourself for that. So, is this your 'spot'?

Yep. I'm here all day every day – if I wasn't I'd be in trouble, I'd end up in jail, so . . .

Why would you get into trouble? What would you do to get into trouble, if you weren't doing artwork?

More than likely fighting.

Why would you fight?

It's fun! I'm a boy!

Yeah, but you've got a bloody detached retina – you *can't* fight. If you fight and someone wallops you . . .

You can't say that – look at the Paralympics – there's geezers out there with no legs and still running around.

But you need your eyes for *this*. *You have to protect your head*: Don't fight – it's daft.

I do protect my head – with my fists. If someone's going to punch me in the face, I'm going to hit them back, aren't I? That's the way it is.

You bloody better, or you're screwed.

Trust me.

How much could you make in a day – a good day – from selling your artwork?

£20 – eight, maybe nine pictures, if I'm lucky.

And this is your money? Yours? You earned it? Can you get any social benefit at all?

Refuse.

You refuse to take it or they refuse to give it?

I refuse.

Why?

Because the government fucked me over for twelve years of my life, they are *not* fucking me over for any more. The government – all these David Camerons and Tony Blairs – they're all upper-class wankers and they don't do anything for the homeless, for actual people, you know what I mean?

But benefit is your *right.*

I don't care. I don't want it. Then all these people would be saying, 'I pay for your benefits, my tax goes towards your benefits,' well I'm sorry, yeah, but there's not a person on this planet who can turn around and say, 'I give you money.' No – you *don't*.

Is that important to you?

I *earn* my money. I make *sure* I earn my money. People say, 'Oh, you're a scavenger' . . . er, no I am not.

In general what do you think all these people, whizzing by, think of you?

That I'm a con artist. That I'm not actually homeless, I'm just doing it for money. They think I'm either a scammer or a druggie, that I'm a smackhead, that I would sell my grandma for my next hit. Do you know what? At this precise moment, do you know what I am saving up for? I'm going to see my daughter, she's nearly one year old . . . it's her birthday in eleven days' time and she lives in Harlow and I can't afford to get there – it's like £60-odd to get there.

Oh, you've got a one-year-old daughter?

Yeah, and she's the biggest pain in the butt going! Just like me!

And who's she with?

Her mum. Her mum and her grandparents 'cos they all live in the same house. The last time I saw her was 27 December last year.

You're joking – so you haven't seen her since she was a few months old? Have you got a picture of your baby girl?

It's on my phone but my phone's dead, otherwise I would show you!

[When I was telling my husband, Steve, about Chuckie's life and I mentioned his mobile phone, Steve was quite surprised that someone without a home might have a phone. Actually, many are given mobiles by some of the charities, often for safety reasons, and others buy them.]

Is she gorgeous?

Yes! Like me, ginger hair and green eyes! There's only one per cent of the world has ginger hair and green eyes! And I'm blind in one of them!

I would guess missing her is very difficult, kind of painful?

Basically, I always said to myself that I'd make sure I'd be the best parent that I possibly could – my parents were fucking shit, yeah? In those words, yeah? I will be a better parent than my own. My daughter, I'll make sure she does full education at school, I'll make sure of it – she's grounded until she is fifteen, I don't care!

No boyfriends till she's thirty!

Never! No, *never*! First boy that broke her heart, I'd kill!

So, tell me about your art. When did you know you were good at it?

When I was about nine, ten. Then it all got more and more detailed and now I can do night skylines of London city blending the river with something that looks like a boat going across the top of it. I drew the biggest Minion in the world as well, I can proudly say it, eighteen foot big in Trafalgar Square. And once, I drew – with charcoal – a black figure on the floor and I used white chalk to flick white light behind it, so it was like a 'shine', you know what I mean?

Was it published?

I don't actually know . . . I don't read, I can't read very well, but what it meant to me was that there is always light beneath the shadow . . . no matter how hard life is there is always goodness and love inside someone, it just needs time to bring it out.

When you first hit the streets when you were young . . . and be honest, yeah, I don't want bravado . . . were you frightened?

At night . . . I'm scared of the dark.

Where do you sleep at night now?

Right here, or I'm down in my 'hidey-hole' – with about thirty-five other people. Down the back of the Savoy Hotel – a right little spot.

Are you safe?

Of course we are! We're at the poshest hotel in the Strand!

But that doesn't mean jack, does it?

Well, it does because police are always patrolling around everywhere and there are security guards back, front, side and even security cameras.

But when you were first on the street, when you were younger . . . ?

I used to hide in bushes. Woods were the best thing for me, 'cos I'm small, I could 'dig' myself under a tree. Three and a half months I spent in Epping Forest. I survived. I used to be quite good at hare coursing, you know with dogs, so I was able to make snares and traps. Get rabbits and stuff like that. I can feed myself like that, could live off the land if I had to. They do those 'challenges' don't they? – 'I'll give you a million pounds but you can't spend a penny for three months'? – piss easy, mate. I'll eat pigeons.

Oh, stop it!

Why? It's food. It's meat.

How *do* you survive for food?

People normally give it to me, or I buy it.

What kind of food do they give you?

Pret A Manger . . . and it's horrible!

But that's all cold food, sandwiches?

Yes, that's mainly our diet. We eat a lot of sandwiches. And coffee. Tea, coffee and sandwiches is mainly a homeless person's diet.

What do you think the effect is on your physical health?

Over time, it hurts. And I've got a hole in my hip . . .

Why?

Er, you know the spiked fences? I thought I'd be a smart-arse and I jumped it and slipped and now I've got a hole the size of a twenty-pence piece, going all the way through my left hip bone.

Can I ask what you were doing, climbing over a spiked fence?

I was being a criminal. Not going to lie – at the end of the day, honesty is the best policy! I was being a criminal. Got caught. Literally!

You did, didn't you! Nasty!

I was stuck there with my pants down for like forty-five minutes.

Oh shut up, shut up.

Well, you wanted to know . . . !

Yeah, I did, but not that much detail.

Why not?

Because it makes me queasy.

Having a strong stomach is the best way to be, especially if you are homeless.

[I needed to stop for a bit so I could find somewhere to go to the loo, banned as I now was from the nearby McDonald's. I left Chuckie guarding my stuff so I could go and find a cafe. Over time I would develop this technique of hurrying into a cafe, looking confident and scanning the tables as if for someone I was clearly meeting and then sidling off to the loos. When I got back Chuckie had finished the picture he'd been working on and was sorting through his suitcase.]

How many homeless people do you know that have got a mobile phone, portable speakers, mobile-phone charger and over a hundred and fifty quid's worth of art gear sitting in this bag [pointing to his little suitcase]?

This is important to you, isn't it?

Yeah, I lose this and I'm *fucked*.

What's in the bag?

Mainly sketch pads, pens, pencils and another set of clothes. That's it.

Can I take a photo of your stuff, or is that too personal?

No, no, I ain't bothered . . . all you will see there are me undercrackers!

Hang on, it's too noisy. [Screaming sirens go by.] **How do you bloody live with that?**

You get used to it.

So, this bag is your life?

It's everything I have. It's like those old people's trolleys! 'Go-Go' trolleys, I call them!

How do you protect it?

Sleep with it. Sit on it. Bite your face off if you try and take it.

But aren't you scared that somebody will take this while you sleep?

No, I've got a reputation for being a bit of a 'nutter' around here!

This is your life, right?

Yep. I don't own a lot.

Why, do you like it that way?

No, I *hate it* that way.

Why?

Well . . . I used to run around in clothes that were worth like £200 – tracksuits and stuff like that – and now I can't afford a pair of joggers.

How *did* you afford that, dare I ask?

Please don't! Long story!

How did you get them? Nicking?

Yes, I used to be, erm . . .

Hmmm, a 'thief of the parish'?

Yes!

Do you not live with a certain level of fear out here?

No. This is a dog-eat-dog world. It doesn't matter how big you are or how old you are . . . all it takes is eight pounds of pressure and you're all out cold.

Yeah, but you have *a hole in your hip*.

Even with my hip, I can still spring up on my feet quicker than most people. I played football for most of my life so I *had* to be quick. And I'm small as well, and I got bullied at school for being ginger . . . I got to be quick and agile, and I did a lot of street fighting when I was a kid, always fighting in school.

How far ahead do you think?

One second at a time. At the end of the day, you can't live any more than that.

Why?

If you think ten years down the line, yeah, you could die in ten seconds' time – it would take a second, bang, you're dead. You walk in front of a bus, yeah, *boof* – gone, that's it, you're dead, know what I mean? You can only live life one second at a time.

But for yourself, you don't have a vision for yourself?

No, I didn't have anyone to push me, you understand? Everyone needs that kick up the arse. I never had that kick up the arse.

But you have a talent, you are very articulate and you are quite funny.

Yeah, funny-looking!

No, you're just *funny*!

Funny-looking! I'm ginger.

No, you're *not* funny looking . . . so, a dream? For yourself?

I get called 'Chuckie' from the *Rugrats* movie, 'cos I've got bright ginger hair, I wear glasses and I can't do my shoelaces up! So my dream is called 'Chuck us a Chance' – a charity for disabled, visually impaired and homeless people. Everyone needs a chance in life, you know what I mean? So, chuck us a chance, mate.

Why are you so positive when you have every reason not to be?

If you can't be positive, what's the fucking point in living . . . my parents, I don't know if they give a monkey's about me, but I am me. I am Darryl John Junior Borden. That's me. That's my name. I am this crazy kid that's got a big gob. That's it. My first nickname was 'Button' because I was so small. I was the short, fat kid with the chunky-monkey face!

But you must have been told that you radiate charm?

I've been told by these people who chat and waffle that I have a very good aura about me . . .

I would say so . . .

I'm positive because I like to make other people smile. Once, it was a girl's thirteenth birthday and she was in Trafalgar Square and she stood next to me – I'd seen her big thirteenth-birthday badge and I said, 'It's your birthday, isn't it?' and she was all shy and that, and I said, 'What's your name?' and she said, 'Amy' . . . and I did her name for her, on the pavement outside the National Gallery – *massive* – and I did a 'Happy Birthday Amy' all in big writing with flowers and butterflies on!

[Darryl seemed so animated, so joyful that it seemed impossible to believe that someone with such energy and passion could disappear forever into the streets. I wondered if he himself thought this was all a passing phase in his life or if it was how he saw his entire life playing out.]

Do you see an end to this lifestyle?

[Suddenly quiet and serious.] Unless I can get the money for a deposit [for a flat], no.

How would you get the money for a deposit?

I'm trying to get a canvas.

What? Is it more important for you to be able to express yourself this way than it is to put a roof over your head? If someone said, 'I can give you a flat or all the artist materials you could ever want,' which would you take?

Artist materials. You know why? Then I could make myself a house! Artist materials also means cement, brick, everything. Art is part of everything. Even the cracks in the pavement slabs are still art.

Why is that art?

Because it is a pattern. It is a continuous pattern.

[I was trying to take a photograph of the pavement, as he saw it.] **God, too many bloody people, all these** *feet . . .*

Listen, this is what it's like for us till three or four o'clock in the morning. When the weekend comes, it gets very rough here. Do you know what would help me more than anything? A dog. I. Want. A. Dog. You could say, 'I'll give you six months' rent to live in the Savoy Hotel or I'll give you a dog' – I'd take the dog, all day long – because a dog will *always* be there for you, no matter what.'

[There was a shadow that crossed Darryl's face. He suddenly seemed deflated. Exhausted. Perhaps it was as simple as that, but he seemed momentarily overwhelmed by a wave of sadness and I thought I should leave him alone with it. It was pretty clear to me – I could have fun with some of the people I would meet – but the life itself? Not fun at all.]

Being 'Othered'

When I'd said goodbye to Chuckie, I needed the loo and something to eat. There was a nice cafe in Neal Street and I was desperate to get warm. As soon I walked in I knew I was being looked at, sized up and found wanting. I wasn't quite 'right', and there was no friendly smile or eye contact from anyone. When I'd finished my cappuccino, I stood in my 'I've totally given up' clothes and asked a waiter where the toilets were. I could see panic cross his face. He asked me, politely, to pay (everyone else seemed to pay at the counter, just before they left) and when that was done, instead of telling me they were downstairs on the right, he escorted me all the way there, in a very uncomfortable silence. Once in, I could almost feel his ear against the door. What was I going to *do* in there? Must be drugs.

I was in a quandary. If I said, 'Ha! I'm not *really* homeless, I'm just writing a book about them,' it would have been tantamount to conceding that I shared his view that homeless people are not to be trusted but that he needn't worry about me, because I wasn't really one of *them*. But if I let him think I *was* homeless, and said nothing, it would give him the sense that he had cowed me, humiliated me and forced me to accept his lack of respect. I chose a third way to deal with what had happened: I confronted the waiter's arrogance and – offering no information on my housing status – had my second public row in a week, and left.

Outside, the temperature had dropped and feeling a bit upset and jibbery I went to an Accessorize to buy a thicker scarf. I was aware of the shop assistant's gaze on me the moment I stepped inside. It had to have been because of how I looked – scruffy, edgy, and with an angry face, after my experience in the cafe. The girl made a pretence of folding things up and straightening out jewellery and never left my side while I rooted around trying to find a scarf for under a tenner. She was plainly thinking that the only reason anyone who looked like I did would come into the shop at all, would be to go on a shoplifting spree.

I had just experienced being 'othered'. I was not a decent, righteous person: I was something else. Something untrustworthy, unpleasant and unwanted. Neither the waiter nor the shop assistant knew the *first* thing about who I was, yet in the space of less than an hour I had been made to feel as if I were a drug addict and a thief. It wasn't so much that neither was true, but as a white, middle-class European it was the first time in my life that I'd had a brush with bigotry and prejudice.

Part of me was angry but I didn't know how to express this feeling of alienation. Another part of me was hurt, quite deeply. I was surprised by this reaction and by the fact that I was sure I would cry if I opened my mouth.

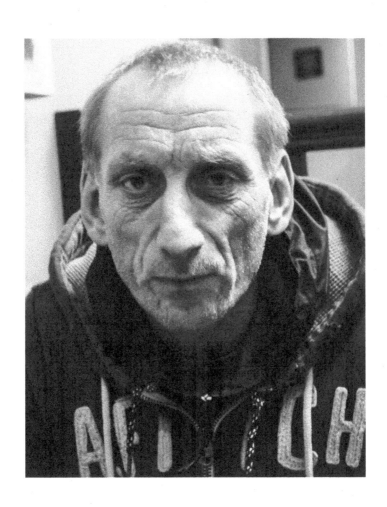

Scott Randalls McDonald

'It's the most disgusting thing I've done,
the lowest point in my life. I've cried at times'

The day I met Scott, I'd woken up feeling washed out. After less than a week I was tired most of the time and had an almost permanent head-ache. I guessed it was partly all the sitting outside in miserable weather but also because I wasn't eating well and had spent a couple of nights on the trot, out and about with the camera. I'd been keeping weird hours and was generally too wiped out to shop or cook. I was surviving on Indian take-aways and Tesco crumpets.

That morning, the West End seemed too far to walk so I opted instead for Camden which has a lot of homeless and troubled people living on its streets. I could also save my weary legs by catching the number 29 bus as a treat. I'd been walking virtually everywhere up to this point.

It was a bright but cold day. Scott was sitting outside a Gap store on the main road, wearing just a sweatshirt and jeans. Just sitting, shivering. He had no plastic cup and wasn't begging. As I walked towards him he looked up and smiled. He had a worn, wounded look about him. I started talking to him, explaining the idea behind my project. He sounded like a Billy Connolly impersonator. Stories sound better when told by a Scot or an Irishman, so I was hooked from the start.

He struggled to his feet and we went across the road to a coffee bar near the Jazz Cafe. Like Melissa, he was anxious about coming inside, but he did, and we cosied down into two over-stuffed leather armchairs next to a radiator. Ordinary enough for me but a luxury Scott said he hadn't had in months.

Scott had been a European coach driver, taking the likes of the England under-21 football team and the Croatian squads around the continent to their matches. He had met loads of celebrities including Ronaldo. He spoke of his job with passion. He generally worked an annual season from March to November, and then had time off. This set-up worked brilliantly for him. Having turned forty-five eight months previously, he needed to have a medical to renew his PSV licence and thus his job. No problem.

Except that shortly before he was due to have this medical, he lost his home (*not* his job, he was at pains to tell me). With no address he could not be issued his special licence and with no licence he couldn't work. He said, 'I could get a job straight away but if I've got nowhere to live, how do I keep myself clean? I have to be immaculate for my job – a suit, tie and polished shoes – and the medical certificate costs £110 – where am I going to get that kind of money now?' He was more ashamed about not working than he was about not having a home.

For Scott life was – literally and figuratively – just rocks and hard places.

Scott Randalls McDonald

Everything was fine, I was living in south London and I had a flat above a pub – the manager of the pub was my friend. I was with a girl called Julia. But when I was at work, Julia was trying to get him into bed and that, so he told me, 'Get rid of her, or you've got to go, Scott.' So, I told her what he'd said to me – what she was up to – and said I wasn't interested any more – 'Get your stuff and go,' basically. She went. She came back about half an hour later and wanted back in and she caused a scene, so I let her in. The next day I was pulled up by my mate and told, 'Listen, you've got to leave at the end of the month 'cos I can't have that . . .' So, that was my falling out with her. I lost my home.

It's my own fault, you know what I mean? If I hadn't been thrown out of the flat I would be working right now. I'd still be in the flat and have my job.

I made a bad choice, right. I'd never make that choice again. And I'll tell you why – 'cos no woman will ever live with me again. Ever. And that is dead, 100 per cent, certain. Women! I should maybe be gay! Ha!

After that I came here. One week you are in your home – the next you are on the street. It's hard to comprehend. Very, very hard to explain. It's a shock. I can still remember my first night on the street. I remember *exactly* the spot and how scared I was . . . *how scared I was* . . . waking up and there were all these guys, drunk, running and jumping all over us, filming us with their phones and throwing stuff. I'll never forget it. And I thought, 'God, that's going to be on the internet and somebody will see it and recognise me.'

Somebody stole all my stuff two weeks ago – what you see me standing in now is what I own. I lost two full bags. I lost all the pictures of my dead dad and everything. I went *mad*, off my head, like I've never been before. I can't replace any of that stuff. I don't even want to talk about that now. [Scott had become terribly upset, turning away from me so I wouldn't see him crying.]

That first night out was horrible. Disgusting. The place stank of urine. The streets are horrible. It's not any different now, now that I've been here for eight months – it's the same as that first night.

I sleep wherever I can find shelter. There's a place along there with scaffolding and that's windproof. I'm always thinking, 'Is it windproof and waterproof?' or '*How* can I waterproof it?'

I sit there everyday, yeah [pointing through the cafe window] and that's what they call my 'spot', right – do you know how *degrading* it is to sit there and ask people for spare change? It's disgusting. Disgusting. And there's National Insurance in Britain – we shouldn't have to do this. And the government – all that bull that they spew – how they are going to help the homeless? They're not interested, they just sweep them under the carpet – out of the way – so nobody can see them. That's the government.

This is the first time I haven't worked. I'd always wanted to be a coach driver . . . always. I went on a coach when I was a little boy and that's what I wanted to be! And I made it happen, yeah. As soon I was twenty-one, I passed the test first time and I've done it ever since.

My childhood was fantastic. Me and my two older brothers. I was brought up to be a gentleman. I was told to always hold the door open for a lady and never use any bad language in front of them. My parents never drank or smoked. I loved school until I got to big school and then I didn't. I just turned rebellious and got kicked out, so I never finished the last year and a half of school. I was forever fighting – just a typical lad.

My first job was in a woodyard – pulling wood off a machine that a man was feeding the wood through – a 'double ender', that's what it was called. That was 1986. I can still remember my first wage – I'd done two nights' overtime – and I got £43! In 1986 and I was sixteen! Woooh! I gave my mum £13 for my keep.

My mother is seventy-four years old and she could *not* handle me being on the street. I'm a forty-five-year-old man – I don't need to be going to a seventy-odd-year-old woman and asking for help. I'm proud. There's no *way* my mother will ever find out about this. No way on God's earth – it would kill her. None of my friends know – nobody. I just keep it going, like it was when I was working on the coaches – they think I'm still working – nothing's changed. But to lie, you have to remember every lie you've told, so I have to watch what I'm saying to people or I'll trip myself up and then everybody will find out. I'd kill myself if my mum ever found out. [Scott was now crying and very distressed.] . . . sorry . . .

[I turned off the recorder as Scott wanted to go to the loo and sort himself out a bit. It was awkward because this cafe – like so many – has a system where you go to the till, present your receipt and ask for the code to the toilet, which you then punch into a keypad on the door. This is to prevent the homeless and non-paying customers from using the facilities. Scott asked if I would go and get the code for him – he was too embarrassed, with his tatty clothes and his tears. When he came back from the loo he started telling me this story about what he and his friends had experienced recently.]

Wardens come and kick you out of wherever you sleep – 'You can't sleep here. If we catch you again, we're going to arrest you.' Good! We'll come tomorrow night and you can come and arrest us! So, the next morning, we were saying, 'Fantastic! You're here to arrest us! We've got our stuff ready!' But they wouldn't arrest us! Anyway, they kicked us out and we went up to Primrose Hill, right at the back of the park. There was a wall with bushes so we got all waterproofed and that – and then we got kicked out of there.

So, then we made signs, 'Homeless and hungry. Can you please help? We've been kicked off the street, kicked out the park, kicked off the field and we don't know where to go now' . . . and people were coming up and . . . we were saying this is *all true*. Where do we go and live now? This is why I ask for money for a hostel but you can't ask people for £11 for a night in a hostel.

I'm sick of phoning the Safer Streets Team and I'm sick of phoning No Second Night Out – they don't come to you, they *don't* come to you. They have to find you three times in the one place and *then* they put you in a hostel, but that's been changed in the last month 'cos the police have got sick of the amount of homeless – it's absolutely unbelievable and it's getting bigger every day – now they've only got to find you *once* and they're supposed to come and get you off the street.

But I've *never been taken off the street*. They've *never* come. On Saturday night a Safer Streets Team were going around everybody that was sitting begging, but they never came near me. I shouted at them, 'Here! I'm sick of phoning you lot – how long have I got to be on the street before you will help me?' And then they say, 'We'll come to you when it's time.' I said, 'How long's "time"? I've been on these streets eight months. You told me you'd get me off the street – I was lying in the damp, on stones for *three months straight* and you never came to see me.'

These people say they are going to help you? These people aren't here to help you. Just there, doing a 'job'. Outreach are the worst – if they come, I'm downright rude to them – and I'm rude to nobody – I tell them to 'f— off', because they are the biggest liars ever. All they want to do is move you on – they don't want you sleeping here. They don't want you begging but they'll not arrest you because you are homeless. I'd be happy to go to sleep in a police cell every night, honestly – more than happy. Just anywhere to get warm, I mean.

One man he tried something – he was obviously gay – but I put him straight in about thirty seconds! Can I say anything on this? [the recorder] I battered the fuck out of him – he was trying to violate me when I was sleeping. When I came round and realised what was going on, I went crazy. Crazy. And that's not me. But this is what the streets have made me.

Before this I was the most generous, happy, outgoing person you could meet. I loved life and I loved to share. If I'm happy, I like people round about me to be happy. I was always smiling – I think it's good for the soul.

I feel angry. Most of the time. Because of my situation. I'm so angry, sad and lonely. I feel violated, to tell the truth.

At seven o'clock at night you're setting up your bed for the night, right – *seven o'clock at night*. I'm off up to the bridge there, on Kentish Town Road . . . wet, cold, damp stones. And there's nobody else there. Just me. And I've got to lie there till seven o'clock in the morning so I can come back and beg. [long silence and sad face] And when it's cold and wet and the rain is *soaking* you in that tunnel, because the wind blows one way or the other, it's horrible, horrible. I can't even explain to you how horrible it is to be so cold . . . and lonely. And scared. Some days you get so low – suicidal thoughts – but I don't know if I would carry it out.

In the tunnel where Scott sleeps

You go out there now and ask anybody – they'll tell you I'm a hard man. I don't take drink or drugs . . . nah, nah . . . I'm a European coach driver – I cannot take drugs! No thank you!

I drank when I was eighteen and I put a boy in hospital for seven months and I've never drunk since. The boy was almost dead and the boy was my cousin. [long silence] Drink? Never. Two days later, when I realised what I'd done and I'd been to see him in the hospital and I'd seen the state of him, I swore – on my knees I was – I swore that I would never ever drink again. And I've never drunk since . . . and that's twenty-seven years.

When I beg and get £10, I stop. I don't need any more. £10 is enough to keep me alive in a day – I don't need to ask people for more. If I've got enough, what do I want to degrade myself for, by asking for more? It's disgusting. It's the most degrading thing I've done, the lowest point in my life.

I've cried at times, when I've been out there, 'What am I doing? Why am I sitting here, asking people for money? Why?'

Some days, I go without food. I've been five days, six days with nothing. The first three days, it kills you, and then you just get used to it. But the first three days are horrible, horrible. But what can you do if people don't want to give you anything?

So I'm constantly tired because when you're sleeping on the street it's cold, it's damp and that stops you sleeping properly. I wake up about every hour, hour and a half. Leaves me feeling angry. And the noise – it's constant.

My body aches all the time. Did you see me, when I got up off my sleeping bag? It takes me forever to straighten out. You feel like you're seventy. Before I went on the street, back in March, I was fit as a fiddle. I had my weight and I had my face about me. Some days are *so* hard, you don't make anything, you can't get anything to eat.

There's a couple of homeless that I talk to, like, but I don't trust *anybody*. People have stolen everything I had, when I was sleeping. If people can steal from someone like me, who *can* you trust? First thing you do, when you wake up, is look and see if you've got any money and if you've money for food, you're *so* happy but if you wake up and there's nothing there, because someone's taken it? Disgusting.

Homeless people will steal off homeless people. No loyalties. The only loyalty is this legal high. Oh my days! I've seen people going off their heads for it – have you seen it? It says, 'Not for human consumption. Do not inhale.' They banned it, in Scotland – they'll need to build mental hospitals in Scotland to deal with the addicts.

[He sighed, and was silent for a minute or so.] I don't have a plan. I have hope. I hope this is going to end before Christmas – that would give me the next three months to get myself back on track – be full size again, healthy, and go back to work again next year.

All I need is to be off the street – if I could get into a hostel, I could go to work from there and I could pay rent. I've got nothing now. This has just got to end. It's got to.

There are two options, right? It either ends the way I want it to or it ends the horrible way – you can die in these streets, easy. The street? It's probably the most dangerous place you could live, in the world. The jail is safer than the street, because when you're in jail you have prison officers looking after you constantly. When you're on the street, you've not got police officers looking after you. You could be killed by one of those psychos who've not got anything to smoke and comes and attacks you in the night.

There are many people out there with mental illnesses, smoking this Spice, and that is scary. Very scary. One of them out there, they call him Bam-Bam, his name's Paul – he's a huge guy and all the soles are coming off his shoes – he's been in a mental hospital, he's that bad and now he's down here, homeless and a mental case – very dangerous. [Later, we were to bump into this guy in the Sainsbury's car park – he was a truly frightening figure.] Camden Wardens, the police, the community coppers – they do nothing! They watch him going about all day, screaming and shouting – why are they not helping that man? They give him a forty-eight-hour ASBO – he doesn't even know what an ASBO *is*! [Anti-Social Behaviour Orders restrict where a person may and may not go in relation to a particular area.]

Everybody tells you, 'We're here to help you. We'll do this, we'll do that' . . . they don't know – come and speak to real people on the street – they'll tell you the truth.

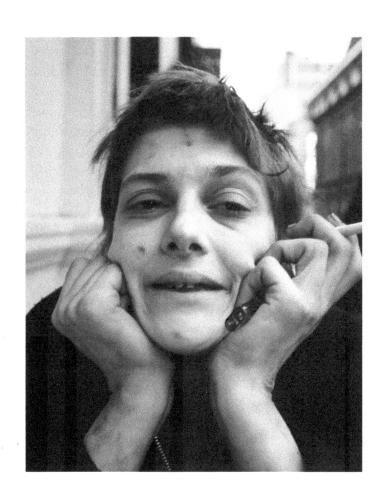

Beth Langham

'I've been raped so many times I can't even count'

Beth had been damaged beyond repair before the age of nine. When I met her she seemed to be lurching rapidly towards an early death in the back-streets of Soho. Her destruction was nearly total and entirely public. I saw her in the middle of Greek Street, barely clothed and spinning in frantic circles, clutching her sleeping bag, sobbing and screaming at passers-by.

I approached her, trying desperately to think what to do to help but ter-rified of making the situation worse. I reached to touch her and her bony arm whipped out and grabbed my wrist. We had, at least, connected.

Up close I could see weeping sores on her face, ears and neck but mostly I saw her startling blue eyes. I held her tightly and stroked her head until her crying subsided. There were about a dozen bystanders staring at us and not one of them came towards her.

Calmed but still spooked, Beth let me take her to a cafe where I prom-ised to buy her food and drink. It wasn't very many degrees above freezing but she wore only a teeny, paper-thin, filthy T-shirt, and enormous sweat-pants. No knickers (I was to see later when she showed me her various injuries and infections) and no bra. She held a little empty cloth bag.

Under her ruined face, almost toothless mouth, scabbed and infected limbs and savagely chopped hair, Beth was a beauty. Exquisite bone struc-ture, huge eyes and a frailty that it almost hurt to look at.

I wanted to get Beth inside the cafe but she resolutely refused to cross the threshold. We sat outside at a table for a few minutes until her breathing settled and the sobbing had subsided. I had absolutely no inten-tion of talking to Beth about the book, but she asked me about the camera, which I now kept in my hand when I was out and about. I told her what I was doing and was surprised when she said she wanted to tell me her story.

In spite of her terrible physical condition and her wretched emotional state, Beth made it quite clear that she had very little time to spare for me, she did not like to be interrupted or have to repeat things. At a stroke she had made me feel like an inexperienced cub reporter interviewing a world stateswoman on a very tight schedule.

Beth was her street name, her 'working' name, but she was born, twenty-six years ago, as Elise Ruth Christine Langham. I bought her endless rounds of jam on toast and she smoked nearly all my fags and pinched my lighter. It was, I think, the shortest 'long' conversation I had with anyone for the book. Her speech was surgical. Clipped, scalpel-sharp sentences delivered without a single adjective to describe *any* aspect of herself at all. It was as if she had already ceased to exist and all that remained was her story. Its content was so horrific as to be numbing.

Beth Langham

I was taken away from my mum at the age of nine. I was raped by a babysitter. [silence] My mum had ordered a female but this man turned up and he said he was from the babysitters. He was lying. [silence] He's dead now, thank God. Yeah. Anyway, I was put into care.

I used to run away from school – at thirteen – to run home to my mum's and watch a movie! And then I'd get taken back into care. My mum's visits were cut from every day to once or twice a week. They just said it would be better for me, better for my 'growing up'. I was in one foster home and I was in a secure unit as well because I ran away one time, from my foster family. I lasted three weeks.

Not wanting to come inside the cafe

Turn it off now. [the recorder] I want to drink my drink.

They sent me to the secure unit because I'd met some Spanish guy . . . with muscles everywhere! I mean *everywhere*! [laughs] I was fifteen, or fourteen. I went shopping one day, for me and him – you know, milk, bread, fags, booze – and as I was about to go across the road, a copper comes over, 'Elise Ruth Christine Langham?' . . . I'm like, 'Oh, no, no, you've got the wrong person' . . . and he went, 'We're taking you home. You're not in trouble, but your mum, your foster parents and social services are worried about you.' Got took back to the secure unit. When you get in the door there, you have to do a wee sample, they have to check your hair for head lice, you have to have a bath, chuck your clothes away and they give you some clothes from the unit.

That's how I found out I was pregnant. [from the urine sample]

Most of my pregnancy I lasted, and then a member of staff from the secure unit, called Roger, said, 'You're too ugly and immature to have kids', and, 'If that baby survives, which I hope it doesn't, I hope you never see it.' My baby died an hour and a half after birth. 'Stressful circumstances,' they said. Whatever that means. I was fifteen.

Can we stop now? [crying]

I ran away straight after the birth and I said to them, 'Look after the baby please. Don't do too much exploratory stuff on the baby . . . make sure she's looked after' [Beth began to crumble here, tears spilling onto her cheeks] and then I just ran away.

Yeah, I've been living on the streets ever since – since I was fifteen, on and off. I've been in and out of certain hostels but only been in them hostels a couple of months . . . 'cos they're full of drug users. Now I live in a phone box at the bottom of Dean Street.

I've had a crack habit since I was fifteen, sixteen. I beg or I have to sell my body. I used to be a prostitute on Brick Lane, in Commercial Street. I used to stand in the red light district and wait for cars to turn up. I've been raped so many times I can't even count. I got raped by three black geezers three years ago – I'll show you this – they beat me to a pulp, near enough to death – see? It's a lump on my hip. I started smoking crystal meth after Brick Lane.

Beth's home

The hardest thing is not knowing what is going to happen to me when I go to sleep at night. That's the main reason I take drugs. I'm scared to sleep at night.

My teeth are coming out because of crack addiction and not brushing my teeth enough and sweet stuff.

I can show you my legs as well, from picking. Can I show you my legs, from the crack? I pick with the crack. I *hate* spots – I have them because I don't have a bath enough. I'm *dirty*. I hate spots – let me show you a big enough one. I hate things with [showing me her wrecked calf] pus in them. I hate pus.

Most other homeless show me respect and if they don't I call them a cunt or a dickhead, you know what I mean? How would you like it if you were sleeping in a phone box? Or sleeping on the street, yeah?

I'm sure you would take drugs if you were raped, yeah?

I've had enough of begging money up, asking people for money ... spending it on drugs and then doing the same thing again. I'm supposed to go to rehab on Thursday – my mum's coming up, finally! [looks happy] To pick me up! Yeah! [squeals with delight] I'm gonna be mummy's little girl again! I'm sorry. [apologising for being happy, it seems] Saying 'sorry' – it's a habit.

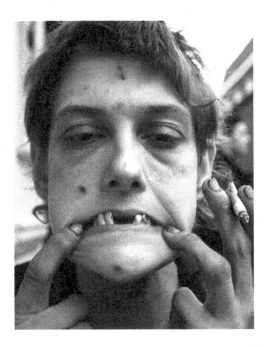

I don't know how much I sleep. I'm not that good with maths. I got kicked out of school at twelve. I sleep during the day. Either in the phone box or on Rathbone Street – I was asleep there all night, last night, and woke up at five o'clock this morning. I missed all my dealers of the evening! I missed all the money-making on Saturday night [prostitution].

I woke up this morning with a £10 note next to me! But £10 don't get you one bag of 'brown' [heroin] to help you wake up. You know what I mean? And I like my raspberry cheesecake cookies from Subway.

I ain't got much longer. About five, ten minutes left, then I need to get . . . I need to beg. For a bed. I need enough for a hostel – I'm trying to get four or five nights and sort out my life.

I want to stop now.

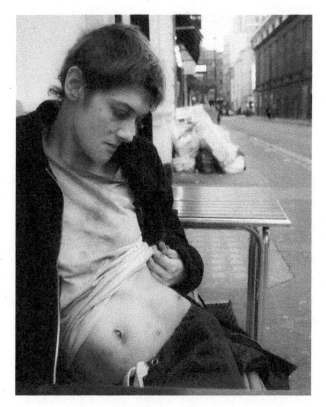

Beth's wounds

My Camera

My camera was an important part of both the action and the stories and it needed sensitive managing. It was now always in my hand, wherever I walked, so that everyone would see it as a *part* of me, and not some threatening game-changer that I'd whip out at the last minute and blindside people with. It had to seem ordinary, friendly and not something that would drastically alter the dynamic.

Friends kept asking me, 'How did you convince people to pose?'

The answer was, 'I didn't.'

Ever.

There are two common – and unpleasant – circumstances in which homeless people typically have their photos taken. One is in the custody suite of a police station, when they've been arrested for whatever (begging, fighting, being drunk and so on). The other is when a member of the public, a passer-by, says they will give money if the homeless person 'performs' in a way that is belittling or humiliating ('Go on then, do a jig . . .') and then that person takes a snap or a video on their phone which they may put on the internet. It was described to me by one victim as the 'dancing monkey trick'. So, small wonder that associations with picture-taking weren't exactly positive to start out with and I had to be careful, respectful.

Was what I was doing ethical?

I did take photographs of people who were asleep or passed out without their permission, but only if they were totally unidentifiable, even to people who might know them. I was harangued a couple of times by members of the public who shouted things like, 'You should be ashamed of yourself, he's asleep for crying out loud', or 'Who the fuck do you think you are?' I was never given a chance to reply but I would have said that these kind of images can be important: they can affect sensibilities, can make people see familiar things in a different way. I took lots of them because I saw lots of homeless people and I wanted people to know this.

In most cases, I would first see a homeless person from a distance. Sometimes the sight of that person would touch me, move me, and I would take the shot. If the person's face was visible I would go up to them and – whether or not they went on to agree to talk – I would tell them I'd taken their picture. If they were happy about it, I would keep it, and if they weren't, I deleted it in front of them. Everyone whose face is towards the camera in this book, whether I interviewed them or not, gave me their informed consent.

It was often a potentially 'lose-lose' situation when I was in the middle of listening to someone talking – take a picture and risk being offensive, or don't take the picture and lose the moment, that crucial moment, when a person's face is saying something greater than the sum of their spoken words.

It was the portrait that I took of Beth, as she talked about the death of her baby, that gave me pause to think about what I was doing. What Beth was telling me was appalling, and looking back, I have absolutely no memory whatsoever of taking that shot. I honestly believe I took the image unconsciously: if I'd been thinking about it, I wouldn't have taken it at all. That she didn't smash the camera out of my hands and scream abuse at me, for what could so justifiably have been perceived as an offensive and insensitive act on my part seems, now, incredible.

I then thought back and recalled that when she'd refused to come into the cafe – and I'd taken that sad image of her in the doorway – I had immediately given her my bag and the camera to look after outside, while I ordered for us both at the counter. She was able to hold and touch the camera. Perhaps that had connected her to it, in some way?

I did encourage people to hold the camera and sometimes created reasons for them to engage with it – as I scrabbled around in my bag for a lighter or when I went off to get us coffees, asking them to look after my gear while I was gone. I decided never to be afraid that one of the people would steal my stuff. No one ever did.

There was never the opportunity to set scenes, sort out lighting, remove annoying things from the background or do retakes. It was plainly unacceptable to say, 'Oh, would you mind looking defeated/sad/beleaguered/despairing *again*, 'cos that bloke's leg was in the way?' I am very happy with the images – often technically off the mark – because somehow they are *true*.

Whilst many of the people I approached over the weeks would not let me record them, and some went on to refuse permission to take their photograph, not once during a conversation that was agreed on and underway did anyone say, 'Look, do you mind not pointing that at me. Get it out of my face and just listen to what the fuck I'm telling you?'

Credit to them all.

The Crack Connection

A few days after talking with Beth I'd met a homeless guy called Micky. He was probably in his forties but looked much older. During my time in the West End, I'd occasionally see him around the bottom of Shaftesbury Avenue, where he lived in a tent at the top of the stairs down to Piccadilly Circus underground station. He refused to be photographed and didn't want to participate in the book other than to give me what I believed were useful insights. I remained wary of him as he seemed to know all the young homeless girls, including Beth and Jade (who you'll meet later), and took a keen interest in their welfare, saying he gave them food, money and shelter. I've read my Dickens so I was never sure if he was a modern-day Fagin, exploiting these young girls, or a genuine benefactor.

A piece of crack. This photo was taken inside a hostel, one night

Crack is popular with young girls of fourteen and fifteen who come down to London to escape whatever nightmare their life was at home. Often this involved sexual abuse from their mothers' partners. It seemed a tragic irony that after escaping an abusive 'old life' these girls had to turn to prostitution in order to survive the 'new life' that was now theirs. The reality, said Micky, is that these girls are getting raped regularly because they are so desperate for the drug – 'chasing, chasing, chasing' – as he put it. They'll take a tenner, five blokes will 'do' them and then they take the drugs to get 'out of it' – now caught in a whole new cycle of horror.

Micky said he'd got Beth clean and off the crack a while back. He took her to a mate's hostel room and kept her there for two weeks during which time he 'poured tons and tons of vodka down her' to get her through the cold turkey. She apparently stayed clean for three months, but only because her drug dealer hadn't seen her around. Beth was no use to the dealer without her habit, so eventually he went to find her (dealers tend not to wander around being visible – you have to go to them), and gave her drugs for free. The temptation was too great, as the miseries of her life hadn't suddenly evaporated, and in no time at all Beth was hooked again. She had to go back on 'the game' to raise the money for the dealer who, now, most definitely wanted paying.

John Matthews

'I was eighteen at the time and
my life just got switched for another life'

He will always be 'John in the leaves' to me, and not John Matthews. A blustery day, when London was dry and dismal and no cheer was to be found, I saw him sitting under a thick furry blanket on the Euston Road. He was pulling on his woolly hat and the wind was swirling the late autumn leaves all around him. We had to shout at each other to be heard above the thunderous traffic.

Before I turned on the recorder, all I knew about the sweet-mannered and self-effacing John was that he'd had a shave the day before, came from Bedfordshire, was twenty-five years old and had been homeless for the last five months, since being released from prison.

By the time I turned it off, some time later, my heart had broken for him.

John Matthews

So, you went to jail because you were stealing food. Why?

To sell.

And what were you going to do with the money?

Drugs. I got myself addicted to a drug, essentially.

Why?

I suppose there's an element of withdrawing yourself away from life and the reality of the situation. But for me, personally, I've used drugs since I was thirteen.

Thirteen?

Not Class A's. Heroin and crack I did when I was nineteen.

Why did you start? What was the impulse?

I was involved in a bad car crash in 2009. I was working and I had my own house – with my missus and my son was just born – spent our first Christmas there, my life was, you know, really, really good . . . and . . . then . . . me and my missus were coming home from a party and the driver of our car fell asleep at the wheel and we had a head-on collision.

Killed my missus.

For the love of God.

I nearly died. I was in intensive care for a couple of months. Broke my back in four places, had my spleen taken out . . .

What's this horrendous scar on your throat?

A tracheotomy – I punctured both my lungs.

Your body would be covered in scars I would imagine. [shows me his torso] **Jesus!**

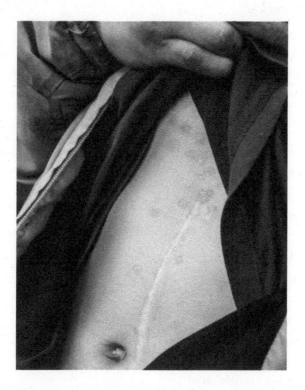

Do you not have to take medication?

Yeah, I did – I was in hospital for seven or eight months, but my age prevailed. Saved me. I was playing rugby at the time, for my town, and I was really fit – eleven and a half stone and now I'm nine and a half stone. To keep your weight on, on the street, is fucking near impossible because of the problem of food intake but I'm doing quite well. Most of the people that I know, they don't look after themselves at all.

And your baby?

He's seven now, he's with the family and that, with his aunty. Since then my life has just been chaotic.

So, you came out of hospital – what were you doing, what happened, what was your life?

When I first came out of hospital, I carried on, and I did really well, but I don't think I dealt with the mental side of it . . . for three years I brought up my son on my own, in our house, and then it just started getting on top of me and I asked my mum if she would look after my son, because I wasn't coping . . . and then . . . yeah . . . I just fell apart, more or less.

Why weren't you coping? Tell me what you were feeling, what was happening, during this descent?

The emotional loss. I was eighteen at the time and my life just got switched for another life, that's what it felt like.

Overnight?

Yeah. Then I got £258,000 [compensation] two years ago. I spent that.

What did you spend it on?

Drugs, hotels, cars, motorbikes.

And what have you got now?

Nothing. [A long, tearful silence as John turned his head away from me.] I lived in Brighton in 2013, all through the summer. I just didn't want to 'establish' myself with that money – I saw it as 'blood money' because of how I got it, you know what I mean?

Yeah, I absolutely understand that.

I did what I wanted to do, and I spent it. I just wanted to get rid of it and then go from there. That was seven or eight months ago, I spent the last of it. I was in a real bad way at the end, when the money was gone, because I was using a lot of drugs. I had that money for two years and I was in a different part of the UK daily – one day in Scotland and the next I'd be in Brighton, sleeping in hotels. I was picking up blokes off the street and taking them for three-course meals, getting drunk with them . . . and yeah . . . 'sharing the love' [delivered with irony]. That money brought me a load of pain and anxiety, so in return I wanted to, you know . . . bring a bit of joy, even if it was short-lived.

So, you gave other people happiness.
Yeah, yeah.

What drugs do you do?
Heroin, crack.

What's good about crack?
It just goes with the heroin really. It was fun, but for me, now, I only take it because I have a physical addiction. I really have got to that point – there is no pleasure in it. I don't enjoy it any more.

Yeah, you 'have to' – I smoke – I don't particularly enjoy smoking, but I wouldn't go out without a packet of fags. What do you do for money?
I get some money from the Job Centre and begging.

And where does the money go?
Everything. Mostly drugs but I do spend some of the money on food – McDonald's, cheap you know, a loaf of bread and that, ham and I love fruit. And obviously you get quite a lot of food as well. I do look after myself – I like to think I do. There are public toilets in St Pancras and you can have a wash and that in the mornings, brush your teeth.

What is the effect then, physically, on you?
Well, I broke my back – I've got metal rods in my back and I do get a shitty back with sleeping on the streets, so yeah, not very good. And I'm addicted

to heroin – without it, I'd be too ill to do anything, you know what I mean? *Physically.* It's different for everyone but you get hot and cold sweats, you can't sleep, your body is all aching – walking ten feet feels like a mile – it's dreadful.

Is heroin just physical pain relief or is it mental pain relief?

I don't know, I'm not a psychiatric worker, but I'd guess both. There's got to be, certainly, elements of both in there.

Where do you sleep?

A bench . . . chopping and changing – somewhere different every night. Up at King's Cross, doorways and that. Places out of the way, behind buildings . . . I mean, I'm twenty-five. I feel the physical effects from the car crash, but all in all, I'm pretty fit.

And what about your emotions, your feelings? What's your mood, most of the time?

It's sort of like, a lot of uncertainty. Just not knowing what tomorrow is going to bring, what I'm going to be doing . . . I mean, I don't stay anywhere for too long, I do move about quite often. I was settled, I *was* settled, you know, before the car crash, I had my life and everything was all in order, and since then I haven't had that stability. Nothing's been set in stone and I'm just somewhere different every day.

And what about loneliness? Do you have friends?

That's why I move about a lot, as well. I'm a very social person, and I don't like being on my own. I mean, I'm used to being on my own and I don't mind it but it gets to the point where you want a decent chat and to socialise.

How would you describe your character?

Outlandish! Very unpredictable but in a good way, a good way. A bad way for society! This is *not* the way they like to see people march.

How do you think society looks at you right now, as it walks by?

Society is one thing, but people, individually, are completely different. People's individual thoughts are nothing to do with society – the thoughts of society are put into people's heads *by* other people and they are *other* people's opinions. Nine out of ten people sort of understand that any one of us could be here – homeless – one day to the next.

What do you think of them?

I don't know them! You can't build an opinion of someone until you've met them. Everyone is different.

What do you think of your future?

I take it day by day at the minute. I'm coming off my driving ban at Christmas, that's what I'm looking forward to . . . as soon as I'm off that I'm going to get enough money together to sit my test and get working again. I'm pretty diverse at the minute! I'd do anything but I wouldn't mind getting a job with some sort of driving.

So, long-term plan would be what? Give me a five-year plan.

Be well established in employment and have my own place.

And your boy?

Obviously – that all goes hand-in-hand with getting my own place, but of course.

Do you feel OK knowing that he is being looked after by your family?

He's in the best place. I made the right decision at the time . . . if I had denied the fact that I was struggling, you know, things could be much different now, you know, my son could be in care, God forbid . . . but he's happy. I haven't seen him for a few months because right now it's a bit . . . with prison and that. The only fear I've got really is my son not doing well, and my son not being looked after, or . . .

How long were you in prison? Remind me?

Six weeks. I got twelve weeks – did me the world of good really, I got clean and I came out on a methadone script [prescription].

But you're off methadone and back on the real thing?

Yeah – methadone is just as bad – you're still addicted. You still have to get up in the morning and go to that place which is the same as getting up in the morning and going to a different place for the real thing.

[Screaming police sirens and traffic noises were reaching fever pitch.] **Christ, does this get on your nerves? Do you not have a permanent headache with this?**

If you took everything on board at once, your head would explode! Living here in London, you have to let it wash over your head, you know, especially doing this, begging . . .

How do you deal with the stresses of all this?

Same as everyone. Same as everyone deals with the day-to-day stresses. I don't doubt for a second that most people that I've seen today have a lot going on in their lives, a lot of hardship – they may not have to sleep in the street but that's the one thing you can be sure of . . . everyone is struggling.

But do you not think you are struggling rather more than most of us?

Sure, yeah, maybe . . . but not more than *everyone*.

So, your mood is what?

It changes all the time. Happy and pissed off are about fifty-fifty at the minute. It's either going all right or it's a bit 'dragging'.

Are you worried about this winter?

No. I've been through twenty-five of them, I'm sure I'll do all right.

But not out on the *street*!

No, but I'm hardcore! I used to be in the Army Cadets at school, I've lived in fields! I've done all that as fun, but it's prepped me.

You have lost everything but it doesn't seem, at this, point, to have defeated you . . .

No.

How do you hold all this together and not just . . .

Well, I mean, it's a bit of both. Being here is sort of 'slamming down' . . . but if you can keep your sanity you are still just holding it together. You know, to be here one day, or one month, one year . . . in ten years' time, if I'm set up and working, this'll be just another 'chapter'.

Brad Lemon

'What happened to me was unbelievable, really. I couldn't see that coming, you know what I mean? You don't *see it coming'*

No, it wasn't his real name. He was mortified at being homeless and couldn't bear the thought that anyone he knew would find out. His favourite actor was Brad Pitt, and after a mate who was passing by at the time said he was a 'lemon', we settled on Brad Lemon.

Shortly after dawn on a Saturday morning Brad and his friend Patrick (who is also in this collection) were in a shop doorway on Southampton Street, near Covent Garden, waking up and sorting out their bedding. The thing that drew me to them was actually Patrick's big brown dog, who didn't seem to want to get up at all. The three of them looked a little dishevelled.

Patrick said he'd talk to me another day but Brad – who was going to get a coffee and then go off to sell copies of the *Big Issue* in the piazza – said he would sit and talk to me for a while beforehand. He'd been homeless for three weeks, following the collapse of his business and his marriage.

I think Brad – probably in his fifties – was still in shock at the speed with which his perfectly ordinary life had come crashing down around him. He was a man who was hurting, but he had a huge work ethic and was very optimistic about his future. I met a lot of people with this powerful belief in a good and decent future – maybe it's because nobody can take the hope away from you, and without it what's to stop you jumping off Hungerford Bridge?

And – sometimes – dreams do come true.

Brad Lemon

When you've had a business and then you're homeless, it's not a good thing. People might see me and it's embarrassing, isn't it? My kids are grown up and they don't know I'm in this situation. I just tell the kids that I work away every month and then I go and visit. I saw them two weeks ago. What can you do? Nothing you *can* do. But I *will* get out of it.

I was a painter and decorator and I had my own painting business, lived in a half-a-million-pound house. Then I got divorced and had a lot of bad problems with my legs. I've had bones taken out and put in, both knees replaced and I nearly lost my leg – it got infected.

So I've had four years of hell and I couldn't work. My knees went just through work . . . just a lot of different things, you know. Bad luck. And my wife – she left, yeah. And I lost the house.

I could never go for another woman again in my life, because of what happened. I was married for thirty-eight years. What happened was she was having an affair and I found out when I was in hospital. I told her to leave. And that has affected me badly, really – 'cos you keep thinking about it, all the time, what was going on and that mucks your mind up. I got depressed, tried to commit suicide . . . [long silence] . . . but sod it . . . now I'm strong . . . you know? And that's what I've ended up with [the contents of his rucksack].

That first night I slept in Lincoln's Inn Fields, under the bins . . . *under the bins* . . . I just wanted to kill myself. It was horrible, horrible. [Suddenly his face changed and he looked very troubled.]

I'm sorry, is that distressing to talk about?

Yeah. [long silence]

We won't talk about that, I can see that you are very upset.

I had nothing. I didn't even have this [pointing at the rucksack]. All I had was cardboard. All I had was these clothes and cardboard. Nothing. No money. Nothing. Horrific. Sleeping out? *It. Was. Horrific.* The first night I couldn't sleep – then I met a couple of people, which was better. When there's two or three of you it is safer. I'm not frightened – I can look after myself . . . but . . . I'm just saying, you don't know, when you're asleep, someone could come and . . . you hear things, don't you? They set alight to people. I'm not a little man, but when you're asleep, what can you do?

Someone nicked my jacket last Tuesday . . . there [nodding towards a shop doorway] with £100 in it. This passer-by saw me and he took me and bought that rucksack there and he bought me a sleeping bag. The kindness of strangers.

I've never signed on. If I can't earn £10 a day then there is something wrong. I saw someone, last week, and they said, 'Do the *Big Issue*, you'll be good at it,' so I started doing that. I work twelve hours a day selling the *Big Issue* now.

But I don't drink, I don't take drugs . . . I won't go there. No, never. I've never done it. I've always been a law-abiding man. I would never do that.

I miss all my stuff, all my possessions, all the things I had, you know what I mean? You get used to it though . . . possessions are nothing, you'll get them again. It's just . . . somewhere to go at night, really. Watch a TV. It's horrible. I'm only in my third week.

I do get lonely. It's not so bad now I'm with them [he means Patrick, and another guy, Alberto] but the first week was bad 'cos I was on my own all night. It was bad. Bad. I felt really cold, freezing. I woke up at 2 a.m., it was that cold. I slept under a dustbin for six nights and then I found this place and I sleep here now.

I'm tired all the time now. Everyone who walks past me wakes me up. You feel physically drained and sometimes in the afternoon I get dizzy and that, you know what I mean? It's just not good, so I just stop for a couple of hours. It does make you very wary – like when you are asleep, something makes you go like that [making a startled wide-eyed face], specially after I got robbed. If I hear someone walk past, I just wake up. Everyone watches you waking up. I'm still upbeat and I will get out of it – it's going to take about a month. I'll just work hard.

You feel tired all the time and because you are on the street you can't go home and go to bed . . . [pointing to his doorway] we can go there after 8 p.m. and sleep, and then today we were up at 5 a.m. because the shop opens . . . and you can't have a wash . . . it's horrible. I book myself into a hotel [one of those hideously depressing quasi-hotels you see in the back-streets of London, where rooms can be rented by the hour] twice a week so that I can have a shower and that's like fifty quid each time.

What do I own? Nothing. That's a sleeping bag and copies of the *Big Issue*. No mementos. Nothing. But my photos are in storage with my kids. This is what I have.

That's my whole life there. And I've worked hard in my life, I had a brand new Mercedes every year . . . that's not important now, I'm just saying. I can make a living doing this [selling the *Big Issue*] but you've got to get good at it, work hard. I've no money coming in, so like now, I'll be selling these *Big Issues* till 7 p.m. tonight. You know we've been awake since two o'clock this morning?

My plan is to work – around Christmas time I will smash it [sell a lot of papers]. I'm saving a little deposit for a room . . . already got £200. I'll go from there to a flat and build myself up . . . without a doubt, love. Look [he shows me a roll of cash] – this is money made from selling the *Big Issue* for two days . . . now that's not bad, is it? If I've got to work twenty hours a day, I will do it – trust me, I *will* get out of this situation.

I'm strong-willed, as I think you can see! There's nothing that's going to stop me getting back to where I was. Nothing. The thing with this is that I've started at rock bottom. I couldn't get any lower – on the street with nothing. Last week I bought a pair of boots to keep warm, I'm going to buy a pair of trousers, and slowly I will build it up.

To cope mentally, you've just got to blank everything you had before, you just blank it out. Because if you don't, you *will* go mad. If you don't, you get depressed and depression will . . . and then you start drinking . . . I blank it out . . . today is today and you start today. Rome wasn't built in a day. And I'm pretty strong – the first night that I had to go to Finsbury Park, to the *Big Issue* office, I didn't have the money to get there . . . I had to walk from here to Finsbury Park and then walk back. And I left at 4:30 a.m. to go there.

To me, now, it doesn't matter what you've got – it's if you are a nice person. It's the people. Now I don't care about TVs, I don't care about cars. Now I value a warm bed, you know what I mean? Or a shower – something that you took for granted but now you can't do. I can't go to the toilet – I have to find a Pret A Manger!

The people who walk past me think 'tramp'. You wouldn't believe what people think. Some of them are just idiots. One woman said to me, 'Why don't you get a proper job?' – but you don't get involved, just got to swallow it. There are a lot of good people about. I've found a lot of good people but there's a lot of arseholes about too.

It's still my fault. I should have known what was happening. You make your bed and you lie on it. I just didn't see what was going to happen, and I should have done, because, you know, the signs were there. Other people have lost more . . . there's a picture there, on the *Big Issue*, of a man with no legs [an injured soldier] . . . what's worse? At least we're walking, aren't we? What's worse? What's happened to me, or what's happened to this man? You tell me?

It's taught me that I can survive anywhere. It's taught me that I don't need anything, that I can go and make something from nothing. And that's hard. I know now that I can go anywhere and do anything and I don't need *anyone*. That gives me a good feeling because I know I can do it. I'm not a young man, either, but I know I can work ten, twelve, thirteen hours still . . . I'll get there in the end. I never even knew I could do this 'selling' thing.

I actually think this is going to make me better and much stronger. In two years I'll have my own house, go back, put the TV on, cook a dinner . . . here, you can't cook, you can't . . . it's horrible. I wouldn't wish this on my worst enemy, honestly. Because living on the street, there's no privacy, that's what I'm trying to say – and sleeping with him [jokingly, points to Patrick who had wandered over and is a very large man], he takes up all the room!

I'm stronger and wiser. What happened to me was unbelievable, really. I couldn't see that coming, you know what I mean? You *don't* see it coming.

Homeless? Tough Luck

I was worried about my cough – it was quite bad and now I wasn't sleeping well at night. There was a lot more to do for the book and I didn't want to be laid up in bed. So, I went to a local GP even though I know there's not much you can do for a cough. Especially if I insisted on spending days – and some nights – out in the pouring rain, chilled to my marrow. When I told the doctor I was sometimes cold and a little weak, and often damp and very tired, he said it was probably bronchitis, gave me antibiotics and advised staying cosy and warm. As if.

He asked me what I was up to, and no sooner had I said the 'H' word than he sat up and said he needed to check for TB – which I thought had died out with the Brontë sisters. Not so, and much more common among street dwellers than you might think. He said if the cough hadn't gone in another week to come back and he'd do a skin test for tuberculosis. Blimey, I thought, that'd scupper my plans for the book.

And that got me thinking. About Brad and John and how things can just come out of the blue and send you down a road you hadn't intended to travel, with consequences you'd never foreseen, let alone planned for.

So, my cough? If it *was* bronchitis then I was in a lot of trouble, because I wouldn't be able to keep going with the book. I was living on coffee, crumpets and apples by now – nobody's idea of a good diet unless you're a supermodel or on a hunger strike. I smoked, so was the cough all my own fault? Did I deserve everything I got? Or was it bad luck?

Luck, I began to wonder – what part does it play in the world of the homeless? And how does it tie in with the decisions *any* of us make?

You see those signs on salesmen's desks saying, 'You make your own luck!' I tend not to agree. You're lucky if you have a loving, inspiring, nurturing family. You're unlucky if you don't. You're lucky if you are bright, with an IQ on the right side of the distribution curve. Unlucky if you are not so smart.

And what about those among us who have little self-confidence or who mismanage our lives and make bad decisions? Scott's decision to let his girlfriend Julia back into his life cost him everything, and from that point his descent into homelessness was swift. John's wife being killed in a car accident – how does *anyone* deal with that, let alone a lad of eighteen? Did he somehow fail to come up to scratch as a human being because he fell apart with grief and despair? And little Darryl – his entire childhood in an inadequate 'care' system with no one who really *loved* him, tipped out onto the street at the age of sixteen. Why would we be surprised at the outcomes?

We control our destinies. Maybe. But only to a point. How many times have you made a rubbish choice or decision and seriously regretted it? Think about how you clawed back from that place (or didn't). Many homeless people are hopeless and chaotic, with no idea how to manage their day-to-day lives, never mind thinking about how to move forward.

I've made several lousy decisions that have gone on, in one way or another, to colour the rest of my life. I've also not managed my life terribly well at times. But here's the thing – I was born bright, white, middle class, have supportive friends, a good education and was brought up to be confident. Periodically, I suffer from existential gloom but have no other mental health issues. I was able to more easily recover from my errors of judgement.

So I asked myself – how hard and for how long are we going to punish the homeless for theirs?

Charisse

'It's not like you've got anybody to cuddle up to at night and say,
"Hey, babes, love you. Nighty night" – you miss that'

Zero degrees and a caustic wind coming off the Thames had just absconded with my *third* bloody umbrella, snapping it out of my hand as I crossed Waterloo bridge towards the station. It was nine o'clock on a Saturday night, I'd just walked the length of the Strand, I was soaked through, and my feet felt like they were two sizes too big for my trainers (and how useless are *they* in the rain?). I'd got water spots on the camera lens and was faint from hunger. I just wanted to be *gone*.

I was staying for a few days with my friends Chris and Margaret in their super-deluxe house in Clerkenwell – total luxury. Two things were at play. One, I wanted to give Alice a break from my comings and goings at odd hours – she did have to go to work at a normal time, after all. Secondly, much as I love her and her flatmate, Rachelle, I found their whole *Sex and the City* sense of housekeeping a bit of a depressing homecoming after a day on the hoof in London. I couldn't relax with piles of dirty dishes, laundry drying everywhere and men in white paper suits and masks dismantling the germ-warfare lab in the bathroom (that last bit is not true). Chris and Margaret's place was heavenly – all scented candles, Farrow & Ball paint and *tidiness*. A miracle, frankly, that I ever got out of bed there at all. That arctic night I felt the pull of their house like an iron filing to a magnet.

I was feet from the entrance to Waterloo and just minutes from bliss when I saw Charisse, sitting on the ground, leaning up against a railing by the steps up to the station. I saw her first from behind and the sight struck me as so desolate.

Having said she'd chat to me for a bit, I went and bought us both enormous hot chocolates with cream and marshmallows on top from inside

Waterloo, and sat down next to her. The ground was icy, and the pair of us were really not very well at all, coughing, shivering and aching.

Charisse was thirty-seven, had been homeless for nine months and was coming up to her first winter, one which was showing every sign of being very harsh. It was as if a suburban housewife had simply been picked up and put down on the streets of central London with nothing but the clothes she stood up in to learn to fend for herself. Which she appeared to have done.

Charisse

Do you know where you will be sleeping tonight?

I try to get into a hostel on a Friday and Saturday night because there's a lot of people out here that are vile. I've had people kick me, spit on me, pour alcohol on me and light a lighter – I've had it all, trust me – that's why I don't sleep down at the IMAX [the huge circular 3D cinema at Waterloo] no more, because of that. Because I sleep on my own, I'm safer up here, by the train station, in the tunnel. Over there, that's where I sleep.

Jesus, but there's constant light there.

Yeah, but basically there's always somebody coming through. It's safer for me.

Have you been attacked or assaulted – apart from this horrible stuff with people?

Yeah, yeah [soft voice]. About five weeks ago I was zipped up in my sleeping bag, down at St John's church, round the corner, and these guys thought it would be funny to start kicking the shit out of me. They thought, you know, 'Oh, a homeless person, they're a bum,' and when they realised that I was a woman, they stopped and were gobsmacked. But I had two black eyes and . . .

You're joking.

Nope, and I had a head injury and ended up in hospital. For three days.

How did you get to hospital?

Somebody was walking up and saw them and called an ambulance . . . but out here in general, I'm actually safer – because of where I was when I had my home – I fled through domestic violence and the council refused to help me.

Tell me as much or as little as you want about how you got here.

I was in a relationship with a complete arsehole . . . he broke my jaw in three places. I put up with him for eight years and one day I just got up and walked out and didn't look back. I went to the council and asked for help and they turned round and said, 'Sorry. There's nothing we can do for twelve months because you've made yourself intentionally homeless.' I just thought, 'Well, you know what, I'm just banging against a brick wall. They're blatantly not going to help me.'

So you go there with your broken jaw and your . . .

Yeah and my hospital records – I had everything, everything. If I'd gone to them *before* I left, they might have been able to do something.

What about women's refuges?

Well, the guy that I was running from found out where I was, in one of the women's refuges . . . so I couldn't stay there. He broke windows and that – he was stalking me and everything. The police were called, I think it was seventy-four times . . . it got really bad . . . and so I decided to come out on the road and it's actually been safer on the street than it was in that situation.

So even men beating you up in the street and pouring booze on you and being disgusting and spitting, you're telling me that that is better than . . .

. . . than where I was, yeah.

And what was your upbringing, your childhood, like?

Basically, my mum was the only one who brought me up – my dad was never a part of my life – he wasn't a very nice person. I don't even know if he's alive or dead. I'm not interested. Yeah, it was just my mum. She struggled bringing me up.

Were you an only child?

No, I've got a brother – I had a brother, bless him, he died from drugs. He was brought up by my nan, because he was scared of my mum's epileptic fits. It was really weird, my brother would run, whereas I would stay by my mum's side. People who made fun of my mum, when she had a sudden fit, would say, 'Oh, look! Another alky,' or something, I'd give them 'what for' – at the age of six this was – and say, 'Hey! That's my mum, you know, she's having a fit but she'll be all right,' and I wouldn't leave her side.

Is your mum still alive?

No, she's not.

I'm sorry. What was she like?

She was amazing. She done everything she could for me. Every penny. She ended up in hospital because my dad wouldn't give her any money for food and the money that she had to live off, for a week, wasn't a lot and she ended up giving food to me, to keep me going – and she'd starve for herself. Then she ended up in hospital because she lost so much weight, you know? But she was amazing and she put me first. And I wish she was here now . . . so I could put her first, to say thank you, you know? I know she's up there watching me and keeping me going.

Don't answer this if you don't want to, but did you have to leave your children when you left that guy?

My children are with their real father – he lives in Folkestone and they're all grown up now, they're going to university.

Did you have them young then?

Yeah, I had my first when I was eighteen and the next one at nineteen.

So, they're safe and they were never a part of this horrible dynamic with your violent partner?

No, no, no . . . and as long as they know I'm OK, and they get that call every day saying, 'Hi girls. I'm all right', that's it, they're happy. They've said to me, 'Mum, if you can get through this, we can get through anything, just by seeing you get through this.'

Can you not go and stay with them, and your ex-husband?

No, he's married and got another life.

How does it make you feel, that you once had a home and a life and a relationship?

I never had a home and a life, really.

Is that how you see it?

It was all controlled and taken away, you know . . . I had no confidence. I couldn't speak to anyone. If I was ten minutes late down the shop, I'd get beaten up.

How many years were you with this animal?

Eight years, eight years . . . yeah . . .

And what made you think he was a good idea?

I don't know. I seem to attract the wrong man all the time and that's why I've sort of given up on men right now.

But your husband, was he OK?

Yeah, but we just didn't get on . . . just didn't get on at all, so no point staying together if there's nothing there.

Do you think your personality has changed, then, since living on the streets?

Makes you stronger, being out here.

In what way?

It's made me . . . well . . . it's made me learn that I can survive, you know, and that there is a different life out here than there is with, you know, a front door . . . and being 'controlled'. I can say 'No!' now, you know? And it makes me feel good.

How do you find the money for the hostel?

Begging.

And how much can you make on a 'good day'?

It can take me three days to make £22 for the night in a hostel. It just depends.

So you spend most of your week begging for money to get inside on a Friday and Saturday night?

Yep . . .

. . . because you're too scared to be out?

Yep.

What do you do about food?

There's always food – you never go hungry in London. [A man bends down to give Charisse some coins.] . . . Thank you very much. There's so many people in London that bring you food, there's soup kitchens, day centres and you can have showers.

And do you use them?

Yeah, I have done, I have done.

Because you look clean and ordered and your sweatshirt is all beautiful and . . .

You have to keep your hygiene, no matter what.

Why is that important?

There is no excuse for being dirty. There is no excuse. Because there's always somewhere you can go to have a shower.

Yeah, but you've got to hike your stuff around.

Yeah, but it's not too bad, you know.

What do you keep with you? What are your possessions?

My sleeping bag and . . . er . . . just underwear, really. Clean underwear. You've got to have clean knickers!

[We stopped so I could run back into the station and get more hot drinks – the temperature had plummeted even in the time we'd been chatting. While she was stirring the whipped cream into her hot chocolate, a group of office workers walked by, within inches of us, looked down for a brief moment, and then went on their way, not missing a step.]

And a lot of people, they just don't acknowledge you.

Tell me about that.

Nine times out of ten, people will stare and look, but as soon as you smile at them, they'll quickly turn their heads and look away and like, 'Oh, I wasn't looking at you', and carry on walking. But then you get the ones that actually stop and say, 'Good morning, how are you today?' or 'Are you all right? Do you need anything?' . . . it's the people who do that that still make me feel that I am human, normal.

And the ones that don't, how do they make you feel?

It's make you feel like . . . you're invisible, invisible. That's how they make you feel – you're not here. It's because people have got a thing about problems – my problem is out there, in their face. Everybody has problems but they tend to keep them in a little box, locked up, and just forget about them, but *my* problem is out there, it's like, 'Oh no, no, no . . . we can't have that', you know?

But nine months living like this, for crying out loud ... I couldn't manage nine bloody days ... What effect has it had on your physical health?

My physical health has deteriorated because I have COPD [chronic obstructive pulmonary disease: an umbrella term that describes lung conditions that make it difficult to empty the air out of the lungs, leading to shortness of breath or the feeling of being tired]. Being homeless has made it worse but I still have to carry on with it. I'm lucky because Boots, in the station, have got my nebuliser in there and they don't shut till 11 p.m., so ...

What's a nebuliser?

It's an oxygen mask that you have to put liquid in ... three times a day I've got to take it. I went in and asked them if I could have it here, and they said, 'Yeah, that's fine.'

Ah, how nice.

Yeah, so I was really pleased with that.

Do you have anybody looking after your health?

Yeah, I've got a doctor at Lower Marsh, just down the road. They see me every week; I go in and have a check-up and make sure everything is all right.

And what else has deteriorated in your physical health?

Probably my looks! When you've got to have the same clothes on for a few days, it's not good ... but you've just got to put up with it.

As a woman, how does that make you feel? Not having make-up, not having a mirror, not being able to wash your hair when you feel like it?

Plain. Plain. That's the only word I can think of. Plain. I don't feel like I'm 'me'. Like, when I've got little jeans on and that, Uggs and a nice top and hair done ... yeah, brilliant! That's me! But when it's not, I'm just plain.

You seem like a quite strong, clear-headed woman, but you've obviously drastically changed from the woman that was living with that animal.

I've made myself – promised myself, not made myself – I promised myself that I would never ever let a man intimidate me or bring me down again. And it's made me a better person for it, I think. So, he's done me a favour! In a way.

Charisse, as I first saw her

This is so hard . . . it is absolutely bloody freezing out here – my arse is numb – and yet you had the courage to make this choice.

Yeah.

How do you feel about yourself, now?

Well, I'm still trying to get there.

How would you describe the 'me'? What's she like, this Charisse?

She's fun. She's happy. Everybody loved Charisse, you know. I'm one of those people who just love life. And you have to grab it with both hands and just take it, you know? And I'm never going to let anyone take that away again. And when I get back to that, I'll be like, 'Yay!'

Do you think about the future? How far ahead do you think?

I don't – not while I'm out here, I don't. I just think, 'Right, today's today, let's see what happens,' and I go day by day. I don't think ahead.

Why not?

Because out here, you can't. You can't.

Why?

You've got to think, 'Right, today I've got to make sure that . . . I've got something in my tummy, I've got clean clothes . . . I've got this and I've got that . . . try and make a bit of money towards the weekend, to get in to a hostel.' And that's the day-to-day life – it becomes a routine out here.

Does it leave you any free time for thinking?

Yeah, you get a lot of time to think, especially if you're sitting here or you're in the Festival Hall [just a few hundred yards away], and I've got a couple of books, as well, that I read, so, yeah . . .

What do you think about?

My kids, mainly. Just hope that they're OK and they're happy. Just that.

You never think about yourself and your future?

No, I've never put myself first.

Is this not the time?

No.

Why is this not the time to put yourself first?

It's not – I still have got to get indoors. When I get indoors, then that's my time. Because then I've got my roof, I've got a bed.

When you say 'get indoors' do you mean the Friday and Saturday nights?

No . . . when I get into a hostel, permanently.

Are you expecting that to happen?

Well, hopefully, yes, because I've been put on a list now, so . . .

How long might you have to wait?

They said it can take up to twelve months.

But there is a whole winter to get through.

Yeah . . . if it's below zero for . . . I think it's three days, four days . . . then they'll open 'cold weather shelters' and they take everybody in . . . but it's got to stay low – it has to be three consecutive days below zero degrees and then, as soon as it hits one degree above zero, they close them all back down again.

How does that make you feel?

I think that's wrong, because there's loads of empty buildings and everything.

What do think the difference is between 'one' and 'zero'?

Not a lot!

Can you feel the difference?

No! [laughs] Honestly, no!

What effect has all this had on your mental health?

I don't think that's changed much to be honest.

What's got worse and what's got better?

I don't think anything's really got worse, only the fact that, as I say, I've got to just get on with it . . . keep doing it . . . if you give up, out here . . . I've seen it, you know . . . I've seen people give up – they end up on drink and drugs – and then that's another thing in their life that they have to deal with, another problem.

Do you take drugs, or drink?

No.

You are very unusual . . . most people, in the end, they can't keep up the fight.

I understand why, and I do get it – because it is horrible out here – it's not nice. But you've just got to keep going, and have the faith that you're going to get out of it. If you really want to, you'll get out of . . . you'll be onto the next stage of your life.

What do you imagine as your future, if you picture it in your head?

I don't really. To be honest, the future could be anything. It could be a really good job and all that and then it could be really shitty and stuck on benefits, you know? It depends how you make your future.

Do you get lonely out here?

Yeah, you do. Everybody does, you know . . . it's not like you've got anybody to cuddle up to at night and say, 'Hey, babes, love you. Nighty night' – you miss that. You miss the little things as well, like switching on a light switch, and putting a kettle on and cooking a little meal or doing a sandwich and that . . . you miss them all, you do. And the things you take for granted, you don't realise and when they're gone, it's like *wow*.

Right, I've got to leave it there and stop – I've really got to make some money tonight!

What Charlie Told Me

On another one of my 'I feel ill' days – which were now nearly every day – I again decided to go to Camden. I don't know why I seemed to think this was somehow an easier day for me – nearer than the West End, true, but God, once there it was like being on stage in *Hieronymus Bosch Hellscape – The Musical*. Scott had talked about what a zoo the place was, and he was right. When King's Cross was being tarted up for the Eurostar, all the hapless and hopeless that had lived there for aeons were 'moved on', north into Camden, and were left to fend pretty much for themselves.

Walking around was, on one level, quite exciting, but it's a short step from excitement to alarm. I was looking at Camden in terms of people forging a life out here, and not as one of the many tourists who just saw it as a hip, thrilling, vaguely anarchic place to go shopping for vintage clothes and punk memorabilia.

I'd come across a very good-looking homeless guy called Charlie that morning and we'd gone and had coffee together, in the Costa on Camden High Street. Unlike Melissa or Scott, he'd looked at ease and comfortable in public company and I supposed his looks and style afforded him a certain protection. I only found out he was homeless because I'd seen him come out of a day centre. He looked like a male model – beautifully groomed and immaculate. Never would I have known that he owned nothing but the clothes he stood up in, a mobile phone and nail clippers (he told me he was a bit OCD about hand hygiene). His hands were indeed beautiful, like a surgeon's or a pianist's. He let me take photographs and record him but then changed his mind so I promised not to publish any of the material. And his name wasn't Charlie.

He said he had things going on in his life and wanted to focus on them. Other homeless people I spoke to but couldn't record or photograph had also been concerned about attracting some kind of unspecified fallout. I heard this, or versions of it, again and again: 'Hey, I'm sorry – can I change my mind? Can you wipe the recording? I'm worried about what might happen later, you know? Is that OK?' I never pressed this point as I was conscious of the fact that they were already anxious and vulnerable, so I just told them I was grateful for any knowledge that would help me understand how they felt about their life and I'd leave it at that.

What Charlie *did* share with me was how to find his mate, Edward.

Edward

'I would love to be able to put pictures up on a wall, to look at'

Finding Edward was like a treasure hunt. Charlie had given me step-by-step instructions to locate him, warning that Edward would almost certainly be asleep, but I wasn't to worry – all I had to do was find him and shout out the code word 'Frodo'. I was surprised that he might be asleep as Camden is phenomenally noisy and it was about midday by now. But all would shortly become clear.

As someone with a fixed address I am familiar with directions like, 'It's second on the left, off Argyle Street, number thirty-four. Ring the bottom bell.' Less so with, 'Keep walking that way for a bit till you see the railings round Regent's Park, by the zoo. Cross over and keep going till you see the Matilda Fountain. Then – and this is tricky, yeah – climb over the railing right under the statue. Sling your bag and stuff over first and reach up and grab one of the rocks at the bottom of the statue, and haul yourself up. Clamber down to the right and walk down the grassy slope . . . he'll be by the bridge. You can't miss him.'

And I didn't. Edward lived in a bright red tent.

He sounded very posh and he looked so young I half wondered if I needed his parents' permission to talk to him. He assured me he was thirty-seven years old.

The code word 'Frodo' worked, but unfortunately for me, Edward needed a large strong coffee before he could face talking, so I had to do the whole army-assault-course thing all over again, but with the added problem of navigating the home stretch whilst holding two tall takeaway coffees. Was I really doing this?

Make no mistake: being homeless in a tent is *not* same thing as camping in a crap place without your mates. It's a total fag. And another thing – despite the fact that Edward himself used the term 'rough sleeper' I absolutely loathe it; it makes homelessness sound vaguely optional or, worse, as if the homeless are nothing more than feckless Outward Bound extremists.

Edward was unlike any of the other homeless I got to know. Tormented and deeply analytical, homelessness was, for him, as much an intellectual conundrum as it was a practical misery. He was torn between the things that he saw as positive about his life and ordinary things – like a house and a family – that he yearned for but which remained beyond his grasp.

Edward

Can I smoke out here? I'm petrified of burning your house down.

Yeah, there's the ashtray [an old Coke can].

You look about twelve. Why don't you have wrinkles and lines?

I think it's because I smoke a lot of dope! Honestly! And I kind of 'live young', you know. I live outside the norms, the stresses of society. I like to think that I've emancipated myself.

How many years have you been living without an address?

I first slept rough ten years ago and the first six months it was hard – but then I found my whole paradigm changed about the world and how I see it . . . why do I need to panic about this? I can use this to my advantage. So, I went travelling for seven years to France, Italy and Australia – the same thing, just living in a tent or in hostels, you know, nowhere permanent. I lived in northern Italy, in Monza, for nearly two years and that was great fun. Then I came back six months ago and I'm in the same situation. I've been homeless, technically, for fifteen years.

So how did it come about?

My mum passed away, bless her, and the house where we lived was sold by probate and then I didn't have anywhere to live, basically. After a few years of renting, I didn't have the credit to get a deposit for a place. I moved into a squat about ten years ago and came up against a particularly nasty property developer who hired people off the street to threaten me with drills and all that and changed the locks. There have been other squats but they're not the nicest, cleanest of places . . . you get 'people who live in squats' in squats, so in a lot of ways it's easier and nicer to be on your own, if you've got a tent. At the moment I'm trying to build credit at an address that's not mine, so that I can then purchase property down the line or whatever.

Do you not feel vulnerable?

I used to. But now I just don't have time! The stress you get from the police or security guards hassling you or people taking your things – that's when it's 'stress'. There's quite a lot of junkies around who just shoot up and leave their rubbish lying around and go to the toilet, like, anywhere. You've no idea of the depths, of the things you see, when you're homeless.

What's the worst of living like this?

Not having running water and, you know, a toilet, things like that. If I want to use the toilet I have to go to McDonald's or I go to St Pancras. [We were in Regent's Park, so a fair distance away.] I know that there's a couple of Portaloos they keep at the church down the road, and they've given me the pass code for the doors, so I can go there. There are places to wash at the day centre – we call it the Asylum – it's cuckoo, that place.

Why?

Just the people there – they are mentally compromised by their living situation, by the fact that they have been ostracised by society – they've been pushed out.

So how old were you when you left school?

I finished school. I've got a degree in marine biology and a diploma in music technology. I've travelled the world and now I've come home. For me, being homeless isn't so much a barrier as a way to free myself from all the things that are going to tie me down – things like council tax, rent and things that I don't need.

Staying 'off the grid' – has that got appeal?

Yes – all you need to do is go to London Bridge at six o'clock in the morning and see all the people crossing the bridge or see all the people on the tube . . . What are they *doing*? A lot of those people aren't happy. I'm not saying mine is an ideal situation, but there is a compromise, and some things have to give and that's just the thing that's 'given', for me – I don't have anywhere to live.

Aren't you terrified that your stuff will get stolen when you leave the tent?

Well, that's a problem. But again, that's an emancipation thing – I don't really attach myself to those things, because I know that they can go. Easily. I take this kind of Buddhist philosophy that everything is transient and changes. You hope for the best but expect the worst. I don't expect my stuff to be here when I come back in the evening, so I'm not disappointed if it's not here. I just get on with it. I've got more interesting, or better ways to spend my time, than worrying.

How *do* you spend your time?

I like museums. I'm trying to get myself into a mode where I can write and I volunteer for Thames21, doing water quality testing and eel monitoring.

You count eels! What?!

Yeah, I count eels, and monitor fauna – that's for the Zoological Society.

The best thing about your life is what?

That I'm free. I can go anywhere – do anything – I want. I don't have any responsibilities to anyone, except that I get Support Allowance and that's my only obligation, to report to them.

And the worst thing?

The worst thing is not being able to accumulate, not to own any possessions. Anything that you can put somewhere, and keep there. I would love to be able to put pictures up on the wall, to look at, or have a TV to turn on. But there is a sense of spirituality that helps you to transcend materialism and be happy in that, and not worry you are missing out. I've still got devices and gadgets – I've still got all that stuff – I'm still really an eighteen-year-old!

What are you reading?

Conan Doyle's *Tales of Unease.*

What do you worry about most?

My needs are immediate – obviously, as you'd expect – but things like the cold – I'm waiting for the cold – so my next problem is to work out some way of getting solar power to power an electric blanket so I can keep warm at night. That's my biggest worry at the moment, really.

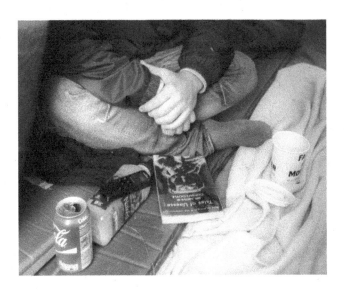

Yeah, I understand . . . so, not what's going on in the Middle East, then?

No, I couldn't give a monkey's to be honest! In a certain way it makes me feel free – OK, I might have to wrap up a bit warmer one night, but I'm fairly resilient. This isn't hard – roughing it like this is not hard – if it was in the Antarctic, then it would be hard, do you know what I mean? I've got a corner shop, I can go to the library, I've got the day centre. The services are good – people always complain about the services but they're there and you've got to be grateful to all the people who have set those things up for people like me.

One thing that it has taught me, being homeless, is not to be pessimistic and to give thanks. I walk around and I look at street lights and I think, 'I would like to thank that person who put that street light up because now I can see.'

What about the emotional aspect?

What, not having people, attachments, family? I have my grandparents who live in a home and my brother is my only other immediate family, but he lives in Australia. So, really I don't have any family. I don't have a wife, children.

Your dream for your future looks like what?

OK . . . [long silence] I'm not delusional in what I want. I'm realistic, so my hopes and dreams for the future . . . [long silence] to be honest, I don't know, because I don't think about the future too much.

Why not?

Obviously, I want to live in a flat or a house of my own just 'cos it would make life a lot easier. Even though I may look like I'm more independent than a lot of people, I still rely on government and services. Obviously, I couldn't have a family like this . . . so I have to think about that kind of thing – if I want to have a family I have to have a house or a flat to live in.

Have you been in love?

Yes. [long silence]

It's painful for you to talk about it?

No, it's not. It's amazingly joyful, actually, it was an amazingly wonderful thing. [long silence] For whatever reasons, I'm not any more. You know, the brightest flames burn fastest and hardest and in a lot of ways it is wrong to hold on to something when it has burned down a bit, so I'm not at all bitter or think back on that with any regret or nostalgia, even.

How would you describe your character?

Easy going to the point of complacency! Obviously, you don't end up like this without being negligent to your own needs, in certain ways, but then you have to compensate. Everybody has their challenges in life, and I just happened to have fallen through the cracks when most people wouldn't, because of lack of support or whatever other reasons. And I've ended up like this. This is the situation I'm in and I have a lot to be grateful for – there's a lot worse things to complain about for many people. I'm still able to work my way out of my situation here – it might be difficult but it's still all possible, and in a way this is just part of my story, part of my life story – and here I am.

What do you think about when you go to sleep at night?

[long silence] The same as everyone else – I have a very free conscience – that's one thing I am happy about. I sleep very easily and I'm comfortable in myself.

How do you think other people see you?

Probably as a vagrant, as a delinquent . . . but that doesn't worry me in the slightest.

What do you think your greatest talent is?

I speak four languages – French, English, Spanish and Italian. Well, my Spanish isn't great actually, sort of mediocre, sort of intermediate. Yeah, I went round Europe and I studied . . . and I can juggle!

Wow, you can *juggle*! How many things?

Only three, I'm afraid!

What about your physical health?

I have some old injuries, snowboarding and whatnot, that come back to haunt me. And it doesn't help, you know, living like this. Probably when next summer comes I'll get a hammock!

And your mental health?

A lot of people's depression, when they are homeless, is triggered by the fact that they haven't got anywhere to go back to – they aren't used to it. For me, I'm kind of used to it, you know, it's been ten years, so the depression side of it isn't such an issue for me. I've been through depression and it's really debilitating. There is a sort of realism that comes with living like this and I've got a depth of experience of the world that allows me to see this for what it is and not panic or not be in any kind of delusion about my own space and my place in it. I don't have any idea that I deserve anything. A lot of people who are homeless feel that the world owes them because they are out there and they don't have a place or whatever. I live a hand-to-mouth existence and my needs are immediate and not much more beyond that, so my everyday problems are probably far less than most people's. I have a different set of worries but my worries are very easy to satisfy – my worry is 'where am I going to sleep tonight?' – and they never last for more than twenty-four hours.

Do you miss the community of people?

No, I've got friends and I still socialise and my friends don't judge me. I don't beg and I don't do those things that put me in that bracket. I fill my time up with biology and stuff like Conan Doyle and things that allow my mind to stay away from these [mental health] problems. I'm over it, basically. And I don't think I would choose a different life to be honest. I have a measure of freedom.

An Asymmetrical Assembly

Edward was middle class and university educated – the first (but not the only) homeless person I met with a degree. Patrick O'Neil, who appears later on in these pages, has a languages degree, and there were three other people I encountered who had been undergraduates, although they didn't want to be in the book. Nevertheless, a high level of educational achievement was rare amongst those I met.

And there was something else that struck me. In all the weeks on the streets of this cosmopolitan metropolis, I had met only one black homeless person – Patrick – and he said I could use his picture but not interview him.

I encountered no Asians at all.

I met few women. Aside from the women you see in the book, there were just three others – two women in their twenties (both of whom had good reasons not to want to talk which, frustratingly, I can't share) and a very much older woman suffering from serious delusions and paranoia. Perhaps women are better hidden from view, and/or are less likely to walk away from their families. Or perhaps I just didn't happen to come across them when I was out and about.

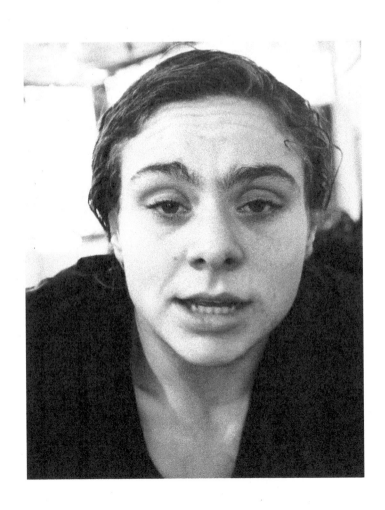

Jade Price

'I do go through the bins, I do pick up pizza off
the floor . . . all that . . . it makes me feel horrible.
I look around, like, "Is anyone watching me?"'

Micky, who had by this time – unbidden, I should add – styled himself into my aide-de-camp, put me on the trail of Jade. He described her and told me where I'd be likely to find her, which was anywhere in the backstreets of Soho. Eventually I caught up with her and we went to (yet another) tawdry cafe, this time on Rupert Street.

Over the coming weeks I regularly ran into Jade – she became important to me for the short time we had together, and I grew very fond of her.

Some nights, if I was just out with the camera, searching for pictures and not people, I would look for her and we'd sit together, usually outside Leicester Square tube station. It meant I could rest my legs and enjoy her company for an hour or so. She was engaging – a fighter, small, tough, scarred inside and out, and so brave. Her courage was only fractionally greater than the violence she lived with.

On our first meeting, she wanted doughnuts to eat. Homeless people seem to have a sweet tooth. She ate with the unabashed gusto that small children have, and her words came fast and furious, mingled with little puffs of icing sugar.

Jade had been homeless for most of the last eight years – a lifetime when you are only twenty-three years old. Before I turned on the recorder, I was asking general questions about her childhood and that was when I first heard her say she was 'daddy's little princess'. She said it with a smile.

Had I left it at that – walked away then – I would have thought, what a shame things ended so badly for her, but at least she'd had a loving father. And that would have been a huge, huge mistake.

Jade Price

I was raised by my nan and grandad because my mum was really young and was in a violent relationship with another man. Every Christmas I had with my mum got ruined . . . she just ended up battered . . . blood . . .

Once, when I was meant to go to *Stories from the Web* and Jacqueline Wilson was going to be there at the library, I remember him hitting my mum – I'll never forget it – he just lost it on her. And as he's hit her with the ashtray – 'cos the swing was that hard – my mum fell and it caught me in my face. My nan had to come and collect me and even though I had a black eye, I was still determined to go to the library. I *loved* Jacqueline Wilson books, I *loved* them!

I loved my nan and grandad. They raised me brilliant – basically, bed at seven and I had to do my homework. I was allowed contact with my real dad but he was always in and out of jail – theft, petrol robbing and criminal offences like that.

Yeah, when I was young, I was 'daddy's little girl' – he used to take me shopping and spoil me because when he used to commit crime it paid good money. He worked as a postman and was robbing all the people's Visas and cards. No one stopped me seeing him 'cos I never used to tell them nothing about what he did.

He's never abused me. Never. Never touched me. But the way my dad sees it, if we do smoke, drink or do drugs, he'd rather us do it in front of his face than behind his back. In case any of us died, or anything, he'd be there to phone the ambulance.

So, 'cos of watching my dad's lifestyle, that's how I fell into that lifestyle, from a very young age. I smoked my first cigarette at eight with my dad and I started hanging around with all the estate 'losers' . . . I was thirteen, fourteen, fifteen – smoking, drinking. Back at the age of ten, I found my dad using crack and I kept thinking, 'What's he doing?' We was in, like, a B&B, one room – that was all the council gave us – I didn't know he was using crack. [long silence] My dad gave me my first crack pipe at the age of ten. In my eyes I thought it was a good thing because it brought us that bit closer.

I've had my dad in the next room when I'm doing prostitution and he's going out and getting customers and then bringing them back. He had a £300-a-day habit. This is the worst thing – once he gave a man my number, saying it's this man's birthday and him and his mates, they wanted a girl – my dad told me to go off with the man who took me round to the churchyard, spunked all in my face, pissed all over me and left me there.

Altogether, my dad has got eight children from seven different mums. And I was the only one that had contact with my dad, all through. His other kids all dropped him, 'cos they all knew what he was like. My older sister has got cerebral palsy and she's blind. I don't even know if she's alive or dead. Her mum was my dad's first baby-mum and she lived on the same street as my mum did, so he started seeing my mum 'cos she was a little schoolgirl, only twelve. So, my mum got involved with him, skipped school, messed up all her exams, got pregnant and then comes me, when she was sixteen. He was twenty-three then. My dad has always gone for young, young girls. Then my dad met a young girl, she was thirteen but she turned fifteen by the time she had the baby. My youngest sister, Shelley, her mum was his youngest baby-mum, she was twelve. Shelley's a qualified hairdresser and everything and that's all because my dad weren't in her life.

It's only me, 'daddy's little princess', that went downhill. All the others have got a brilliant life.

I finished primary school and I was the first person in my whole year to get into one of the top schools in Birmingham and our headmaster, Sir Dexter Hutt, was knighted by the queen. But then, eight years ago . . . I went off the rails, and back on the street . . . but . . . that was only like for a couple of months and then I went back to my nan and my grandad's. [Jade got pregnant during this period, aged sixteen, but didn't want to talk about the father.]

I've got a little seven-year-old daughter, living with my mum! Got pictures of her on my Facebook! I'll show you one, I've got to show you one . . . there's a McDonald's up the road and they've got a tablet there with free internet . . . so, we'll pop up there.

My mum messed up with me – she weren't my mum – my nan and grandad were. My mum's just turned forty. I was her only child, before, but now she's just had a little baby and my daughter loves her to bits. My daughter does dancing with the dance group, she got silver for tap dance. She does tap dance, ballet and disco and now she's just been taken on in a school theatre!

My mum wants me home, to live with her, but . . . with the way I am at the moment . . . yeah, I'm off heroin, I'm off crack . . . rephrase that . . . I'm off heroin and I'm off alcohol . . . I'm still on crack . . . it's . . . the way I am.

I know I'm going to die soon. I've got two blocked arteries, a damaged heart valve – all through heroin – it clotted all around my heart when I was injecting in my groin.

I'm petrified. I'm petrified of dying. But I try not to think about it. I just can't think about it, but I know when I die I'll be with my grandad . . . I won't see my little girl, but I will know that she's in safe hands with my mum.

Six years ago, I lost my grandad – just before Christmas – that ripped me apart. Even to this day I can't get over it because I was so close to my grandad. Before he died, he got the chance to see his first ever great-grandchild! And I'll never forget when he first saw my daughter, he goes, 'Jade, I've seen the way you are around her – you are a fantastic mum, keep it up.'

When I lost my grandad, I put myself on a life-support machine by injecting heroin. I put myself in a coma. They told my mum I wasn't going to see Boxing Day. I just wanted to be with my grandad – even to this day, like, I miss him *so* much. I'd do anything just to be with him. With my grandad dying, I've gone really, really down . . . emotionally, physically.

I've been pretty well homeless for eight years, since I was fifteen. On and off, but my longest time now is the last two years. This will be my second Christmas straight on the street.

I think I was the one who went downhill because my dad is a bad influence . . . he's made me like this. He's got quite bad psychosis – he's stabbed the bed when I was *sleeping* in it. I wasn't scared. I was 'daddy's little girl' and I was young and I didn't care.

But even though I've gone through this episode of going downhill, I *will* succeed and I'm going to push myself.

I'm going to work with disabled children. Or the elderly. Because my sister, she's disabled. And also because everyone slates disabled people, but do you know what? They are fantastic, amazing proper people. I'd never put disabled people down, ever.

It's like, on the street, I met a disabled boy two weeks ago . . . he was only about four, five and 'cos it was Halloween, I made, like, a little scary creature and everybody called it Harriet. It was like a pumpkin, but it had legs on the side, like a spider, but a furry one – and it was fantastic, it was – and I let the little boy take it home.

Truthfully, the last seven or eight years I've just had to try and survive. I've been emotional. It's just horrible . . . it is actually horrible, outside . . . *everyone* just walks past you. I've cried through the night, some nights . . . you're *that* hungry and you're *that* tired and because it's been raining and you can't sleep and you're really, really cold as well, and I've had no blanket . . . I've survived a lot of my homeless life with no blanket. Straight up.

And there's people coming out of the pub and weeing all over us – it's drinkers coming to the pub, coming clubbing – they get drunk and think, 'Oh, let's do this little silly thing.' I get weed on, so then I have to throw my blanket away – and when you lose a *blanket* . . . I break down. Emotionally. I just start crying. And the worst thing is, when that's happened, it's always the next day when you're hungry and you've got no blanket and everyone still walks past you. Not caring.

I've been set on fire. And I'm just a young girl that was asleep. I've got a few little scars from it, to this day, where the zip caught on my knuckles and in the cold, all of that still gets infected, to this day. Also, bottles of vodka over my head.

There's been days when I've been really, really hungry and I've asked people for 99p for a cheeseburger and they say, 'You're a tramp – go through the bins.' Like this morning, it took me five hours just to get £5.

Sometimes, there's nice, genuine people that buy you a McDonald's or they go to Tesco and do a little shop for you . . . chocolate and bits and bobs. But, yeah, when I can't get food, I *do* go through the bins, I do pick up pizza off the floor . . . all that . . . it makes me feel horrible. I look around, like, 'Is anyone watching me?' Sometimes, I have bought food. If somebody gives me money and says to buy food, I respect their wishes and I do buy food.

For money, I sleep with dealers and then they give you the ten-shot [a £10 syringe of heroin]. Some of them will smoke all night with you and look after you and *not* want sex.

And prostitution – it's the only way to cope for money out here – for the simple fact that when we beg on the street, which I find *so, so* hard 'cos everyone walks past, looks down at you – and not one of them has taken the time and said, 'All right? How are you?' A little 'Hello' would be fine, it makes you feel stronger. That's what I recommend to people – if you don't want to talk to the homeless, at least say 'Hello' and smile because that will make them feel a little bit stronger.

Showing off her newly donated shoes

Believe it or not, people give more to the men beggars. But the *women* beggars . . . men want something for it. It degrades you. Makes you feel worthless – but at the same time, when you can't get the money, the only option . . . it's either prostitution or robbing people. And I won't go out there and rob.

When I first come on the street I was bad for drugs, *bad*, and I was doing like six men a night. The money depends. £20 – that's just a quick handjob. A blow job, £40, and £60 for sex *and* a blow job. Some have offered me an extra £100 to go without a condom but I will not risk my life. Like with needles – I've *never* shared a needle – there's so much HIV out on the streets.

I don't have a bank account so I can't get benefits – 'cos I haven't got ID. I've never had ID in my life.

The drugs block it all out. The thing is, when you're doing prostitution, there's no feeling, no thought – you just lie there. I done a man, the other day, and I was lying there with him on top of me – we went into a 50p-for-twenty-minutes toilet round the corner, a little cubicle on the street. He took me there – he just said he wanted a blow job and sex and would give me £50 and I thought, 'Yeah, I'm hungry, I'm tired and I need a new blanket . . .' We got in the cubicle and he's passed me the money – and the deal was sex and a blow job – but he was big and he told me to lie down on the floor and he shoved it straight up my bum. He put his hand over my mouth and said that if I moved, he was going to take the money and come in my face. But then, when he came, because the twenty minutes weren't up and there were ten minutes left, he went, 'Nah, I'm not letting you out,' and he's literally grabbed me by my hair and put me over his knee and spanked my bum *that hard*. He's just one man that works around here. I was screaming, crying and shaking and no one heard because it was the early hours of the morning and it's surrounded by, like, a building site.

I don't sleep at night. Because with everything that's happened to me, I'm petrified. I *will not* lie there at night, asleep. I try and sleep in the day. I go to Oxford Street, sometimes outside Boots, but when you are asleep no one gives you a penny, or, if someone *has* left money there, another homeless has come and taken it, so you wake up with no money anyway. It helps if I do my Sudoku – I love it! I've finished four books of 500 puzzles and I read the newspaper.

[Jade had such a glorious smile, and I wanted to know where it came from.] It's hiding everything. It hides my whole life, all the pain, the hurt, I just sort of smile through it. That's what I've had to do. The only time I've had a real smile was with my nan and grandad, and giving birth and being with my daughter.

[When we had finished talking, Jade mentioned again her love of Sudoku and that she had once had one of those 'adult colouring books' – full of complex and beautiful drawings that you colour in – that help people to relax. I offered to take her shopping for one . . .]

Fantastic! They kept me off drink before – got me off heroin before – and I miss it now, I'd love a colouring book again. Yeah, straight up, one of them ones with the patterns! They like, keep me from getting emotional, keeps me from stressing. I can just sit there and colour . . . I don't even *care* if anyone gives me money!

Language and Loneliness

Back at the flat with Alice, the night after I met Jade, I was subdued and uncommunicative. I felt a species of shame – how could Jade and I be living within five miles of each other and yet experience life in Britain so differently?

So I was trailing around the flat, feeling gloomy and trying to find space on the radiators to hang up my laundry. Alice said, 'You're not saying much – you OK?' and I realised how taciturn I was being. That led me to think about why we deliver our speech in the ways that we do and why the same words can come out sounding so different. There are so many ways to arrange spoken words, to deliver them, accenting them with silences or pauses and decorating them with tone. So difficult to convey all that when you write them down on paper.

I recorded thirty people for this collection, but I spoke to more than twice that number 'off the record', as it were. I suppose it's just as well they were all happy to talk but unwilling to appear in these pages – you'd have needed a low-loader to get the book home.

I had thought a lot about *what* the people I had been spending time with were saying, but not very much about *how* they were saying it. Nomadic, largely alone and ostracised, I started to notice that the homeless sometimes spoke in ways that were unfamiliar to me.

A funny thing happened almost every time I met someone new. Before turning on the recorder, I would have already explained about the book and we would have introduced ourselves. Then, when I pressed 'record', I'd ask them to repeat their name, for the tape. At this point they would say, 'Simon Blythe, 18 November 1987' or 'Claire Watts, born 7 July 2001'. Jade even wrote her date of birth next to her signature on a little note that she wrote for me (see the Fault Lines chapter). It dawned on me that this was how most of their discourse began, because most of it was with the establishment. When they're arrested for something they know that the first thing they're going to be asked by the police officer is their name and date of birth (the rest of us would also have to give an address but, well . . .). The same sort of thing applies when they go into a day centre or stay in a night shelter – they must give their name and date of birth – it's just an automatic response.

It was unusual for them to have unofficial conversations of any length. So many homeless people had told me how good it felt to sit and *talk* – and not with an outreach worker, a doctor or a cop, but just an interested human who had no expectations and was happy to sit and chat in a companionable, relaxed way about anything and everything. When I was younger I lived briefly in Moscow and learned Russian – I spoke it well enough, with a reasonably extensive vocabulary. When I came back to London, I stopped speaking Russian because there wasn't anyone else around to talk to in that language and now I've entirely forgotten most of it.

Is it the same dynamic with the homeless? With less opportunity for conversation, in the sense that you and I have, do they lose the knack of free-flowing, reactive and organised speech? Is their natural lack of trust limiting the subjects that can be talked about? Is conversation reduced to logistics, offers and acceptances of help?

Jade's speech had been virtually unpunctuated; a friendly tirade of events – connected but still a little random. She had a huge amount she wanted to say, and it all came pouring out, one idea never quite finished before the next started. Almost like she felt I would suddenly stop being interested, so she had to tell me absolutely *everything* as fast as she could. A lot of people talked to me like this.

Beth was more staccato and spoke as if she were reading a potted version – a timeline, almost – of her own life. None of the 'I suppose I felt that I . . .' or 'I wondered if . . . ?' There was a notable absence of self-description.

Others, like Edward and John Matthews, were self-aware and self-analytical, and talked in the general, almost existentially.

All the characters in this book were, however, masters of under-statement.

Words uttered almost in passing left me slack-jawed and saying things like, 'You *what?*' and 'Sorry? What did you just say?' so many times you'd have thought English wasn't my mother tongue.

I can't imagine how damaging it must be not to have people to talk to; surely it would erode your sense of self? With the ruination of time, illness, cold and misery, the homeless become distorted and the exterior they end up showing the world is a sort of shabby, angry, run-down and wounded *un*person. Who wants to talk to someone like that?

It is difficult to discern the power of a pause or the choked pain in a voice in the written word. These stories you're reading can't easily convey the halting voices, the uneven delivery of those unused to talking logically and at length, or the sobs and silences. All arising, I suspect, from a long, lonely and largely isolated existence. I must have said, 'Take your time, there's no hurry at all' a hundred times.

A word or two on loneliness and isolation. The American military has a little book called the *Army Field Manual* – a sort of 'how to torture people and get away with it' guidebook. It describes the best way to destroy a person, to break that person down – physically and emotionally.

Their method?

Keep a person separated from other people and foster a *'feeling of futility'.*

Manu

Manu was hard to miss. He was sitting on the pedestrianised area in front of the National Gallery, drawing chalk flags of seemingly every nation on the planet. Dozens and dozens of them, in colourful serried ranks. They were remarkable, really, and over the coming weeks I would find that his detailed and painstaking work attracted lots of crowds and admiring passers-by. Children especially liked to be with him as he encouraged them to take the chalk and add to the great unfolding masterpiece. I will remember Manu for his flags and the laughter he created around him.

He came to London from Algeria thirty years ago. He was just out of his teens and here illegally but found work and, for the next twenty years, he slaved away as a chef in kitchens around the country.

He had a job, a girlfriend, money in the bank and a nice home – 'I was happy. I was very happy. It was beautiful my life, beautiful.' Then, in 2005, the Home Office learned of his illegal entry into the UK, decades before, and took away his passport while they decided what to do with him. Bad enough, but then they lost about 175,000 people's documents. Manu was one of them. Now undocumented, he couldn't work and, as he puts it:

'In a split second, everything went downhill. I had been working illegally – fake name, fake ID – fake everything. I can't get another home now because of my immigration status. I'm still waiting for my passport. It's been ten years now.

'You never know what's around the corner. In the early days I slept behind Tesco in Piccadilly Circus. I was scared. I'll be honest with you, I was shoplifting to survive. These days I've got the day centre helping me out and I'm doing some volunteering for them now – looking after new clients [homeless people], showing them around.

'I don't get any benefit and I live on the money from doing these flags and street art. Because I earn my own money I don't do handouts – there's free food in London but I don't go there because some people have no money and I don't want to take their food, you know? I'm not greedy.

'I lost my kidney in 2011 [pulling up his top to reveal a long, savage looking scar] and I was diagnosed with TB from sleeping in the street and eating shit food, being cold – plus I was drinking and taking drugs, but now I'm healthy and I'm feeling good. I was in hospital for a month – they gave me medication and the TB was gone. But, I lost my kidney, I think it was on the Friday, and on the Sunday I was back on the street because they hadn't space in the hospital for me to stay.

'The worst is the cold. And people – they kick you. I had a friend, he was set on fire, and a friend who was kicked when he was sleeping – myself, I was pissed on. Can't get any worse, can it?'

[I interrupted] . . . **Yet I watched you with the kids earlier – getting them involved in the drawing – where are you getting that sense of joy?**

'I've been doing this for seven years now. I'd been sitting in here in Trafalgar Square, drinking and acting stupid and I saw a guy, a young man, roughly twenty years old, and his mum and dad pushing him along in a wheelchair. I looked at him and smiled and he smiled at me . . . I looked at my friends and said, "Look, I'm forty-plus. What am I doing? Let's do something."

'And I started doing the flags. Make everyone happy. Make me happy. Talk to people.'

Stain Removal

A little before each daybreak the council's men and machinery wash away the human stains of the homeless and their lonely nights.

Manu was always fun to be with – upbeat, indefatigable. If I'd been out all night, taking pictures or chatting in that neck of the woods, I'd sometimes look for him just after sunup. We'd sit on the steps of the National Gallery and share a smoke.

But he didn't really have time to talk much after 8 a.m. because every morning, before the tourists and groups of schoolkids all started arriving, he had to redo everything he had painted the day before. During the night, the council would have scrubbed away all traces of the work he had so lovingly created – a reminder that he didn't really exist, not *really*. He was Sisyphus with a piece of chalk instead of a rock. Punishment without end, for sins committed more than a quarter of a century ago.

Steve Young

Things went very badly wrong with Steve Young before they got better.

Steve and his mate, Paul, had been sleeping on the pavement outside Charing Cross Station a few feet up from a little glass-fronted coffee bar. I came along at about nine o'clock in the morning, and noticed the paintings that Paul did, lined up against a wall just up from the coffee bar, which he was selling for a fiver to passers-by.

Paul agreed to talk to me and so we moved over to one of the tables outside the bar and sat down. Steve disappeared round the corner while I explained to Paul my ideas for the book. Steve returned ten minutes later with two things he hadn't left with: one was a large bottle of whisky, and the other was the now certain belief that I was going to upset his friend, Paul, by letting him open up and talk about his life.

Alarmingly quickly, Steve became convulsed with rage. He was saying, not unreasonably, that once I'd gone, it would be *him* who had to pick up the pieces of Paul, who he predicted would be an emotional wreck after talking about his past. So I said to Paul, 'Look, Steve's got a point . . . when we're done talking, I'll walk away and you'll be the one who's upset after opening up all your old wounds and Steve'll be the one who has to look after you.' Brilliantly handled, I thought – giving him the choice *in front* of Steve.

Not so brilliant when Paul said, 'Well, Steve can fuck right off. It's none of his fucking business and I can make up my own fucking mind.' Great. Now I'd caused a row. Steve was now choleric and started circling around the table and putting his face very close to mine, spitting with fury. I was doing my whole UN peacekeeping thing, using a relaxed, conciliatory tone and trying to keep the idea of a punch-up at bay and casualties to a minimum.

Stupidly, I only noticed that about one third of the bottle of whisky had been emptied into a used plastic Coke cup at the point when the *second* third was being poured. This was over the space of about fifteen minutes and nobody *seemed* to be pissed, but Paul's words were now getting a little slurred. He was also becoming what my grandmother would have called 'fresh'; quite liberal with his embraces and rather too many kisses planted on my face.

Steve abruptly backed off, saying darkly, 'You stupid cow, you don't know what you're starting.'

He reappeared soon after and seemed to have abandoned his role as Paul's protector as quickly as he had adopted it.

He stopped patrolling around the table and announced – to my surprise and, if I'm honest, horror – that *he* wanted to participate too. I could see a hundred ways that this could go badly wrong, so I said gamely, 'Look,

I'm not being funny, yeah, but I think you're a bit pissed and I don't want anyone saying later that I took advantage of a bloke who wasn't exactly sober. You know what I mean? Plus, I'd feel bad if you said things you might wish you hadn't, you know, later on . . .'

To which he replied, 'Don't be fucking daft – I'm a paranoid schizophrenic and I did twelve years for attempted murder. And look at these machete scars! *No one* takes advantage of *me*!' This was getting worse by the minute. Steve then proceeded to stand on one leg for about five minutes to demonstrate his sobriety. I was absolutely baffled and sat mute, with no idea of what the appropriate response was: should I smile encouragingly or pretend this wasn't happening? In the end, I did what I often do: I took a photograph.

Eventually, I turned on the recorder and handed it over to Steve. Empowering, I thought.

Just as we were about to begin, a couple of men turned up, apparently looking for a fight with Steve. He seemed quite happy to oblige. There was a brief scuffle with a bit of pushing and shoving but nothing too dramatic. I managed to get a couple of shots of the scrap. Steve saw off the aggressors with some menacing threats but wouldn't tell me what it was all about. While I was a touch tachycardic he seemed totally unfazed. We picked up where we had left off.

I told him to hold it close to his mouth while he told me about himself.

I think Steve must have crushed the recorder in his hand during the earlier ruckus because when he gave it back to me it was a slightly different shape and it never worked again. I had to recall our conversation later as there was no recording for me to transcribe. I'd have to buy another one at the Argos farther up on the Strand. Good job I always checked the recorder after every conversation.

Steve was thirty-two years old when he realised that his mental illness was a danger to those around him, so had walked away from his wife and family. He was educated, had O-levels and said he was creative and loved music – especially soul and rock – which calms him.

He managed his schizophrenia with booze and drugs and lived in a permanent state of fear that he would 'kick off' – a concern I wholly shared. Mostly, he said, he was lonely – 'I wake up at five o'clock and by half past eight I'm not sure I even want to live. No one can help me.' When he wasn't lonely, he said he was angry. He had worked as a manager at a well-known chain store but couldn't hold down the job. He'd had flats in the past, but could never stay in them – the walls closed in on him and he panicked. He has to be constantly moving or he would go mad.

Eddy Copeland

Eddy was slumped against the wall, outside McDonald's at King's Cross, so exhausted he couldn't hold his head up. He had a thick beard and a crooked smile. He hadn't slept in days and there were only pennies in his begging cup. That afternoon he was too shattered to talk to me, but he told me to come back in a day or two.

When I did return, it was simply too cold for me to cope with being out so I dragged the poor man into McDonald's – the homeless are sick to death of McDonald's – because it was close and Eddy was still exhausted and couldn't manage to walk very far. We settled down in a little booth and as we ploughed through our burgers and Cokes, Eddy took me quietly through his life.

When he was fifteen, he came home from school and found his mum dead on the kitchen floor.

She had overdosed on heroin. That was more than twenty years ago. Eddy never knew who his father was but had adored his mother and never recovered from her death. It precipitated his descent into failed relationships and then homelessness. 'When I think about my mum I know she's safe now and watching over me. It's not time for me yet, so she's keeping me alive. She was in a lot of pain, my mum, yeah.'

He worked as a roofer and started a family. Now, he wanted to get that life back:

'It's hard being without family. I'm still taking the heroin but that's to stop me thinking about my mum. I used to be an alcoholic but I've been sober now nine months. I spend about a tenner on the heroin, every day, like. I smoke cannabis as well, and that helps.

'I can make quite a lot of money begging – a good day I can make £80 or £90. I just sit down and ask nicely! Being polite, have manners. [Eddy thought he might now have a place in a hostel.] That will be a step forward for me but it's still sleeping on a floor with loads of other men and I'll have to pay for it each night.

'Sometimes I am lonely, it's hard. Hard. You've got no one to talk to – it's not nice at all. You're sleeping on your own and there's nobody there to talk to. With the other homeless we just talk about what's happened in the day, how much money you've made or whatever. I just wish I could have my mum in my life and – if I could – my wife and my children back. I've got two kids. I was fifteen or sixteen when I had my first child – I have two, they're twenty-three and twenty-two now. I haven't seen them since they were eleven years old – because after I found my mum it all just fell apart – and then the drugs. I could get in touch with my kids but . . . I don't know . . . I just don't want them seeing their dad being homeless, basically. Sometimes I phone them. Now and again.

'All I've got is a sleeping bag. Nothing else – what I've got is what I've got on me! Literally. Being in the same clothes all the time – it's not nice.

'But them, out there [looking through the McDonald's window, onto the street] they just think, "Look at that person on the floor, homeless, filthy, stinking." Some people do have respect, come up to talk to me . . . but the others? Why don't you try it for a night and see how you like it? The world is pretty crap, to tell you the truth.'

Jason

Despite the diversity in people's stories, there was only one profession I came across more than once amongst the homeless I met: soldiering. It seems a disproportionate number of war veterans – in comparison with other professions – end up penniless on the streets.

Jason's story was similar to most of the other ex-military men I would meet (with the notable exception of Darren O'Shea, who appears later in this book) but these men felt too ashamed to be recorded talking about their lives and loves which had disintegrated when they came home from war.

Jason left South Africa when he was thirteen years old and was adopted by another family. He got married and had five kids – two sons and three daughters – and had lots of pictures of them on his phone. He stayed married for twenty-five years.

He spent seventeen years in the Parachute Regiment. His last posting was in Afghanistan, where he'd served before. He loved his life in the army and came out as a staff sergeant, ten years ago.

'I had mental problems – seeing what I saw out there – I really don't want to talk about that . . . I can't . . . I was shot . . . [shows me the wound, on his neck] the bullet hit the floor and then broke into pieces and one of those pieces hit me. I wanted to stay in the army, but they offered me a desk job with Army Careers – I'm a front-line soldier. I saw a lot of shit. You know? I was out in Angola and you people don't hear about it, you know? We did a lot of shit out in Africa – not good. I was born in Africa so it was like a homecoming except it wasn't . . . like when I came back here.

'I see the kids all the time. My daughter, the one you just saw a picture of, she lives in a hostel – because when I split up with my wife, she came with me. The kids aren't happy about my situation – they think the government should be helping me a lot more. The army hasn't helped me. Not at all. I did ask for help. I started doing a bit of counseling and that but it wasn't for me – a waste of time – a load of bollocks if you ask me! So, I got up one day, from the session and said, "Sorry, you're talking shit. Goodbye."

'All I'm glad of is that my grandchildren are grown up and all lovely. My ex-wife hasn't got all of the house – I left her 35 per cent of the house – and the rest of it I signed over to my grandchildren. So, whatever happens to me, their college is paid for.

'I'm an ex-heroin addict, but I've been clean now, five years. When it all fell apart, I was on the street in Brighton and then I came back up here. This was only a few years ago, darling, I haven't been up here that long but I've been homeless on and off for ten years.

'Now, I'm someone who *can't* be inside. Believe it or not, I got given a flat, by a charity, over in Maida Vale, because I've been on the streets so long. I went there for two nights – but now I can't go in, because I'm too used to being outside. I don't feel I can . . . all the walls coming in on me, and everything . . . I can't even sleep in a bed no more.

'The drink, it just blanks things out. I started, first of all, with amphetamines and then heroin. When you've got a bit of gear inside you, you don't give a fuck, and I suppose the alcohol is the same as well. I'm a recovering alcoholic – I have had a couple of drinks today, but that's just to stop me rattling. I don't drink to get myself off my face, you know what I mean? I drink just to keep myself level.

'If you'd talked to me last year, you wouldn't have been talking to me, Jason – you'd have been talking to "J the Idiot", who was paralytic up there [on street level] on three or four bottles of whisky or vodka a day. Seriously. And then I had a heart attack, walking across Oxford Street, coming out of Tesco with a bottle of vodka in my hand. I was fighting with the paramedics and the police – just to get my bottle of vodka back, yeah!

'I stayed in hospital for three weeks. When I came out, the silly thing was, I came back straight on the street. I did go to a night shelter but I bumped into a couple of mates, and I went back on the piss again, didn't I?

'If I'm lucky, I'll get three or four hours sleep a night, and if I'm really lucky, I'll get five. I don't like sleeping in the day – I like keeping awake. Don't feel safe.'

The Side Effects of Sound Effects

Within days of starting out I was exhausted, had a permanent headache and a nasty cold. When I came up to what would turn out to be the half-way mark of my trip, I was really starting to struggle. It was mortifying. I'd started out well-nourished and healthy, and every twenty-four hours I'd be in a soft, safe, dry bed. Hot water whenever I wanted. What was wrong with me?

True, I'd done loads more walking than I was used to and the head-aches were probably from the exhaust fumes which feel much thicker at ground level. But I suspected they were also related to the sheer magni-tude of what I was hearing.

I heard two types of sounds, ceaselessly, it seemed: the voices of the homeless and the sounds of the street. Each took a different kind of toll on me.

On one level I was enjoying the psychological space I occupied, and the mostly good-natured and hospitable people I was hanging out with. The homeless are really interesting to talk to but I was also soaking up all their stories of injustice, pain, rage, loneliness and hurt and it began to weigh heavily on me. It made me care about them more, respect them more. It also made it harder for me to get to sleep – even under a goose-down duvet.

As for street noises, there is no backing track I can let you listen to. Just believe me when I say the only way to replicate the sound effects (sirens, bus air-brakes, screams, traffic, feet, building works, lorries loading and unloading – just for starters) would be to stick your head inside a Dyson vacuum cleaner, turn off the eco setting and dial it up to 2,000 watts. The sounds are migraine-inducing during the day and unsettling at night.

I was perpetually chilled, sitting on freezing pavements in dirty, dusty gusts of wind. Some days I thought my cheekbones would splinter from the vindictive wind nipping at my face. My clothes were filthy (especially my cuffs, for some unfathomable reason) by the end of a single day. For the first week my feet were raw with blisters and thereafter felt like two lumps of wood superglued to the end of my legs.

I can't remember one day of decent weather, but that could be my faulty memory. I was forever washing my hands in cafes and my clothes and hair smelled funny, like a blocked storm drain or a swamp. I folded with exhaustion as soon as I got home.

And there's that word again. Home.

Jane Durham and Kenny Green

'We do have arguments . . . But we can't be parted – everywhere she goes, I go, and everywhere I go, she follows me'

They were a scream, really. Beaten down time and again but always coming back with their chins up and their teeth gritted. With a combined age of more than 120 years, they were worthy of respect.

I had been heading back to Waterloo to find Charisse and have another chat with her, but had no joy on that front. Needing the loo and yet more coffee, I headed down into the concrete bowels of the brutal rotunda that is the IMAX cinema, where I knew there was a Costa and clean facilities. I was in such a hurry I didn't see Jane and Kenny on my way in but caught sight of them on my less hasty exit.

They were properly bedded down on – and under – several grubby white duvets, alongside suitcases and bags covering about ten square metres. An impressive encampment. I introduced myself and was immediately invited to join them, but not until I'd bought several more coffees for all of us. I was charged with bringing back as many sachets of sugar as I could get away with without attracting the attention of the security guard. (What was happening to London? Security guards in a *cinema* now?)

I've interviewed tons of people in my working life but it was the first time I'd ever said, 'You sure it's OK for me to sit on your bed?' It was a dismal, rainy afternoon, the corners of their bedding were soaking wet, and there were leaves and litter all over the place.

They called this awful place 'Middle Earth'.

Jane Durham and Kenny Green

Jane: My mum was a schoolteacher so I could read before I went to school. I took what were GCEs then and O-levels and A-levels. But I just wanted to be a cook! I've done a lot of 'carer' jobs, as well, and I did train as an SEN Nurse – I wish I'd done the extra year so that I'd be an SRN – but I'm too old now, though. I last worked about nine years ago. I miss the people. And the pay packet, obviously!

I've got four children – I left and came to London with my children. That was years ago, mind. I miss my children. I do. I see them occasionally – when I can. They don't live that far away, but there isn't enough room in their house. They feel really bad about my situation and they think it is disgusting.

I worked in a pub as a manager and had accommodation upstairs, that was part of the package. But then they got in a new manager and he didn't want me living in the flat, so that was that . . . this was just before I met Kenny in the hostel.

Kenny: I was living in a hostel, for the homeless, in Clapham, when Jane arrived. Before she met me, she was sleeping rough, on her *own* in Kenton Park. In the hostel, there was a guy who used to molest her – off-camera, the security camera there – and she got pissed off with it. One day she was crying and she told me what this man had been doing to her. So, when I found out I . . . *retaliated*. I beat him up so I was imprisoned. For twenty-eight days. That's how I left the hostel and that's how I became homeless. This was eleven years ago. I looked after her for six months and then one day, I asked her for a kiss! We've been together ever since.

Jane: Kenny looks after me. Nobody else. I'm a bipolar, I've got heart disease, that tachycardia where your heart doesn't beat as it should, I've got COPD [the same lung condition that Charisse had developed], liver disease and a few other things . . . psychotic episodes.

After the hostel, I was put in a temporary place in east London – it was absolutely riddled with rats.

Kenny: . . . and mice. We were watching the TV one night and she could hear some scratchings and she said, 'There's rats there, Kenny', you know, behind the skirting board. I went into the kitchenette and I could see them on the top of our sink. So I killed one and I put it in a plastic bag and gave it to Jane to take to the housing office – she ditched it on the carpet there!

Jane: They were jumping on their chairs!

Then they gave us a place where you could only stay for two years and then you are supposed to find your own . . . *way*, sort of thing. We left there and since then we've been in 'temporaries' or on the street. The council have assessed us twice and twice they've said we're not enough of a 'hardship' case. People keep coming and saying stuff but nothing seems to be happening. I don't believe them. The outreach teams? We call them the *out of reach teams* . . .

Kenny: Yeah, she's sixty-two and I'm sixty-one, and trying to look after her.

Jane: We went to the council and they said that they have to assess us. The place they put us in? The most *deplorable* place imaginable. Half the roof was falling down, it was a fire hazard, no hot water, no electricity, no heating . . .

Kenny: We've been here for months now, and in the good summer weather, we surface to the 'top', like.

We just cope with what's around us. As soon as I wake up in the morning, Tam, I like to buy a newspaper and a cup of tea or coffee, and read it and be left alone in peace, doing my crossword – then I'm happy. And I read.

When I was a kid I always used to read. My mother used to buy a magazine called *True Detective* and at night when she fell asleep it would fall out of her hand, onto the floor, and I used to creep in and thieve it, go to bed and read it and then take it back before she woke up! At the minute, I'm halfway through a Jeffery Deaver book called *The Empty Chair*. Jane likes Charles Dickens.

Jane: They're all based on poverty and children in poverty, aren't they? It interests me, it does. Because he was a man of substance, and he didn't like what was going on around him in Victorian England – with children and workhouses and things like that. So all his books are pretty traumatic, aren't they?

I like horror too, so I'm very into Edgar Allan Poe, they are terrifying – 'The Tell-Tale Heart' – the guy who kills somebody and thinks he can hear his heartbeat under the floor . . . the man was a lunatic. And I also like one particular book of Oscar Wilde, *The Picture of Dorian Gray*, and that's about a boyfriend he had, isn't it?

[We stopped chatting when I was sent to get more hot drinks. As I walked back towards this elderly couple, I felt such a wave of sadness at how forlorn and exposed they looked. I asked them what they felt like, inside . . .]

Jane: You feel like an animal, actually, don't you, Kenny?

Kenny: Sometimes, if we have to go somewhere, we leave this cardboard here, if it's dry. Sometimes, when you're here and it rains, it draws the rain inside. But underneath your bottom, there's a mat [shows me a bedroll], it's to keep you off the concrete, 'cos the cold gets into your bones. Sometimes, when I go to bed, I sleep with my boots on as well. In case there are any intruders at night.

There's a lot of different types of begging, right? Well, we are *not* beggars – we never ask *nobody* for *nothing*. It's not in my nature to do so. The police call us 'silent beggars' – which we are not, but you do get a lot of good Samaritans who pass by and drop you £5 or some doughnuts or a coffee – which we are grateful for. We eat whatever we get.

Jane: Sandwiches mostly.

Kenny: When we've got money, I go to the fish shop and come back with fresh fish. You know, I like to eat, I like my food. I'm also a carnivore but buying meat dishes around here is very, very expensive. Mostly we eat cold food. But, occasionally, we eat hot food.

[I was curious about how they managed the day-to-day bits of their lives . . .]

Jane: We go to the launderette every fortnight, don't we?

Kenny: Yeah, in Kennington. It's a bus journey, 'cos that's the nearest launderette.

Jane: And we've got permission now to use the Costa Coffee loos, there in the IMAX.

[I noticed Jane paying special attention to one particular bag.]

That bag is important to us. It's got all our paperwork and our birth certificates and the orange bag has our clothes.

Kenny: We've got a suitcase for clean clothes and a suitcase for dirty clothes.

[Kenny started rooting around under the covers and produced a tray of Ferrero Rocher chocolates.]

Jane: We found them on the table, over there outside the cinema – there were three empty bottles of wine and those and I thought, 'Oh, I'm having those!'

[So there we sat, on wet bedding outside this famous cinema, surrounded by litter and leaves, eating very expensive chocs.]

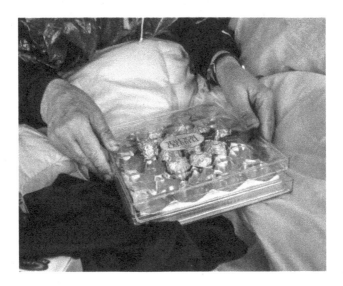

Kenny: I've been robbed and I've been attacked as well, *in my sleep*, up there, in the park, St John's. When it's summer, we sleep there because there's no rain and it's warm. One man tried to smash my head in with a rock but when I woke, I put my arm up, in front of the rock, but I ended up with a big scar on my arm. Someone who was in the park got on their mobile phone and got the cops in.

Jane: Yeah, and there was that man at two o'clock the other morning, walking past shouting obscenities at us . . . threatening us . . . and he had a knife. I was scared!

Kenny: And I was asleep – lying drunk asleep. I think a lot of people are civilised and some aren't. I don't care what they think about me.

Jane: Oh, I do, sometimes.

Kenny: We're pissed off being surrounded by alcoholics, every day! We like to drink – I would call myself an alcoholic – but an *educated* alcoholic, you know? If you can't beat them, join them! It makes you go to sleep quicker and then you get peace of mind. When you're surrounded, every day, by people doing crack cocaine . . . who needs it? We saw a man over there one morning, jacking a syringe into his groin . . . isn't that right, Princess?

Jane: Yeah, and we've been *peed* on. By passers-by. And water poured on us.

Kenny: And people running over our legs – they laugh and think we're two idiots. One night, I was here suffering – my legs were swollen and these people ran straight over me – I lost my temper, but I couldn't get up on my feet, to go and retaliate. I sleep with one eye and one ear 'open' now, put it that way.

[We were surrounded by bags, suitcases, an old supermarket trolley and God knows what else – I wondered which of their belongings were the most important to them.]

What are your most prized possessions?

Kenny: Each other.

Jane: The mobile phone has to come into it because it is a lifeline. I'm not very good at using them! I haven't got an *all singing all dancing* one but . . .

Kenny: And my children. And my mother, who is still alive.

[Jane went off to the loo and when she came back she looked cleaner and fresher, and was saying what a hassle it was having to wash like that, in a public toilet.]

Kenny: Aye, ye cannot really do anything here. And sex? Only *al fresco* sex!

Jane: . . . well, that's practically impossible!

'Middle Earth' at dusk

Kenny: A kiss and cuddle and that's it! But living in the elements, it's not good for our health, living here in Middle Earth – it's what we call this. If someone says, 'Oh, where are you going now?' we say, 'Back down to Middle Earth' . . . she's Bilbo!

But this is not healthy for anyone. Me and her – we've not had a hot bath in I don't know how long. We have 'body washes' but it's not the same as getting under the shower and having a good old scrub around . . . hair gel, shampoo . . . we were always spotlessly clean.

And since we've been living on the street she's not got access to her medication, because her doctor is miles and miles away . . . we can get there but it takes a very, very long time and when you get there you have to make an appointment. So, you might have to leave and they'll call you back two or three days later with an appointment, so you're making the two journeys, just to get one appointment, so she's often without her medicine, yeah.

And I'm suffering with great pain in my hips – maybe too many years sleeping on concrete. My feet are OK. They haven't been washed for about five or six weeks but I take my socks off and wipe my feet with wet wipes, cut my nails and look after my tootsies – because if you don't look after them, they don't look after you.

Jane: This life is not good, is it?

Kenny: She's got a tremendous cough, first thing in the morning. First thing she wants in the morning – before a cup of tea – is a cigarette. Then I lie here, and I can hear her wheezing and coughing, for ten minutes . . . she won't get help.

Jane: The other day someone said, 'You always seem to be smiling,' and I said that it was a 'painted smile' because actually I feel angry. Just angry! It's hard to describe bipolar – or manic depression as it used to be called – you get highs when you are really, really chatty and happy and then you get these absolute lows, where you are tearful, suicidal *and* angry.

Kenny: I'm an independent man, I always have been and I don't want to depend on others.

In my life before, I was a married man, for just over twenty-three years. Two beautiful children. I speak to them, sometimes, on the phone. I don't want them to know about my situation. It's none of their business and I don't want to set a bad example . . . and I don't want them to be here when I die. [dry laugh]

I'm a very nice chappie but when people 'trample on the corns of my toes', I retaliate. My best quality is humour. My worst? My temper!

Jane: And he's mean! Me, I'm fiery – but motherly as well, to everyone . . .

Kenny: Aye, a lot of the people around here, they call us 'mum and dad', 'cos they're very young. They make us feel like dinosaurs!

Jane: But we have our fights, though, don't we?

Kenny: We do have arguments, but it is always verbal. But we can't be parted – everywhere she goes, I go, and everywhere I go, she follows me. I do miss the home comforts of being able to cook, to have a bath or a shower. When I used to have teeth, I brushed my teeth! But that's in the past . . .

Jane: Getting a proper wash, you know, a bath or a shower when you want it. Go and make a cup of tea, when you like. Hot food. Oh, and watching the telly.

Kenny: Yeah we loved lying in bed, watching the telly! We loved sharing a bath together and listening to music and I love the smell of my own cooking, in the background. 'Cos I'm quite a good old cook.

Jane: Yes, he's not a bad cook.

Kenny: I do 'one pot' meals where I throw in what's the best and it always comes out brilliant. I do casseroles, I do spaghetti bolognese.

[As he popped the last chocolate into his mouth and wiped his hands on a tissue, Kenny said, quietly:]

Hopefully, at the end of the day – there will be an end to this life.

Logistics

Jane and Kenny had talked about the complexities of getting to the launderette, to their doctor and the risky decision of whether to leave their possessions, or cart them around on a necessary journey. It drove home the point about the interminable logistics involved in keeping this dreadful, spartan life just ticking over.

So many considerations for people already hungry, worn out and fed up – is this building closed at the weekend? Can we sleep here in the week? Where can I leave my stuff? Are there security cameras? Is that a good thing or not? Will it rain tonight? Will those thugs come back to this spot again tonight? Where is the nearest twenty-four-hour toilet? Is the disabled toilet in Rupert Street still out of order? . . . on and on it goes.

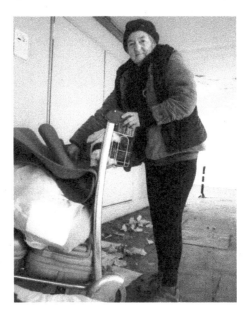

Thought has to be given to where and when to eat and drink, to be sure of getting to a public toilet when needed and not getting caught out. If a food run is coming to a certain place at 7 a.m. on a Wednesday, you need to find a place for Tuesday night that's near enough to get there in time, that's safe enough . . .

For Jane and Kenny the practicalities of a life lived outside were tough enough, but for the next person I met, Brock, these little 'complications' landed him in court.

Brock

'You feel very small . . . very, very small'

I first saw Brock sitting in the recess of an air vent at the Palace Theatre and took a photograph of his legs poking out onto Shaftesbury Avenue. When I went up to him, to say hello and tell him about the picture, the poor man nearly had a heart attack. He'd fallen asleep, sitting upright, chin on chest.

Brock sat at the centre of a shrine he had dedicated to Mr Grumpy. He was surrounded by dozens of drawings of his interpretation of this famous *Mr Men* character, penned on bits of old cardboard boxes.

He agreed to talk about his life on one condition. I had to go and buy – yes – coffees, but also had to return with a 'surprise cake' that would be acceptable to him, or he would withdraw his cooperation. I left him guarding my stuff and set forth to meet expectations.

Brock had come out of prison in 2008 and had been homeless pretty much ever since. He was fifty years old with twinkly eyes, and having just woken up, was a little disorganised. Nevertheless, he managed to maintain his rather aristocratic air throughout our time together. We were both rather bumbling that day as if some internal IED had blown apart our centres of coordination. Coffees got spilled on pictures, chewing gum got stuck on my bum, people knocked into us, and we couldn't get comfortable no matter how hard we tried.

Brock

Why were you in jail?

I got done for GBH, section 18 [causing grievous bodily harm with intent to wound]. I got three years, but I only did thirteen and a half months.

Was it very difficult being confined? It would kill me.

That was my first time in and I was *highly* stressed.

Did you get hassled?

A bit – but you put your head down, accept you can't get out and get on with it. Unless you do that, you'll suffer, mentally.

You don't look terribly 'GBH-y'?

I'm not. I don't fight, as a rule, but I was protecting my family. Life was pretty good, back before I went to prison – I was happy – I don't take much pleasing, to be honest.

I went into the army in the eighties, the Falklands, came out in eighty-five . . . I spent *all* my time in this country. I was single when I came out in eighty-five. And then I had two kids with someone – before my wife. I got married to someone else, after my kids' mum.

So, you were living with your woman, your kids, you had a job – life was perfectly ordinary. What happened to make it *not* ordinary?

Drink, I think, happened – I was drinking too much.

Why?

I don't know if there is a 'why' . . . I don't know why I drank too much, but it became a problem, which I noticed, but didn't do anything about, as you do . . .

Was it like from depression, just existential depression?

I was diagnosed with a borderline personality disorder. I was actually trying to access help, because I *was* depressed, I *knew* I was depressed, but because I hadn't been 'labelled' I couldn't get the help. When I got help, I did a CBT [cognitive behavioural therapy] and actually gained quite a bit . . . and I did stress and anger management. When I was being 'labelled' I went through a whole range of different tablets, to see which one worked. I didn't actually get one that worked until I got into jail – I found one that I put loads of weight on with, one that I lost loads of weight with, one that wound me up and one that calmed me down – but I didn't find one, until I got to jail, that *let me sleep*. Mirtazapine [an antidepressant] was the only one I actually got on with.

And what did you feel after all of that?

Relieved. It worked, so much so that if I get a problem now, I can go back to it and take what I learned from the CBT and the anger management and use it.

What used to make you angry?

When I was drinking? Anything. If I was drinking, *anything* would trigger me. Now it takes a lot to trigger me. A helluva lot. Anyway, I met my wife – I didn't have kids with her but she had eight! I married into eight!

Brave man!

I used to cook dinner on a Sunday, for a minimum of twelve – minimum! And it's the easiest dinner I've ever cooked.

Are you a good cook?

Yes – a piece of piss.

Really! I can't cook, I'm terrible. My husband has to do it.

I love cooking Sunday roast . . . *love* cooking Sunday roast.

So, when did you become homeless?

I came out of prison in 2008 – the wife wrote me a 'Dear John' and left me when I was inside. So, I went to my sister's, on tag [electronic ankle tag to monitor an offender's movements which will have been restricted to particular places].

And how did that work out?

Not very well at all. They were going through a lot of problems at the time and her husband was running a tyre company which was going down – not for want of trying – he wanted to work.

And how long did you manage to stay with them?

I did four and a half months with them and once I got off my tag, I got a flat – this is back in Wiltshire.

So all your homelessness had been in Wiltshire?

Yeah, over there. But the flat . . . I found I just drifted . . . drugs, basically – the hard ones.

Like heroin and crack and stuff?

Yeah.

Why? Why do you think you did that?

Thing is, before I was in prison, I was only drinking and smoking a bit of pot, a bit of coke on the weekends but after I was out of jail, I got heavier into the drink. Then my mate's brother came around and washed up a gram of coke into a rock and that went down a treat, I loved it. I wouldn't know anybody that wouldn't like it — it's one of the best buzzes you'll ever get.

And I guess you were doing this because you were unhappy?

Yeah, you could put it that way, yeah. I only managed to keep the flat for about a year.

Because what? You fell apart with drugs and drink?

It wasn't the flat, it was more the company. I kind of got into the drink and drugs quite heavily — so rather than stay on in that way, I moved away from it. I just gave the flat up. I actually moved into the woods for a year.

You lived in woods for a year?

Yeah! In my tent . . . I *loved it*!

How on earth did you manage? How did you live?

Same as everybody.

What about cooking and lights and . . . electricity and being warm?

Cook on the fire and get under a blanket if I'm cold. I had a tent!

Were you not worried about other people coming by and creating trouble for you?

No, no. And you wouldn't have found me!

And what did you do for money? Did you get any social benefit?

Yeah, yeah, I was signing on.

So you had enough to buy groceries and stuff?

Yeah, yeah. Or go 'skipping'.

You actually went *skipping*? [I mimed skipping with a rope.]

No, you go down to the skip and take the food out of the skip.

So, that finds you stuff to *use* or finds you stuff to *sell*?

[in a very small voice] It finds you stuff to eat.

You go into skips to find *food*?

Mmm. In supermarkets, they throw it away in big bags – perfectly good food. It's not actually *touching* the bin, it goes into the bin in big plastic bags.

So, you were doing your Bear Grylls impression, for this epic year in the woods – what happened then?

I moved in with a good mate of mine who had his own flat and he said, 'Look, come out of the woods and come and stay with me.' So I did. I was there quite a while, then he was ill and had to sell the flat, basically – and I ended up in Swindon, back on the street . . .

The bed Brock makes every night with all his artwork on display

It's actually getting to me now, and, sat here . . . and I don't sleep well at nights . . . *zoom, zoom, zoom* [indicating endless traffic], noise, constant . . . I can literally have a footfall *this* close [showing about two inches with his thumb and forefinger] as I'm sleeping.

So how many hours of consecutive sleep would you get?
Not many.

But you have to let your defences down, to sleep – how do you do that?
Carefully. Well, you *don't* do it, basically. You don't do it. I actually trip.

Yeah, the hallucinations come from sleep deprivation.
Yeah, yeah and I realise that. I can sit here and see things that I *know* they're not there, when I'm that exhausted.

When do you beg?
Prime begging time is when the pubs kick out and everybody is pissed.

Oh, really? I would have thought that was a horrible time 'cos they are all drunk and horrible.
Yep . . . they're all drunk and loose with their money!

What's being homeless like for you, for Brock?
[long silence] The worst is loneliness, probably. I'm a loner at heart, but I am a social loner, a bit of a recluse, but I like to socialise as well.

What does loneliness feel like?
I don't know how I would explain it, to be honest . . . I get kind of uptight, then kind of withdraw, and I get very snappy. I bark, I bite and then I apologise.

Why didn't you bite me, or snap at me, when I pitched up and frightened the bloody life out of you?
Because I was in a good mood!

I was just thinking – if a perfect stranger walked into my house and said 'Hi! Can I come and talk to you about your life . . .'

It's not really my house . . .

. . . I would say, 'Fuck off.' Why did you say, 'Yes' to a stranger like me, why would you want to talk to someone like me?

Because it's talking, isn't it?

I actually had a sign out – it's gone now – that said, 'Homeless. Ex-army. Donations towards a hot meal/hot drink etc. welcome. Or just smile and say hello. Or just say hello.' Half the time, we get ignored. We are invisible. And that's frustrating.

What does it feel like to be invisible?

You feel very small . . . very, very small.

[I offered him a smoke and we talked briefly about the cost of cigarettes, which are pennies in Italy but in the UK you don't seem to get much change from a tenner for a single packet of twenty . . .]

I smoke dog-ends.

That's a bit grim. [We both sat in a sad silence for a moment or two.] **How would you describe your character?**

Quite happy-go-lucky, outgoing, good judge of character . . . erm . . . vulnerable . . . but I put a 'front' on it, I have got a 'front'.

But we all have to do that, because otherwise I think we would not be able to get up in the morning.

I always back away from a fight, although I know what I can do, which is why I don't fight.

Yeah and look where it got you last time!

But I did a good job!

Have you learned anything about yourself?

Yeah – I can do it. I'm actually probably fitter now – because I have to walk and carry all my kit – I'm quite happy on the street. I suppose it's because I've got no ties, there's no 'I've got to go and do this' or 'I've got to go and do that' . . . not got to answer to anyone.

Can you get benefit?

I can, but I've actually let it lapse because since I got here, I couldn't find a Job Centre!

Oh, for God's sake, Brock!

I can get it all back, I can get it.

***Will* you? Because you *need* it . . .**

I'm thinking of going back, anyway, to Wiltshire. What's here? I've got nothing here. All my family are back there. I think I need a kick up the arse and get back to reality, really.

What do you *need* to get back to reality? What would be the things you would need for that to happen?

Housing would be a good start, but I don't know . . . see, that's a quandary there, you see . . . I don't actually know if I *want* to be housed, because I am actually quite happy here – I'm not happy '*here*' here . . . but . . .

No, I understand. So you are saying that 'confinement' would be quite difficult in the sense of a fixed address.

I think so – I think I *would* struggle with it. It *is* always something you aim for, something you want – but it is something that I would struggle with.

I've only been wandering the streets for a short period and I go home to a warm bed, but I still have a constant cough and cold, my joints ache, my arse is always frozen . . .

If you get ill out here then you *are* in trouble – there's nowhere to go, nowhere to stay . . . you can't go to bed and wrap yourself up in your quilt, make yourself a cup of coffee or a Lemsip or what have you . . . I just have this [shows me the cardboard as insulation].

And everything that I see here – this is what you have?

This is me, yeah.

What are your most important possessions?

It's my sleeping bag. You've got to be warm . . . and my blankets, yeah. I don't have anything that is emotionally precious. My wallet. With my ID.

Do you see this changing?

Yeah, yeah. I've got to pick myself up and do something. I will do, eventually. It's hard at times – all your stuff is with you – you can't just walk off into a shop . . . I mean, I've got this trolley, like an old granny! The bin man gave me that . . . that's some of my stuff, and the rest is in my rucksack. Basically, that's where my bedding goes.

And what do you think you could make with your future?

Well, to be honest I'm quite educated. Been through college – a City and Guilds in mechanical engineering. I'm a qualified armourer . . . I'm a qualified barman/cellarman, come to that.

[A loud street-sweeping machine came right up against the pavement, not three feet from us, and it was virtually impossible to hear each other.]

That's two or three times a day, that is.

It'd drive me *bonkers*, the noise. Do you not have a permanent headache?

No, you get used to it. It's a bit like living next to a railway line, you know what I mean – you eventually get used to the noise. Eventually.

[A man appeared alongside us on the pavement, his feet just inches from where we sat. He was taking a series of photos of his girlfriend and kept asking her, in a loud voice, to move to the left, look up, move forward and so on.

He kept stepping backwards without even looking, knocking into us – it was as if Brock and I weren't there, or if we were, we were about as noteworthy as a discarded crisp packet. I quickly got angry, saying, 'Actually, you know what, we're trying to talk here . . . and we can't hear ourselves because of you. People show no fucking respect.']

What do you think about our society, now?

I don't. I'm not politically minded at all. It's never interested me.

Because . . . ?

Basically, they say one thing and then do something totally different. They're all liars. Nothing ever changes . . . well, it does change but what they *say* is going to happen, very rarely ever happens.

What are your happiest memories from the past?

Probably all my outdoor activities – being out in the mountains, rock climbing, abseiling, walking the hills. I used to love walking the hills – they used to call me a goat, a mountain goat [chuckles]. We used to go down to the coast . . . to Lulworth Cove . . . it's one of my favourite places, yeah.

Is it? What are your other favourite places?

Cheddar Gorge.

Why do you like these places?

They're outdoors, it's scenic, I suppose. I've always been an outdoor person.

This must be very difficult for you, then, because there's nothing very beautiful here?

There's no 'green', no. This is the worst bit – there's no 'green'.

What does nature do for you?

It relaxes me, really. I'm relaxed when I'm out in the countryside. Don't know, it's just somewhere where I love to be.

And are you looking forward to getting out of London and going back to where you came from?

I'm a bit dubious, to be honest. All the drink and the drugs are back there.

Don't **go back to all that shit.**

All the exes are there, the kids are there, the family's there.

Do you miss your kids?

Yeah – they don't know where I am because I haven't told them.

Why not?

Probably because I'm in a rut at the moment. I split up with their mum when they were young, so they are probably better off not knowing. I know where they are . . . it's not been *that* long since I've seen them. I mean, they're grown up, anyway.

Are you having trouble with your bit of cardboard, there, are you!?

My arse goes numb, honestly . . . I go completely bloody numb. And my bum just got stuck to a bit of chewing gum!

What, is there chewing gum on my carpet!

Yes! But it's not mine!

Get out of my garden, woman!

Do the police bother you?

They have done. I've actually got an ASBO.

You've got an *ASBO*? How d'you get an ASBO?

From down the other end of Regent Street. I only went down to look out for my mates' things . . . and when they got back, all three of us got ASBOs . . . because they didn't like us on Regent Street!

Were you making the place look untidy?

Basically, yeah . . . if you look at the reasoning . . . it's something to do with your conduct, right, so [reading from the sheet he'd taken from his pocket] 'begging, loitering in a public place, littering, leaving bedding or clothing unattended, harassing or intimidating members of the public, obstructing the general public . . .'

Oh, for God's sake . . .

'. . . loitering near banks, shops or cash points . . .'

There isn't much of London left, then, is there?

No . . . 'approaching customers at restaurants . . . spot begging . . .'

And you've got a little art gallery going on here . . .

[I was surrounded by dozens of images of Mr Grumpy drawn on bits of cardboard.]

Because this says 'Homeless, ex-Army', and basically that is begging and I'll get in trouble with the police. These ones [points to the others] are all right, because not one of them says 'give me your money'.

That doesn't say 'give me money' – that just describes that you are homeless . . .

It puts me in a position where I am begging – that's *their* words, *their* words. Whereas *these* – they are just my artwork.

[Brock's artwork earned him a fiver from me as I decided I wanted to buy one of his sketches. It hangs on my study wall now. I tucked it away in my bag and left Brock to go back to the sleep I had so suddenly interrupted earlier.]

A Few Words on Cardboard

I used to make a point of walking around any big city with my eyes cast skyward to look at the tops of all the elegant buildings and admire the care and love that architects and builders in days gone by had put into their craft.

Now, I was doing the reverse – I started looking downward with sweeping glances along the pavements making sure I took it all in. It became my prism for reinterpreting my appreciation of London. I began to see the physical landscape in a different way, with things often taking on a different character, cardboard being chief amongst them.

A recently vacated bed outside The Savoy Hotel

Suddenly, I saw cardboard *everywhere*.

Things I bought and took home, or had delivered to my house, came in cardboard. It was just rubbish that I threw away, something of no use whatsoever.

But I was being re-educated. Cardboard can become a wall, sheltering you from the wind. It can be a carpet, a bed or a pillow, providing protection against the damp and cold, and maybe even a tiny bit of comfort. A cardboard sign that says 'Help me, please' replaces speech and conveys needs. When drawn or sketched on, it's a medium for creativity and can be sold for an income. Sometimes cardboard even serves as camouflage, providing a place of safety where you can hide and no one will notice you.

It is humiliating having to go around collecting cardboard in busy city streets. It's not like driving back with an IKEA flat-pack with all the anticipation of assembling it in the warmth of your home. It's dispiriting and embarrassing. The homeless do all their living in precisely the same physical spaces in London that millions of us move around in, but the *places*

that we see and the *things* we see, may mean something wholly different to them. We see a bench, they see an elevated bed, we see a broken Coke bottle, they may see a makeshift crack pipe.

Turning a broken bottle neck into a crack pipe

Most things at ground level have significance to the homeless, ranging from utility to perhaps a threat. The geography of their lives and their perceived maps of the city aren't the same as mine. They might look at a section of pavement in terms of its proximity to the heating system of a building, its relationship to crosswinds or street lamps or even its suitability as a discreet place to inject drugs. When was the last time you or I even *noticed* a section of pavement?

Dream On

The homeless are, generally, bad sleepers. What Brock had said about being so tired that he would trip made me think of the Sydney Pollack film *They Shoot Horses, Don't They?* It's virtually impossible for the homeless to get anything approaching what the medical community consider necessary for an adult: seven to nine hours unbroken sleep pretty much every day.

This business of getting uninterrupted sleep is seriously important. The problem with short bursts of sleep is that, over time, your body simply *cannot* repair itself. Something called the Human Growth Hormone peaks during deep sleep and without it there are truly calamitous results. Lack of sleep will destroy you, and a lot faster than you probably think.

When people see the homeless slouched against a wall, or slumped over their begging cup, with a vacant expression and half-closed eyes, they might conclude that they're just lying around, stoned or generally idling.

Actually, what they're doing is hovering around the edges of severe mental and physical breakdown. Not as dramatic to observe as a road traffic accident (that'd get people's attention) but if it goes on too long the consequences are likely to be equally catastrophic.

Can you imagine trying to manage your life, your family and your job if you felt exhausted, irritable and couldn't focus on anything much – *all the time*? Eventually, you'd start finding it hard to read, to speak clearly and your judgement would go out the window. A little longer with intermittent sleep (on a pavement, mind, not a bed, and out there in the elements) and you'd begin to feel disorientated, you'd hallucinate (just like Brock talked about) then start drifting into lethargy and eventually complete social withdrawal.

All of the above, without exception, I witnessed in various permutations, in every single person I spoke to on the streets: every single one of them.

When I'd been talking to Beth (who had been sleeping in a phone box), Jade (who sometimes caught a few hours sleep in Micky's tent at the top of the stairs at Piccadilly Circus tube, for crying out loud) and Eddy (who didn't so much sleep, as 'pass out' on the Euston Road), I'd attributed their sometimes scattergun and erratic speech to the fact that they didn't have long, linguistically complex conversations very often: now I was beginning to see it was also very much part of simply not sleeping.

Your energy tank is empty, your brain is spaghetti, but still local councils and government expect you to pull yourself together and get organised so that you can get back into mainstream society. Well, that's never going to happen, is it? How are you supposed to correctly fill in loads of forms for hostels/housing, account for your movements over the last x-periods or remember to take your medications (assuming you've been together enough to get to a GP, collect a prescription and take it to a chemist to get it filled)?

That the homeless can ever manage to stand up, speak coherently and remember their own name or even what day of the week it is, is a miracle. A real testament to their individual strengths. That they are sometimes ranting, wandering around filthy with their trousers half down cannot really be a surprise at all, can it?

If Amnesty International classifies sleep deprivation as a form of torture and Article 22 of the Third Geneva Convention, 1949 (they figured this out nearly *seventy* years ago) says that a person can't be treated like this, how can it be that what is so contentious in Guantánamo Bay is apparently quite OK on the Tottenham Court Road?

Jasmine

'It's crazy how little compassion people have for others'

She never did tell me her real name, and I never asked.

She told me to choose one for her so I decided to call her Jasmine. Most plants are deciduous *or* evergreen but not jasmine. It's one of the most varied flowers there is and it tries very hard to stay beautiful 365 days a year. The name was perfect.

In a rainstorm straight from the Book of Genesis, down near Embankment, Jasmine had been running across a main road wearing only a tiny little leopard-print dress, an anorak with the hood up and a pair of broken summer shoes. Muddy water was splashed up the backs of her bare legs.

When I caught up with her at the entrance to the tube station at around seven in the morning, I didn't realise that she was transexual – only that she was in disarray and very twitchy. She said she was worried about talking to me. She was very polite and very afraid, and then outlined her sexuality and gender issues. I didn't want to scare her but I really did want to talk to her – a woman's (I'd only interviewed five on the record at this point) *and* a transexual's perspective on homelessness was bound to be compelling.

Eventually she agreed to come and have a coffee while I explained more about the book, and if she still didn't want to talk at that point, we agreed she would just walk away. She was clear she did not want any images of her to be taken that would identify her. It was all I could do to persuade her to let me take the picture you can see, of her hands on her lap. It was a shame, because Jasmine had a beautiful face.

On the way to the cafe, she gave me a thumbnail sketch of the catastrophic and horrific event that led her to come to London. She asked that I not print any part of that story.

She was thirty-three years old and had been homeless for about two years. She was barely surviving on the streets, through prostitution, the income from which was intended to pay for her gender reassignment surgery.

She had a wonderful throaty, but feminine, voice, and was painfully self-effacing. Her delivery was at times both scathing and comedic and I really enjoyed her company.

We sat outside yet another unspeakably dreary cafe, shivering in the cold while she told me her story.

Jasmine

You are very beautiful. I can't believe you are – what am I supposed to say – transexual or transgender?

I use 'transexual', but 'transgender' is also fine.

When did you realise that you didn't want to be living in the body you had?

When I was about three, I was insisting that I was a girl and then it just went downhill from there. My mum would have been a bit more onside, but because of my dad it was just not going to happen. So I started toeing the line when I was ten and thought, 'Well, I'll just do this in ten years' time' [transition]. But, of course, it never happened. Then, going up until my early twenties, I had an alcohol problem for a bit and a massive breakdown in my late teens.

Have you paid a high price, to hold on to your identity?

Oh, God, I've lost *absolutely* everything that I could have had otherwise, *absolutely* everything.

And that makes you feel what?

Great . . . I've done it, and you know what? Just being myself is worth it, but I *am* upset that I lost my family and my good friends. So, anyway, I came to London to make the money to pay for my boobs and the rest.

So how did you get the money to pay?

From prostitution. I came down to London before last Christmas but ended up in hospital for six weeks with a collapsed lung – because [laughing] I was carrying my home on my back, like a terrapin! The doctor decided I was smoking crack and heroin and therefore wouldn't, you know . . . they were judging me.

And are you a massive drug user?

I have the odd pipe and I have the odd toot but I'm not a massive drug user.

Is it a worry that someone is going to nick your stuff? [I was looking at her two large bags on the ground.]

It's a big worry – all my make-up was in that bag and it was stolen – that fucked up a few bookings – and it's expensive, especially when you need it for work, and when you're out all the time anyway . . . you're fucked without make-up. And there was the time when my phone got robbed. It's awful, all this . . . proper bag-lady stuff! All my toiletries and God-knows-what are in there. Make-up, perfume, wipes. Pair of shoes I'm trying to fit in. My last pair of shoes got stolen . . . actually I thought they were going to hit me too, the people who took them.

Have you been attacked, on the street?

Yes. I had my jaw dislocated a few months ago.

Who did that?

A punter . . . and, going back ten years, I had five guys jump out of a car and kick me around . . . so it's actually not as bad as it could be. I've had drinks spiked pretty bad . . . I knew *you* wouldn't do that, but . . .

Oh my God, you were worried I would spike your drink?

[I had gone into the cafe to buy us both a coffee while she waited outside and I had noticed at the time that she had been watching me pretty closely.]

God, no, I *wasn't* . . . I just do it [i.e. keep an eye on people near her] out of, what's it called . . . ?

Shit. Who's done that to you, drugged you like that?

God, loads of people.

Oh, for fuck's sake.

To be honest with you, it's just part and parcel, isn't it? It just happens all the time, but . . . I've not been hurt in ways [on the street] that I've not been hurt before, I'll put it that way.

And what did you do last night?

I did some work, but mostly kind of biding my time . . . I mean there are kind of warm places you can sit.

Like?

Like staircases round the back of places – I try to keep out of the way, because you do get people following you around and all the rest of it.

Is that frightening?

It's very frightening, yeah.

What's your fear level, most of the time?

The first two weeks were the scariest – everybody says that. You really do think you're going to get knifed, there and then – you just think you're going to die.

What, from a punter or from somebody in the street?

Well, from both. I mean, going back to the nineties it was real *Clockwork Orange* stuff, people were setting the homeless on fire at the bus stop, kicked to death and all that . . . it's not as bad as it was then. Yeah, and I've had my tooth cracked as well but that wasn't from a punter, that was from a kid in town.

You're very casual about the violence . . . you're not even using that word, you're saying, 'Ah, you know, it could be worse' and I'm thinking 'Really?'

But I did grow up with a lot of violence, well beyond what I've seen in the last two years. Saying that, it shouldn't have happened at all. It's stuff that a normal person shouldn't have to worry about.

As a transexual do you get more work or less work as a prostitute?

I think it is harder – as a normal female you can just get work anywhere, but I have to be very careful. I mean, I've been chased in the street by men 'cos sometimes I don't disclose, and I take a risk.

What, you don't necessarily tell them? Fuck, you're brave.

Ninety-nine per cent of the time I do tell them – and I have to be very desperate *not* to.

I think you are incredibly brave – do you think you are?

I think I am tough. I don't necessarily think I'm brave. I just do what I need to do. I think I am scared of the *other* consequences, the *other* possibilities . . .

And what are the 'other possibilities'?

Failing – and having to perhaps live as a parody of myself, or God forbid, as a guy.

I thought you were 100 per cent 'woman', which I guess you are – you look ten times better than most regular women.

But being six-foot two-inches, I have my work cut out for me!

Can you get any surgery on the National Health Service?

This is a good thing for the recorder – the NHS will not provide that because they don't deem it as important. They'll do the 'bottom' surgery, which considering I've had half that done on the black market, they probably wouldn't touch now.

Black market in England or abroad?

I don't want to disclose that.

OK. Were you not taking a *huge* risk?

Yep. The NHS will give you hormones but they're not the dose I'm taking – they'd be a lot lower. But they *won't* give you face surgery – it's very rare that they will even give you a boob job.

How much more money do you need to save?

About £20,000 . . . I've not got £20 to my name, you know! But, I'm getting 2ks worth of work calls a week. It's the carrot in front of me.

Where are you going to sleep tonight?

I'm not going to sleep tonight because I'm going to hopefully get some punters – it's Saturday night. I really don't know, I'll sleep . . . find a cafe, and sort of do this in a corner for a bit [she puts her head in her cupped hand as if she were thinking, to disguise fact she would actually be resting]. I don't like sleeping outside.

But you can't get much sleep?

No, sort of an hour, two hours at a time. And you've got the buses – with a travelcard you can get the bus for free, so you can go for an hour before they wake you up, and then another hour and then another hour, you know? If I was brave enough, I'd do the Circle Line but I know I'd wake up with my bags stolen, so I wouldn't do that.

What does it feel like, all this?

Sometimes it feels like *absolute despair*, absolute despair. But especially when it's cold, or raining, you know? There have been two weeks at a time when my feet didn't dry out. They were all cracked. You can dry your shoes under a hand dryer [in a public toilet] but you can't *fully* dry them. And then you walk in them for another five minutes and they're soaking wet again.

So, the overall effect on your health is what?

Actually, I think I'm in quite good health at the moment – I take vitamins, I try and eat regularly but sometimes I go three days without eating . . . but then I used to do that anyway because I was anorexic, so it's no actual big change for me, that. And I know when my 'danger levels' are – when my hair is going to start going white or falling out or when I'm going to start puking up stomach acid.

Assume I'm from another planet, which in a sense I am – tell me about the day-to-day hardships of living on the street.

Doing your make-up in public is the pits, but as a transexual it is hard to go into women's toilets – I'm quite 'passable' so I *can* walk into a woman's toilet and not get funny looks or whatever, but if I take off my hood [of her anorak] people clock me and you get the, 'Why the fuck are you in here?' sort of thing.

People are actually abusive?

It's very distressing and occasionally can be dangerous – the best option is a disabled toilet, because you've got your own space there and somebody is not going to walk in at a bad time, you know, and cause a problem. But, even if you are just sat at a table in a cafe with a little mirror, it's the most depressing thing going.

What about washing your body, your clothes, your hair, *drying* your hair – how does all that work?

There's places . . . the Whitechapel did do showers on certain days. And it's so funny because as a transexual you have to walk past everybody and cover up your various bits which is a *nightmare*. Last year I was doing a lot of 'strip-washes' in the toilets, which isn't the best, and your hair does start to get really ratty.

And your clothes?

Oh God, I don't know if you want this on the recorder but I haven't washed my clothes for about four months. I've washed my underwear in the sink and put it under the hand dryer but stuff like that [points to her micro-scopic nylon minidress], you've nowhere to wash it, you can't fit it into a sink at Mackie's [McDonald's], do you know what I mean, or flush it down the toilet.

So, the physical hardships of your day are tough?

There are some days it's been really depressing, but if the sun's shining and you've got mates out on the street . . . and people do look out for you, and a lot of the druggies are actually a good set of people – all they're interested in is getting their money and scoring – they're not interested in causing anyone any problems – and they *will* watch your back.

There's other times when you don't see anybody you know, and you're walking around and it's *chucking* it down and it's really hard. There's nowhere for you to go, you're banned from X, Y and Z, it's just absolutely shit. And your only choice is, you know, walking. It is *absolute* shit. [Her phone rang . . . it was a punter.] I might have something good here, a job.

[Jasmine took the call and made arrangments.]

You are so brave. I'd be bricking it. You don't know who the fuck they *are*?

I know . . . you know, I *never* wanted to do this . . .

Do you charge different things at different prices?

A tenner is normally the last thing girls will do it for because for most of them, it's about the drugs, and to score their drugs, it's a tenner. Call girls, it's more sort of like £60, £100 . . . I do a mixture of all different things depending on how well I'm doing and what I need.

And what's your preference?

Obviously, taking calls. I mean, it's legal for a start.

Do you usually have to go back to their house?

That's the ideal.

Don't you feel vulnerable?

Yeah, and I've had some bad experiences. I had a guy give me a joint that had heroin in it, you know, all sorts of things.

Do you have a plan, like when you go in, do you check out 'how would I escape?'

Exactly. Exactly. You make sure you know where your bags are compared to him, so he can't grab them without you getting in the way and how you can get away, whether there's anybody else around and always let people know where you are, if you can – if not, at least *pretend* that you're letting people know so that he doesn't get any ideas. It's all a bit of a blag, but . . . very stressful, but you get used to it. You'd be surprised, but you get used to it.

So, when you are doing your job, what's going through your head? Do you blank it out? What?

I'm thinking, 'Why don't you hurry up?', you know? Some of the guys think they're great if they've got a big dick or can last for ages . . .

. . . and you don't want them to! Ha!

Exactly! And especially, you know, if you're hurting afterwards, then you can't do the next job, and if you do, it's going to *really* hurt, do you know what I mean? But you have to. You wouldn't do it normally but if . . .

If you could have a wish and make next week your 'dream' week, what would it be like?

I don't think I even think like that any more. I'm just thinking the next step and I'm thinking what's in front of me and what's coming up behind me.

So are you saying you don't think long term?

I used to. I can't now, I think I'm too messed up now to even do that. I was thinking about settling down, that was always going to be the next step, you know, get a new flat, but after all that has happened I don't think I'd feel safe doing that.

What do you think people think of you? People on their way to work?

All the time they judge. They immediately assume you're a drug addict, that it's your fault and that you're a thief – it's really depressing.

What does that make you feel inside?

[long, long silence] How does it make me feel? . . . I can't even answer that.

Am I upsetting you by asking these questions?

No, no, it's absolutely fine – it's very depressing – I'm doing this so I can hold my head up high and every time I do, somebody smacks me back down again. One thing that's very, very apparent to me is that class is nothing to do with how you talk or what you wear, how you were brought up or whatever, it's whether or not you piss on those who are in the gutter, that's what class is. And it's surprising who has it and who doesn't, do you know what I mean? And obviously you have it!

I don't know if anyone's said that before! What do you think about before you go to sleep?

It depends. Sometimes I get chewed up about stuff that's happened.

What about you, emotionally?

I buy my own hormones, but I'm a week late with them at the minute – I'm saving till I can get some more, so I can pick myself up. So for the last few days I've had big mood swings. The last couple of nights I think I felt that I was sort of on the verge of a breakdown.

How would you describe your personality?

I'd probably call myself resilient, now. I have my mood swings as well. I'm incredibly stubborn – I'm dead laid back, but you get me to that one point where I don't want to quit, and I'm very, very stubborn. I won't make any compromises on who I am. At all. I'm realistic. I am aware of my faults, my weaknesses, the things I need to improve on, and about other people – I'm aware that if I hide this [referring to her 'new' gender] then I get less hassle.

Is that why you wear the hood?

Also because one of the things they did last summer [when she was so viciously attacked] was cut all my hair off.

Have you ever been in love?

Yes – a couple of times. But I think I have been betrayed too many times and certainly being on the game now has taught me a hell of a lot more about fellas than I perhaps wanted to know and more than is perhaps healthy to know . . . it's sad, isn't it? But I don't think I could be in love. I honestly don't think it is possible.

Who have you got in your life that you can talk to, like we've been talking? Who can you share your thoughts and feelings with?

[long silence] Now and again I do. If a punter gets me really coked up then perhaps I will say a little more than I should – obviously I don't want to do the whole 'crisis-support' thing with a punter who is paying for my company, but you do tend to run your mouth a bit more when you're asked the questions.

Do you have any girlfriends or boyfriends?

Nobody who I feel I can *trust*, that's the difficult thing, especially with everything that has happened.

What do you think about the world around us?

I think it's revolting, absolutely revolting. It is pathetic. People are more selfish, quicker to look down their noses at other people. Competition for competition's sake, because people feel like they are not doing anything with their lives *unless* they are competing.

Money is a zero-sum game. If you've got more of it then somebody has got less of it. It's like if someone was jealous of my hair – 'fuck off' it is isn't hurting anybody – me doing something nice for myself isn't taking anything away from somebody else. But having a big flash car – that *is* taking away from other people. So smash somebody's Jag up, and you will get arrested for it and it *is* insured so the person will get recompensed . . . but somebody cuts my hair off and fucks with me in other ways, there is no insurance for that, I'm fucked and everybody just laughs because they think it's funny and it's like, 'Hang on a minute – you would be giving sympathy if somebody got their car smashed up.' People have different priorities, people want different things out of life . . . it's crazy how little compassion people have for others.

Assault and Battery

Ask yourself this – how many times have you ever been punched, kicked, urinated on or set alight?

Had I been talking to car owners, beekeepers or hairdressers about their lives and how they experience the world, I doubt I would even have asked the question, 'Have you ever been assaulted?' I learned early on to remember to ask because it was sufficiently common that some people said they wouldn't have thought to mention it had I not raised the issue.

Now, put your hand in your pocket or bag . . . is there a front-door key there? The key to where you live? If you've got one, the risk of your being attacked or abused on the street today is very low.

Not having a home means you are vulnerable to much higher levels of violence than those who do. Before I began these travels, my answer to the question at the beginning of this chapter was, 'No, never.' A few weeks with the homeless and my answer changed to, 'Yes, last night.'

Armed with only my camera, I was in Villiers Street, on one of my sorties into the unsettling world of London at night. It was tiring because I was operating at a fairly high level of anxiety, scurrying in and out of crowds, shadows and sometimes dark alleys with an expensive camera and no idea how to even spell *taekwondo*. (I do now, obviously.)

I'd got to know a group of people who often bedded down around this area and I knew I'd find at least someone awake. So there I was, sitting relaxing and leaning against someone's army kitbag, sharing a beer and a smoke.

A man in a business suit stumbled towards us, brandishing a long piece of wood and shouting abuse. We'd had no warning, heard nothing at all to alert us and suddenly there he was – drunk and enraged, towering over us and battering us. I don't know if it would classify as a 'serious beating' – I've got nothing to compare it with – but it was hard enough that the next day my leg was bruised from my ankle up to my hip and it stayed that way for ages. It seemed to have happened in slow motion but was, in fact, over in an instant. We'd had barely enough time to register what was happening, never mind to struggle to our feet and *react*. He was there and then he was gone. All I can remember is curling up into a ball on my side, protecting my head and covering my camera. It was a random, hateful drunk who thought it was a lark to beat up the homeless.

Nobody was particularly shocked. Seen it all before. Nothing new. And what would they do anyway? Tell the police? Hardly. A few of them checked me over for damage, consoled me and I went on my way. Home. Enough was enough.

I walked east along the Strand and headed up to Holborn. My leg hurt a bit but I wanted to keep moving. I was afraid that if I sat down I'd burst into tears, and walking helped stop my legs shaking, so I trudged back to Highbury, on foot.

No neighbourhood watch or curtain-twitchers along the Strand at half four in the morning.

On the long walk home I replayed in my mind what had happened. I wondered what the man who'd attacked us would say about it in the morning. Maybe he wouldn't remember. Maybe he wouldn't care.

Being a victim is corrosive, and the homeless are victims all day long, and not only as casualties of physical violence. They're also victims of disease, malnutrition and psychological disorders.

Many victims – sexually abused adults, battered women, even children via Childline – have an official voice with an agenda and often members from that group form the leadership. By contrast, decisions about what the homeless need, what they ought to do and where they ought to do it are not made by they themselves but by other people. Perhaps they're not seen as 'fit' to be involved in high-level decision making.

There are loads of big charities ostensibly doing good things for the homeless – although a lot of people I met didn't trust them at all, seeing them as Big Business conning the public into thinking their donations would make a difference. The homeless I met were often extremely suspicious of the larger organisations and their financial motives, harbouring a sense of being scammed, not saved.

The homeless are a totally recognisable, countable group of people sharing common experiences – yet they themselves are not organised as a group. They have no sense of *self*-representation – everyone else is busy doing it for them.

Benji Moss

'You get to the point where you stop caring. Because nobody else cares, do they?... At what point do you have a nervous breakdown, at what point do you lose the fucking will to live?'

Cutting through Soho Square on my way to Old Compton Street, I spotted Benji sitting on a park bench strumming a guitar. I just thought it was nice that a guy was out making music. My antennae twitched when I noticed that he was with two men who were almost certainly homeless (wheelie baskets, sleeping bags *and* drinking beer).

There was nothing about Benji that said 'homeless'. He could have been a mate of mine that I was meeting later on for a drink. Just a regular guy. But a regular guy that had lost his job, his home, his girlfriend and all his social coordinates. He was living with a map he didn't know how to read.

He'd been homeless for eighteen months and the shock had not lessened. He couldn't grasp that this was how society now defined him.

I sat at his feet while he unpacked his life.

As I was walking away, Benji shouted at me, across the grass, 'Hey, Tam – put this in the book for me, will you? "It's a crime to rob the rich. It's capitalism to rob the poor."' I told him I would.

Benji Moss

It's . . . what's that syndrome? When you're in a barrel and you can't get to the top to drag yourself out of it? It's hard because every now and then someone keeps letting a bit of the water out and you get further and further away from the top.

Come on, why are we homeless for God's sake? Yeah, I'm going to chuck all my gear away, empty my bank account and give it to somebody and sleep on the street. Sure. Right, I'm going to do that!

A couple of mates of mine that were homeless were taken off the street and were put in the Sally Army. They'd been there for two years and *eventually* got found a place but you have to get in that position where you get taken off the street first, and then you have to live in a hostel.

But then if you live in a hostel and you get yourself a job – you can't live in a hostel any more! It's a bit of a trap.

You can't have both. You can't work your way out of it, because if you try and work your way out of it, you're on your own. I've got friends saying to me, 'Go on, rough yourself up a bit, chuck some muck on your face, and you might, you know . . .' Well, I can't do that . . . because I've got to be doing something. Because I have a bit of self-pride – I've got some pride.

All my family have disappeared. I lost my parents when I was seventeen. It didn't really play a part in all this, not really. I was going to college at the time and people around helped me. When I lost my parents it was pretty devastating and I did go off the rails a little bit, but my nan and grandad took care of me, but obviously they're gone now. I have got brothers and sisters but they're all over the world – a sister in France, a brother in America, I've got another sister in New Zealand. I haven't spoken to them for years. I *can't* tell them what position I'm in – it's a pride thing. I don't want them to know that I'm on my arse. Why would I tell them?

When my life went tits up, it was probably a year and a half ago. When it first happens to you, you're embarrassed by it, and so you tend not to tell anybody, you try and keep it secret.

I was in a relationship at the time but I make bad decisions when it comes to girlfriends. My girlfriend didn't want to work, she couldn't be bothered and just watched bloody Jeremy Kyle all day, while I was running around.

I was working as a chef. I was doing all right, and then we got hit by the recession and I was put on the dole. I had my rent paid for me, but my housing benefit was capped and I couldn't keep up with the rent. Kept getting behind. They offered to get me a CSCS card [Construction Skills Certification Scheme] you know, to work on the building sites, so I got my CSCS card and went to the agencies, but the work is like two days here and one day there, and then you've got to sign *off* the dole and it's not enough money to pay your rent . . . and then you have to go through all the palaver of re-signing on and . . . and then the 'sanctions' . . . 'Why are you re-signing on? We got you a CSCS card' . . . but they don't understand the way that some of these jobs work, you know what I mean?

Now I don't get benefit, 'cos like I say, I've got my CSCS card . . . I'm ringing up agencies at the moment – working and homeless as well! You'll do two weeks here or there but it's not enough to save a deposit for even a *room*. Even in the East End they want nine weeks' deposit! Where am I going to find nine weeks' deposit from? It's ridiculous. I've still got to eat, I've still got to pay my tube fare. I'm hoping my next job will be for four or five months or something like that, so if I get it and it's like five or six days a week, then I'll be able to get back on that bottom step of the ladder.

At the moment, my income's solely from busking. I've got a book of songs in there [his bag] that I sit and write – it's not all politically motivated, not all homeless motivated – it's just motivated by whatever comes along. A lot of it is just instrumental. That's how I articulate myself, that's how I probably stay sane!

Sometimes I make £20 or £30 a week or sometimes I can have a result, and can make £120, £150. Ha! If I didn't have my 'cash cow' [his guitar] . . . a couple of days ago, I was skint, I was playing away, I'd made a couple of quid when all of a sudden I broke a couple of strings on my guitar and I thought *shit*, so I went down to Denmark Street, hopefully to find a shop that sold cheap guitar strings. I went into one shop and the guy obviously knew that I was homeless and that I'd been out busking and he *gave* me a couple of guitar strings! And I thought, if it wasn't for little handouts like that, I'd be fucked! Totally. Christmas is coming up and I'm going to get some battery-operated fairy lights and put them on my guitar and go busking. There's good money to be made Christmas time but it's very difficult to play the guitar when your fingers are freezing!

The worst is when you haven't got a penny in your pocket and you're starving hungry, and I take my guitar out – and you know, I don't always *feel like* I want to play the guitar for people, so I just strum chords and some people take pity and chuck me a few quid . . . and then it's straight down to McDonald's for a cheap McChicken sandwich or something.

I know it's shit food, but how can I cook? I can't go to one of those vegetarian or healthy food places because a meal is like £7.50. I can't spend £7.50 for a meal when I can fill my belly for a quid. That, and you get to use the toilets! You have to be on the dole in order to get a meal, you know, 'meal vouchers' for the food banks. You have to be on the dole. And I'm not.

Just not knowing what you're going to be doing the next day, it's hard. Every day you take as it comes. It's like, 'What am I going to be doing tomorrow? Am I going to earn any money tomorrow? Am I going to have enough money to have something to eat?' Or 'I'm desperate for a beer because I'm cold.' You know, you just want to forget about it all.

I don't do drugs. I do smoke marijuana when I can afford it or someone else has got it. I do like to have a drink, but that's mainly . . . a bit of alcohol in you keeps you warm, doesn't it? It is a bit demoralising, yeah. It is a bit. But then you have a couple of beers, smoke a joint and you don't feel as bad! A nice sense of euphoria. Things aren't as bad then.

Other people, they smoke crack or heroin and then they can forget about it completely. It's a completely different drug. It's not for me. I know

I've got an addictive nature . . . that would definitely fuck me up, I know it would.

You get pissed off with people's prejudices as well, people sort of looking down their noses at you. 'I'm so much better than you,' but I'm an educated bloke . . . went to a good school up in Lincolnshire, came out with a few GCSEs, wasn't quite sure what I wanted to do, got into catering, became a chef through the old City and Guilds. I worked hard.

They must think, 'Oh, this guy is a fucking useless bum, he's obviously a drug addict' or something like that, or, 'Oh, it's his fault his life is that way.' I'm pissed off for the simple reason that I'm an English guy, I worked really hard, paid a lot of tax and National Insurance, and the minute I'm on my arse and I need some help, it's sort of, 'Well, you put yourself in that position' . . . I *didn't* put myself in that position – I got made redundant. Let's take it piece by piece: I got made redundant, I got offered the CSCS card, I *thought* it might be a way out but two days' work here and one day's work there . . . it doesn't fucking see you through. You've got to eat, rent is extortionate – even renting a room now is ridiculously expensive. It makes it easier for them to ignore me. Definitely.

Last year I bought myself a £7.99 tent from Argos and I lived in Epping Forest for quite a while – you can disappear in there. But you always get the odd busybody dog walker. I'll never forget, me and a friend were sitting outside the tent, and we had a little fire on the go, cooking some grub up – I'd bought a couple of mess tins from Wilkinson and we put our beans and sausages in there – and this woman came past and she goes – excuse my language – 'You fucking Eastern European,' and I'm like, 'I'm from Lincolnshire! I'm not an Eastern European,' and even if I was, would it make any difference, you know? At the end of the day, when you're on your arse, it doesn't matter what country you're from, you're on your arse, aren't you?

I'll sleep anywhere there's shelter, no wind. Shop doorways – you're not allowed to sleep on the pavement – you can get arrested for that, and parks are quite good. Park benches because you're off the ground. That's why a lot of homeless people get cardboard because they need some insulation between a cold stone floor, so . . . you have to do what you've got to do! I mean, sometimes, I've been so knackered, I've sat down, put my guitar down and I've fallen asleep, sitting down! All my sleep is broken sleep.

At the moment, I'm still quite healthy, so, I'm not in a state . . . I'm not as bad as some of the people out there – they are really ill, because they've been sleeping on the streets all the time. Look at my fucking teeth, they are starting to rot. I haven't seen a dentist for three years now. I just can't afford it. I like to think I am quite strong in the mind – you've got to be, because you *can* lose it – I've seen people really lose it.

I go to McDonald's or supermarkets 'cos they've got nice toilets and washrooms in there and you can wash and sort yourself out. If you can get yourself seven or eight quid together, you can go down the launderette and give your clothes a wash, I mean . . . being smelly and stinky is horrible, I don't like it.

My possessions? Four or five changes of socks – definitely, socks keeping your feet dry is always important – a change of underwear, tooth-brush, and some other bits and bobs. I have got a bag, but it's at a mate's at the minute . . . it's just full of bizarre things for work! I keep my hard hat, my hi-viz, Stanley knife, an adjustable spanner just in case I need them for work . . . just silly things like that. I've pretty well lost most of my photo-graphs, all gone, disappeared.

I do think about my future, I do think about it. I try to stay positive – it's the *only* way. If I couldn't stay positive, I dread to think. I really do. I don't know, I don't know. [He lights up a smoke and looks sad.] I try not to think about it.

But planning? A week! Nothing more than a week. Not really, no. Go out busking, make a few bob, if I make £25 or £35 in a day it's a bonus, then I can eat for a couple of days!

I don't get lonely, that's the thing – I'm sat here with my mates [two friends sitting on the next bench] – you don't get lonely. A lot of the home-less people stick together. I think because you need somebody, you need *someone*, don't you? To talk to, to sit there and put the world to rights, to complain and bitch about. You know what I mean! I've noticed in the homeless community, they all bitch about each other, but deep down they all look after each other.

I miss things, from before. I miss security. Being able to go home at the end of the day. Just chill out, switch the telly on, stuff like that, you know, all the things you took for granted . . . being able to walk into the kitchen and bung a pizza in the oven or something, or make a cup of tea. I had a couple of nice guitars, a nice bass guitar, a drum kit . . . I had to slowly start selling it all off . . . all my musical equipment, my laptop . . . for the rent.

I remember watching a programme where they took four or five celebrities and they sent them out on the street, for a week . . . a week . . . do it for fucking three or four months!

The problem now is people's prejudices – one in fifty people'll be nice. It's like when I'm busking . . . I had a result today . . . in twenty minutes I made £15. But yesterday I was busking for four and a half hours and I didn't even make a fiver.

You get to the point where you stop caring. Because nobody else cares, do they? You lose your inhibitions . . . you know, you're not shy to say what you think . . . that's why a lot of homeless people, some of them can be quite aggressive, because they've got *nothing to lose*. You've got nothing to lose, man. You get arseholes out there, especially Friday and Saturday nights, people are out having a drink . . . some people can be really nice and some people can be *right* arseholes.

At what point do you have a nervous breakdown, at what point do you lose the fucking will to live? I could reach that point, probably, yeah, but I don't want to.

But life is worth living. Of course it is. We are given a life – don't waste it.

Daily Bread – Food or Fodder?

Humans need to eat both cooked food and lots of healthy raw fruit too. What they don't need, at all, is junk food. And herein lies the rub.

No home, no kitchen. No kitchen, no cooker. You get the idea.

Cooking food is a pleasant pastime for a lot of people but it is more than a hobby, a preference – it's a prerequisite for staying well. Cooked meat and vegetables are easier to digest so you're less likely to have stomach problems. Breaking down your food *outside* your body (cooking it) means you use less energy than if you're doing that job *inside* (digesting it) and overall you get more goodies from that food. That's the idea, at any rate.

Think about pythons ... or lions ... they eat enormous quantities of uncooked food and they take days and days to digest it, all the while having no spare energy left to do anything else. Like build spaceships or write books. Or find a job and a home.

'Oh, but you never go hungry on the streets – there's always food' is the common refrain of a lot of malnourished homeless people.

'But apart from hot meals some day centres provide – that you have to pay for – don't you eat mostly sandwiches and McDonald's?' I'd ask.

'Well, yeah, there is that, I suppose,' people would say.

The homeless eat crap food all the time. This is because it's either free – like Jade eating pizza she found on the pavement or else from soup runs and so on – or cheap. Cheap food is usually *fast* food and fast food is, well, junk food. This kind of fodder is useless at increasing long-term energy and does nothing for your immune system or your brain function.

Junk food is appealing to the homeless not just because it's cheap but because it can be bought in places where no one looks at them twice as they stand in fast moving lines to order and pay. This is important for them as they are very alive to being noticed, observed and – usually – judged. They don't generally buy healthy little quinoa salads from M&S not just because they can't afford them, but also because they're embarrassed – people stare at them – they don't really belong in M&S. They don't have carrier bags full of food because they don't have that kind of money in 'one go' (because they've not raised enough begging or because they've had to spend it on drugs to make staying alive an even vaguely viable proposition that day), they don't have anywhere to *keep* it, and it's too heavy to carry around along with the rest of their lives.

The homeless eat a phenomenal amount of bread

All pretty hopeless and all very cyclical. Eat rubbish and very soon you feel like rubbish. You're too undernourished and weak to put eating a well-balanced, nutritious meal anywhere near the top of the 'things I need to do today' list. And, anyway, there's a McDonald's on practically every city block in London. Benji had been the umpteenth person to talk about eating at McDonald's. Eating at McDonald's a lot. Like every day, over months or even years.

Maybe you saw the movie *Super Size Me*, in which Morgan Spurlock eats nothing but McDonald's for four weeks as an experiment. It gave him depression, lethargy, headaches and more. And Morgan Spurlock started off fit as a flea and wasn't living on a pavement. His doctors were surprised at how quickly his health deteriorated and advised him to stop. He didn't, and now apparently has irreversible heart damage.

So, why is any of this worth mentioning? Because the homeless are expected to get off their backsides, pull up their socks (if they've got any), get a job and get their lives together – and do it all against the backdrop of their almost uniformly appalling histories, mental illnesses, exhaustion and, to cap it all off, their malnutrition.

Stephen Reynolds

'The only kind of help I'll get is if I hurt someone:
what kind of sick joke is that?'

When I first saw Stephen, I thought he was quite beautiful, still as a statue. He was shy and very worried that I wouldn't want to talk to him because he mumbled. He was sweet and gentle.

It was difficult to reconcile what I sensed from being with him with the fact that he suffered from dangerous and severe personality disorder (DSPD). His only concern during our first five minutes together – on a glacial and windswept Euston Road – was my physical comfort.

He told me his dad had been violent and abusive, and his mum (who he clearly adored) had turned to drink. His dad left and his mum could not then cope with her five children. One day, when Stephen was about nine years old, she dropped the kids off at their father's and left them there. Stephen was beaten by his father, social services got involved and, at the age of eleven, he went into care. He has been in and out of institutions for the rest of his life, culminating in prison.

He had virtually no formal education and said he wished he'd had an authority figure, someone he could have looked up to, respected and listened to – but he never found one. The care system taught him nothing, but he did learn one skill in prison – 'I'm a bad-boy cook now!'

I felt very affectionate towards Stephen and respected his formidable inner strength. It wasn't his fault that he was so dangerous.

Self-conscious and softly spoken, he described clearly the Alice in Wonderland of contradictions that he had to contend with.

Stephen Reynolds

So, when did you become homeless, for the first time?

About five years ago, and it was just a brief spell. After prison I was just too embarrassed to ask family members and that for help. This time around, there are no branches for me to try and reach out to. I just have to try and do it myself.

What was prison like? Did you learn anything positive?

I learned things that you could use positively, like . . . sometimes it's better to give the person 'their moment'. I read a book called *The 48 Laws of Power* by Robert Greene – sometimes it's better to let people have their little bit of power over you.

How did prison change you?

When I came out – I got three and a half years but served twenty-one months – I was the same person who went in, but everyone else had changed! And that was the hard part – like they had all moved on and I was still Stephen who had just been in jail.

So, when you came out, you were how old?

Seventeen, just coming up to eighteen. I was only out for eleven weeks and they sent me back for a year and a half.

What for?

Breaching my licence – I didn't go to meetings. I came out and that was when I really experienced life – 2007 I was released. I got a job in Domino's, making pizzas – I enjoyed it. For nineteen months, I lived the life – I worked, I went out, I had friends – that's the most normal I've ever been, like, socially. That's the only time I've ever saved money to go on holiday, gone shopping, arranged to go ice skating . . .

Who did you live with?

I lived with my brother, he had a flat, with his girlfriend and I stayed with him. And then, what happened was, on 21 October 2008, I drank a pint glass half full of sambuca and half full of Southern Comfort and I woke up in a police station. I had attacked five people. I went to prison for five years.

Tell me about that night.

I was with my girlfriend, Amber, and my friend Brian and we went out . . . honestly, yeah . . . I don't remember. I attacked five people.

How seriously did you attack them?

One was GBH, section 20 [unlawful wounding without intent], with my fists – one guy I hit, he hit his head and he had a bleed and the rest of them I just slapped. I'm not trying . . . it was appalling, yeah . . . all of my crimes before, even the police said that I did them to sort of make some money or . . . but this was a random, unprovoked attack.

Do you have any idea why you did it?

I was on medication and I believe it was because of my medication and being mixed with alcohol . . . risperidone and mirtazapine – antipsychotic and for depression.

What kind of mental health issues did you have then?

Well, I have DSPD which is not really mental health and not really clinical . . . I've got the paperwork here. Do you want to see it?

Yeah, sure, why not . . . what does it stand for?

Dangerous severe personality disorder – there's only 2,700 people with it. I was diagnosed in prison.

But shouldn't you be being looked after?

I was in Highgate Mental Hospital as an outpatient but when I went out one day, I got robbed and I stayed out – when I went back they said, 'But you've discharged yourself . . .'

Hang on, I've got to get my glasses to read this stuff.

You're not in a rush, are you?

No, not at all.

Good! I like a bit of company.

[I began to read various sections of the many documents he had organised into folders.]

You keep all this paperwork for what reason?

Because I'm at the stage where I might climb onto a bridge – because no one helps me – I might make a sign and with red paint and write *'I'VE GOT DSPD AND THEY WON'T HELP ME UNLESS I HURT SOMEONE.'*

[We sat side by side looking at the documents together – each of us pointing out a paragraph here or there of interest.]

It says I can't experience emotions.

I've just looked at a page at random and it says you should be '*prioritised* with the highest level of supervision and treatment'.

I'm a MAPPA [Multi-Agency Public Protection Arrangement], yeah, you know what I mean? And I'm walking the streets! As I said, there are 2,700 people with this diagnosis in the country, yeah – 2,100 are in prisons, 300 of them are in secure hospitals and there are 300 walking the streets – I am one of those 300.

I didn't choose to be like this.

I'm not judging you. You seem very, very intelligent and articulate.

But that's usually the case with serial killers and mass murderers and all the crazy people!

You shouldn't think of yourself as 'crazy' – you should think of yourself as 'you' – with the issues you have. It says you are at 'high risk', you need 'treatment' and you need 'planning' . . . and you're sitting here begging . . . ?

Ridiculous, isn't it?! Honestly. My mum phoned the police and said, 'Look, he wants help and the only way to help him is if he is in prison for a long time.'

How I first found Stephen

But that's so nuts – you've got to *do something bad*, hurt someone . . .

Yeah, lose my liberty to get help – how's that helping me?

Jesus. It's unbelievable. It says: 'Despite the improvements and continued work that Mr Reynolds self-reports in his relationships . . .' So, you *do* make improvements, and then you end up out here?

It's the reason I've got all this with me, is because if I *do* end up on a roof I want to say, 'Look, mate: I'm fucking sick and I want help . . . will you fucking help me *now*?'

What if you just walked into the psychiatric unit of the hospital?

That's what I did at Highgate . . . I said I might hurt someone or hurt myself.

And what did they do?

They contacted Westminster and then they put me in the Highgate mental hospital and I went out that day and got robbed.

[At this point a man walked up and became abusive. Stephen remained silent in the face of this hostility, but I couldn't let it go, saying, 'He's not well' in response to the man's tirade about how Stephen should get a job. The man answered, 'Well, if he's well enough to beg . . .' I couldn't keep my cool and railed, 'You don't know what the fuck you're talking about – you're in no position to judge, are you?' . . . and then, to Stephen . . .]

God, you are way more polite than I would be . . .

Yeah, like I said, you just have to give him his moment.

So, where did you go? Who did you go to when you left prison?

You only do what you know . . . you've got to imagine, yeah, I've just come out of prison, no one's waiting for me, so where do I go? I go to a drug dealer's house. Got smashed out of my face and got a bird round. And obviously everyone else is chatting and doing their shit . . . and that's it – I'm back – within two minutes you forget where you've been for the last three and a half years. I lasted nearly two years and then I broke into a takeaway, drunk, in Coventry and I got sixteen weeks – I served eight weeks – with another £46 . . . [Prisoners are given this sum in cash on release.]

. . . and you're back out again.

And this time I've got addicted to this legal high. My mum was saying, 'How can we get you off this?' and in the end she took me to a field in Essex and in seventeen days I came off it.

A *field*?

Yeah! A field! In Battlebridge – she's got a camper van and I stayed there until I was off the drugs and then she said, 'Look, you're going to have a fresh start, wipe the slate clean and go live with your brother,' so I did. But I said, 'I've tried a million times to make things work so what's going to be different this time?' And, yeah, I ended up back out on the street.

What's it like, living on the street?

Lonely.

Who do you talk to?

Everyone I can.

What do you miss about human company?

Don't . . . you are going to make me cry here . . . [He was serious.]

Oh, don't cry . . .

What do I miss? . . . God, you are going to make me cry . . . what do I miss? General shit. You know when you are sitting at home, right, you don't even think, you take it for granted – you're sitting there in your comfort . . . when I had that chance, in May, I should have just taken it.

But now, literally, I've just come from seeing my mum – I had to tell her that I might do something stupid – imagine what it's like for her? She tried to help me and I fucked it up. How can I stay with her, in her flat? She knows I'm out on the street – how must it be to see your son like that? I *know* it must be hard.

What do I know? I hardly know you, but you seem like a gentle, *extremely* self-aware, compassionate man – you seem to understand your own mental dynamics really well . . .

Yeah, but I don't know how to deal with it all . . . and this is a shitty example – but say you barge into me, walking down here, you'd be like, 'Sorry, sorry!' but I might react differently to it, yeah [he means he might attack me] . . . I have to retrain myself, to *learn* how to react differently – 'cos if I react the way *I* do, it gets me in trouble.

You seem incredibly bright – I can't believe there isn't a future for you that *isn't* this. What do *you* think your situation is?

I'm optimistic that I'll be off the streets pretty soon – but then I think, I'll be in the same situation I've always been in . . . people might think that, 'Oh, Stephen's all right now, 'cos he's off the streets' . . . but Stephen *isn't all right now* because I'm going to have get a job, all of these 'processes', I've got no ID, I've got no clothes, I worry about how people look at me, how I talk – 'cos I talk funny, I mumble and I stumble . . .

Maybe you shouldn't worry about *everything* in one go. Maybe go back to Highgate and say, 'Look, I need to fix this shit. Help me.' If you had an infected leg you'd go to hospital and say, 'I need something for this leg because I can't walk properly.' But instead you seem to be saying, 'I've got this infection, but I'm just going to keep limping.' Don't. Go get it fixed. Trying and failing is fine – you've just got to *keep* trying – maybe you'll fail again, but maybe you won't.

I spoke to these people before and I'm hoping they'll come and find me and take me to No Second Night Out. They said you get assessed there and I'll show them this paperwork and then they'll know I need help.

Yeah – because you could flip at any moment. Tell me how you survive on the streets.

It's only one month that I've been begging. Before that I used to shoplift.

What? And then sell the stuff?

Yeah . . . all day every day. Meat, drinks – anything – toiletries . . .

Did you prefer shoplifting to begging?

I just did shoplifting because it was all I knew – I'd done it before. I was too scared to beg and I was embarrassed. And then one day, I thought, fuck it – now I'm getting braver.

What *do* you do with your money? Do you take drugs now?

I smoke the legal highs but I don't take drugs or drink and all that crap – I'm not high-funding! But I do gamble – 25p each way on the races!

That doesn't exactly sound like a big problem, 25p each way! What does most of your money go on, then?

Fizzy drinks, phone credit . . . don't know . . . bus pass . . . launderette.

Where do you sleep?

Over there, see that Quaker building? There are metal gates and I sleep behind them. There's a camera, right above me [which made him feel safer], and it's wind- and rain-proof.

Do you feel vulnerable, on the street?

One time, I woke up and a geezer had his hand on my chest – I looked at him and fear shot through my head – then I screamed and the guy got up and ran . . . then another time, a big black guy came up – I thought he was going to ask if I wanted to buy some drugs, but he said, 'You want to fuck?' He looked so big and strong – imagine if you were sleeping somewhere and he was *on you*? And that's what made me think I had to get away from Westminster and come here.

I go to bed probably about nine or ten o'clock at night and sleep until six or seven. You wake up a few times. Crazy people waking you up, screaming and that. Where I sleep – I'm allowed to sleep there – the police can't move me on . . . 'cos it's the Quakers – Quakers, yeah, they're cool.

How would you describe your character – your personality?

[very long silence] I . . . am . . . [more silence] . . . I am . . . er . . . I don't know how to describe myself. I would say that I am kind, considerate and helpful but I'm devious as well!

What would you want in your future?

No one chooses who they are born as, right? I'm twenty-eight and really and truly, if I could *just* get some stable accommodation, a mediocre job, *not* go back to prison and have a nice relationship with a girl – I would be happy with that. I don't want anything else, do you know what I mean?

Do you think this future is within reach?

If I didn't, I wouldn't be here.

Good. What's your next step, then?

My first step is to get off the streets. I cannot do *anything* carrying my bags around everywhere. My friend just got a job, giving out the newspapers – £20 for three hours – and I think I could get a job like that but I don't have the ID, so . . .

What do you mean, you don't have ID?

No birth certificate, no passport – nothing.

[A mate of Stephen's turned up and wanted to beg where we were sitting, so I stopped recording and we went to a cafe outside King's Cross Station. Once seated, I turned the recorder on again and we were midway through talking about dogs . . .]

Why do you think people are more sympathetic to dogs than people?

It's animals, isn't it – everyone has a soft spot for some kind of animal . . .
they must see the animal and think, 'Oh, I wonder if they are feeding that
animal?'

**But don't people have them – especially homeless people – because
it's something to care for and to love them back?**

Well, now I've started to hang around with this Polish guy who's got a dog,
I've started thinking it would be a bit of companionship . . .

**How long can you go without a proper conversation with someone?
About stuff *you* want to talk about?**

Days. Unless people like yourself stop and chat to you. Some are really
drug-involved and I try and stay away from them.

Why?

Because they are shit.

What sort of things do you miss talking about?

Football yesterday, football tonight, football tomorrow! I support Arsenal.
Everything!

*[Stephen abruptly stopped smiling and his face became sad and serious. I
let him sit for a minute or two in silence, and then he said:]*

Over time I realised I felt so little and inadequate – I mean, really, you
aren't helping me by giving me money, are you?

I am because at that moment in time, you have a need . . .

But it's like a cycle, and unless something in the cycle changes you'll just be
going round and round in it.

**Yeah, you *are* in a cycle – we are all in our cycles – it's not necessarily
our fault, and you can only live one day at a time, and if, on that day,**

you need the money for drugs or whatever, then that's what you need. I can't look at the bigger picture then – I don't have that right.

Seriously though, if I don't get off the streets – I might go to prison just to get warm . . .

You'd seriously think about doing something to get into prison for winter?

Of course! Three meals a day. I like to bathe and shower and watch TV.

It's tough for you, isn't it?

Well, it's tough for those people coming in on a boat from Syria – so it's not tough for me, is it? They're risking their lives to get away from something – I'm eating, drinking, I'm smoking – I can't grumble, man.

You 'can't grumble'? Are you serious? [We sat together quietly for a few minutes.] **I just saw the tattoo on your neck there – it says** *loyalty* **– is that an important quality?**

Hypocritically, I would say 'yes' . . . because I've lied and been devious numerous times . . .

Do you not think that everybody has?

I admire loyalty and I believe that I am loyal but obviously, in the past, I've done things that aren't loyal – I shouldn't have done that kind of thing, so it's hypocritical – does that make sense?

It does, but I think you need to be less hard on yourself. Every one of us has done things we're ashamed of . . . I haven't gone to prison for the things that I've done that I'm ashamed of, but I have done things.

Yeah – I have to think hard about my liberty – when I'm in a cell I think, 'How did I get here? What decision did I make?' I have to think about my decisions *way before* I get there. The only kind of help I'll get is if I hurt someone: what kind of sick joke is that?

Uneasy with the Unwell?

People with mental illness so often seem to end up on the street and people on the street so often end up with mental illness. What a mess.

Was I afraid of them?

Honestly? No.

It was never the first thing I asked, nor the first thing people told me. By the time it came up in conversation (as it did with Stephen) we had already made a connection with, and formed an opinion about, each other – and had figured out a way to be comfortable together. I never felt unsafe – very few people who are mentally ill are violent or dangerous. They're mostly just very, very sad.

The majority of the people I spoke to did have mental problems – some extremely severe – but they were well aware of them and, at least at the point at which I was talking to them, perfectly articulate. I didn't have any qualms about recording their thoughts and they themselves were quite open about discussing their mental health problems. I never had any difficulty at all in understanding what people were talking about and never thought they didn't understand what I was doing.

I did use my common sense. I didn't get too close if I felt people were protective of their (God knows, limited) personal space, but got very close if I felt it was right to touch them, hold them and even kiss them. They have very little experience of friendly touch and affection, living as they do, and if that was what they wanted from me, then I was happy to give it.

I was alive to tiny changes in facial expression or tone of voice, and I was straightforward and direct. It would be foolish to think the homeless can't spot a dissembler, a liar or a threat – they are extremely sensitive and have very impressive built-in radars. I felt strongly that it would have been

235

wrong to exclude talking to people who were mentally unwell. I couldn't see why this would make them – or their perceptions of their worlds – any less valid. Wouldn't that be similar to saying an alcoholic's opinion is worthless? People with psychological problems see a world, inhabit a world, that looks much as yours or mine does but they just see it all through a different prism.

It came as a huge shock, though, to see quite how many mentally ill people there really are living out on the streets. They are desperately vulnerable and mostly scared so it was ironic that people so often thought I was being 'brave' talking to *them*.

There is no reason to be afraid of someone just because they're homeless and psychologically damaged. It is, however, a very good reason to listen: they have a lot to say that is worth hearing.

Michael

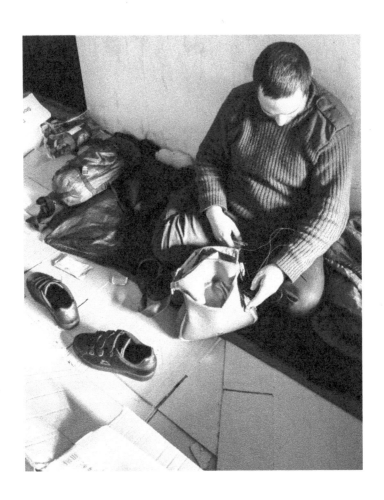

Martins

*'The street will destroy you completely – I saw that
happen within a few weeks with people . . . You can't swim
any more, up the fucking river. It drags you down'*

I'd seen Martins a few times during my wanderings, and we were on nod-
ding terms. Word had got out that a woman was going round talking to
homeless people, so he knew who I was. Even knew my name.

He was living in a small cardboard encampment, in a little tunnel off
Brydges Place, not too far from Trafalgar Square.

He was a big, sturdy fishing boat of a man – on an even keel, strong
enough to withstand big storms and definitely going to make it back to
shore in one piece.

Martins was an ex-soldier. A Latvian, he'd had a tough, loving but no-
nonsense childhood and his command of English was impressive. He'd
been on the street for about a month and didn't want his face to be seen,
but was very pleased to be able to share his thoughts.

Martins

Just getting used to this is very tough. This is really hard. First of all, the safety, because all the time there are people around you, you know? And when you're asleep, you basically don't know what their intentions are. It is tense.

In general, I'm kind of a calm person so I tried to keep it cool. But it was horrible, that first night. I can't describe it to you ... very bad ... very close to a mental breakdown, I suppose. Now I do feel safe, but I'm not able to sleep for long. At night, you have to sleep with one eye open and the next day you feel like a fucking zombie – that's why you have to have a spliff or something, you know?

I haven't been attacked. But my friend here [pointing to a man in a sleeping bag, lying a few feet away], some gypsy guy broke a wine bottle over his head, seriously. They had an argument or something.

Anyway, I got sick and basically I couldn't afford to pay my rent, so I had to move out. And that was it, yeah. I had quite a lot of direct debits and it all caught up with me. I had used my savings to pay the mortgage on my mother's house – she could have been evicted. She's back in our country and it's rather me than her, so ... it's all right, I'll just try to stay positive and I'll try and fix things in another month.

I had a really good job as a bricklayer, here in London. I was earning £20 an hour, roughly. You earn good money but you have to work really, really hard. It was a good life. I had a girlfriend and we were living in Paddington.

Out here I don't feel vulnerable, but I have had to deal with things, you know? You have to prove yourself, out here. Somebody says something to you – you knock him out. Then, if you do that once that will be it, and everybody will be cool with you and nobody will try to get in your head. If you're weak, they will try to fuck you every single day. In any kind of way! Take your tobacco, take your food, whatever. They will just try to take any advantage they can. I see that happen, every day.

I can protect myself and I've tried to step up for other guys who've got abused here. This is really hard, here. The street will destroy you completely – I saw that happen within a few weeks with people. Some go to a mental hospital and some commit suicide – they cannot take this any more. I know a guy – he killed himself. He hanged himself.

I don't believe in luck. Luck is bullshit, bullshit. To be blessed, you have to work really hard . . . you are as lucky as you work towards.

But that can't be true! You did all the right things and here we are, sitting in cardboard boxes. [The guy who'd been asleep near us, woke up. He asked for a cigarette and said, 'I'm listening to you – I totally agree!']

Some people get on drugs, or alcohol and it drives them into depression. The main thing about all this? It's that people *get used to this*, they accept it. That's the biggest fucking mistake they could ever do. I was talking to a guy and he gets £230 benefits, a week, and I said, 'So what the fuck are you doing out here, man? You could just save up and get a nice place, or something,' and he said, 'You know? I don't care – as long as I've got a can of beer and a sandwich, I'm cool.' I think that some people choose to be in this situation. You'll not believe me but I've met a businessman who was really successful, before, he had all these companies, yeah, and he said, 'You know what? I've escaped. This is my escape.' He left his family – wife, kids, everything. There are different people out here. But this is not for me.

Living like this is not much fun, I can tell you. I smoke Spice, but rarely, to be honest with you. One of its components is from jet fuel! Basically, the government let it out, as a counterbalance for weed. I'm not a fan of these drugs and alcohol, I just do it rarely to relax and chill out.

The cardboard keeps the wind out because the wind goes low and this pushes it up so it helps. But it could be worse – it could always be worse – I could be disabled, can't move. Remember there is a saying, 'No matter how fucked up it is, it could always be worse.' And I read books to stay positive – all different really. I like science . . . science and history. I am well educated. I finished military academy and served in the army for seven years.

In a few days' time I will start a shit hotel cleaning job – raise a little bit of a deposit and get some kind of a room and go from there. I'll still be living here but going to work in the morning – I will have to. I have no choice. I'll have to take my stuff with me – but nobody said it will be easy!

This is not permanent. It fucking can't be! You're joking! But this is definitely a sobering life experience – I used to look at homeless people . . . you know, 'Oh it's a fucking guy with a sign or whatever,' but next time I will feel what that person feels – he sits there, he's cold, he's hungry – you know? You never think about these things, you take them for granted. A lot of people take for granted a one-bedroom flat – come on, that's treasure, man! It's your fucking treasure.

And the fucking police run you from here and from the tube station – they come at eight o'clock in the weekdays and move you. At nine o'clock the day centre opens and you can job search. You get housing advice, medical advice, wash your clothes, have a shower . . . you know, all that kind of thing.

The main thing on the street is not to become a fucking animal – have showers, wash your clothes and keep clean like a normal human being. I'm thirty years old for fuck's sake! I can't look like an animal! I still like girls, and stuff . . . !

Some people, they just accept it – they reach a point where that's it – it's over. You can't swim any more, up the fucking river. It drags you down, that's it.

I'm not worried. I am a mentally very strong person. I've been through a lot of things and this will not break me . . . come on . . . for fuck's sake, if the Taliban didn't kill me in the fucking mountains, you think this will? It's just temporary – just one more month and I'll be fixed up.

There is a little fucked-up country, called Dagestan. Very fucked-up people live there, very fucked up, and from time to time we have to do these big operations, you know, against them. It is quite frightening – you got shot at. It's not like they show you on the TV . . . yeah, a few of my friends got killed. I got shot myself, in the legs, and I have bomb shrapnel here and in the back as well.

I was a commander in the army and I always tend to think with my head and not my dick and that's what's good about me, you know? And I got mature much faster than I should have – some kids at ten years old are riding around on bicycles and things but I was working in the forest with my father and grandfather, so I really had a very short childhood. And a tough one because I was always abused at school and I was weak, as a kid.

I was brought up really strict and my mum was really strict about how to treat women, you know, and when we used to watch TV and I would say some rude remark, she would slap me in the face . . . we are a very religious family and this kind of shit is not allowed.

I'll be honest with you. I don't want my family to know because I don't want my mother to worry – she would not be able to sleep if [she knew] her son was sleeping on the street.

I will fix things up and it will be OK, it will. I just need a little, little bit of time. And time is on my side – that's the one thing I have. And you have to be strong or this shit will destroy you – the streets will destroy you super-fast.

Fault Lines

I didn't agree with Martins' views that if you're 'good' and work hard, all will be well with the world. He espoused the view, but didn't seem to exemplify it. His work ethic and commitment to his mum hadn't protected him at all. Why, I wondered yet again, are the homeless apt to be so self-accusatory?

Fault and blame are close friends – it's much easier to avoid personal responsibility if you can blame someone else. *The homeless are just a bunch of useless lazy fuckers, rubbish druggies who could get a job if they wanted to. They've brought this on themselves. No one but themselves to blame. The homeless deserve to be vilified.* This way of thinking allows people to absolve themselves of having to give a damn for those people who are in trouble.

That *anybody* lives on the street in twenty-first-century Britain, for *whatever* reason, is horrifying. It should be a blight on all our consciences. We are a collective, a society, and shouldn't be able to pick and choose when we feel like being a part of it.

Like Benji said, who would wake up one fine morning and simply walk away from a halfway decent life and opt instead to live in pain and penury on a pavement? Blaming the homeless and deeming them to be somehow less *valid* is akin to dismissing a man with one leg as being of no worth because he will never win a marathon, or saying a girl with Down's syndrome is less valuable than you because she can't solve quadratic equations as fast as you can. I've never been able to manage them at all.

And Jade – born to a teenage mum and a father who was a paedophile and a pimp – you wouldn't have needed a crystal ball to see that *her* life was going to end in catastrophe. Still, had to be her fault, right? She could have done things differently, right?

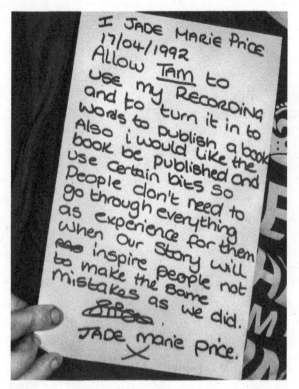

Jade mentioning 'mistakes' she believes she's responsible for

So, we can safely conclude, we needn't feel uneasy about the existence of homeless people. They're not 'us', they're different. They just don't come up to scratch.

The reality? We don't need to blame them. They're busy doing that themselves.

Kerry Evans

'So brilliant, so invigorating, so normal . . . *just to actually have*
an adult conversation and not about homeless issues'

Kerry, Kerry, Kerry – what a mess it all became for her. As a teenager, she'd
come up with a half-baked, poorly thought-out plan to get her own home.
But, like most teenagers, she'd had scant sense of consequences, and
everything went into free fall from the moment she actually got what she
wanted: one horror leading to the next with precision timing.

At sixteen years old, Kerry, who was then living with her mum in a
council flat, wanted to get a place of her own and make her own life. She
wanted her mum to write a letter to the local council saying that she could
no longer support her daughter and was going to kick her out. Kerry
thought she'd then be offered a place in a hostel and from there get a flat
of her own. Her mum was struggling financially and Kerry had (and still
did when I met her) a gusto for life which, instead of being her salvation,
became her downfall. Initially, Kerry's mum refused her request, but eventually, she caved in.

As it all took place so long ago and Kerry had become a heavy drug
user, she couldn't remember exactly what had happened after that, except
that she did get a hostel and then she lost it.

At thirty-five years old, Kerry had spent the majority of her adult life on
the streets or the margins of homelessness. She was tough and you'd have
been a fool to mess with her.

Kerry Evans

Can you remember what it felt like not to have anywhere to live?

It was absolutely terrifying. I didn't know what to expect or what was going to happen next. I was thinking, right, if I go to sleep am I going to get raped? Are they going to kill me? Am I going to land up like the bloke the other day who was tied to a trolley and dumped in the canal?

Where did you sleep on your first night?

I met a guy and he was all right and he said, 'I've got somewhere that I stay and you're more than welcome to come and stay there with me.' It was a car propped up on bricks! It felt safe because I had one seat, at the front, and he had the other side, so there was a little space between us – and the bloody gearstick! I did end up sleeping in the end, but it was so cold. We were there about six weeks.

What did you have with you?

What I stood in. A bit like what I am now. No . . . I may have had a bag with a change of clothes and I did have my underwear! I made sure I brought that! Well, clean knickers anyway!

How long were you homeless the first time?

Eight years at first and a lot of the time it was just in parks, on benches and that was cold. A few times people came and gave me a blanket or something to wrap up in. I've never done a shop doorway – it would probably be more safe because it's lit, but how the hell are you meant to sleep with lights on! And then more or less between twenty and thirty, I was

248

homeless here, in Islington. In between that I did have different hostels for two years and then the flat I've just lost.

How did you lose the flat?

Anti-social behaviour.

And what was your anti-social behaviour?

Well, what it was, the people there didn't want me in the first place. The only reason that I got the flat at all, was because at the time I was in a wheelchair, after I was run over by a thirty-two-tonne lorry – but I got done by quality – it was a Marks and Sparks lorry!

Did they compensate you?

I got £64,500 and then, after a while, I managed to get out of the wheelchair and start walking again.

How long did it take you to get through the sixty-four big ones?

Three and a half months!

Was it good, while it lasted?

In a way, yeah. Mind you I don't remember much of it because I really wasn't sober for hardly any of it, ha! But yeah, the money went. But I put £10,000 away for my boy . . . I've got a son.

Tell me about your son.

He's just turned sixteen. He's a beautiful kid, he really is. He's such a good boy. He's with my mum. About six months ago I found out she moved, took my boy with her and not told anyone where she'd gone. It's been nearly a year now and I haven't seen him.

Do you miss him?

Yeah, [crying openly] he's my world.

It's upsetting you, yeah. I'm sorry. I'm sorry.

It's all right [trying to hold herself together]. He was my world.

How old were you when you had him?

Nineteen.

And did the relationship with the dad go wrong?

Yeah, just a bit! Severely! He was an arsehole. He was terrible.

How does that make you feel about things, that you've been homeless nearly all your adult life?

Makes me wonder where the council are, why the government don't help and stuff like that. I've been kicked out of my address . . . all right, yes, it *was* my fault.

How was it your fault?

I got ASBOs because I used to play loud music all the time. When I put the stereo on, it would start quiet-ish and then get louder and louder until it went full blast.

You seem like a nice person, so what is it that makes you behave like that?

I love my music. I play classical flute and I got up to Grade 8.

So where, in all of this nightmare, did you learn the flute?

I'd asked my mum for a saxophone for Christmas when I was about twelve or thirteen. Wanted a saxophone but landed up with a flute – but never mind! Kept that up – love my music. Mum used to pay for private lessons.

And did you busk, and make money that way?

I could have, but I sold it.

Why?

For alcohol!

So, you were chucked out of your flat recently – what was it that made you behave anti-socially?

Well, towards the end, the last eight months I was there, I played no music – but I did lose my fob-key for the main door so I used to have to ring everyone else's buzzer to get in, so they started complaining about that. They didn't want me there – they wanted me out. Fair play – they got me out.

And what did you do then?

I didn't even know they were kicking me out. I hadn't opened my post. My buzzer went one morning and they said, 'You're Kerry Evans, aren't you?' and there was this woman with two locksmiths behind her and she said, 'I've come to evict you. We'll give you some time to collect your stuff and then you've got to go.'

What did you collect?

I was so angry that I didn't take fuck all. I've got a £4,500 sofa from Multi-york on Tottenham Court Road, from when I had the compensation. I furnished the flat and it was brand new . . . ohhh and a king-size bed. I miss that!

How does that all make you feel?

Angry, annoyed, upset . . . more with myself than anyone else.

So, where have you been sleeping recently?

I've spent a lot of time down at King's Cross – not the best of areas to be, I know, but . . . lots of prostitutes – that's one thing I've never done.

Why not?

That I don't know, because I probably could make a fair bit of money and fund my crack habit, but I'm not selling myself, no. I don't suck cock for 'rock' (crack) and won't go down for 'brown' (heroin).

Where do you get your money from, then? Begging?
Yes.

What's that like – to beg for money?
I hate it.

And that is your only income – no social benefit?
I do. I get ESA [Employment and Support Allowance] and that's £225 a fortnight.

Do you spend most of it on your crack habit?
Crack . . . and the drink is my biggest problem. Been on crack since I was twenty-one.

Is crack expensive? Is it a difficult habit to fund?
I was begging yesterday and then I met a friend and we done £60 on crack and £20 on brown.

So, most of the money that you get goes to support the habits that you've now got?
Drink is my biggest one, my biggest habit.

What do you drink?
K Cider.

Tell me why you started on crack and booze?
I don't know, it helps with the situation I've got at the moment – get a couple of cans down you and you think 'fuck the world'. Bollocks. That's my favourite word, by the way, *bollocks*!

What does crack feel like? I've never tried it.

Really? Well, then you don't want to. I suppose it's the high it gives you – I've never been able to explain it. It's a bloody difficult question! I suppose it makes you feel 'in control', but obviously you bloody well ain't! It's the last thing you are. I mean I can sit and be on my own and feel quite sick with it and then I think, 'What the fuck are you crying for? Come on, girl. Ain't it your fault you are in this situation?'

Is that what you think? That this is all your fault?

My fault that I got kicked out of the flat.

How do you think other people see you?

Well, looking down at me like that, they are obviously disgusted, but, hey, they are higher up and being higher up, that makes them 'better' than me, do you know what I mean? You're better than me? Ha! Fuck yourself, bollocks, ha! Really and truthfully, it makes me feel low. It does.

What do you think about them?

I look at them and I think, 'I bet you had a nice warm bed to sleep in last night, warm, cosy . . . and you might be going to work – at least you can work.' At the moment, one of the reasons I don't have a job is because my leg breaks down and . . .

Yeah, I noticed you were limping really badly. Why haven't they given you crutches, to help you walk? Are you in pain?

Constant . . . are you queasy?

Why?

[Kerry rolled up the leg of her tracksuit bottoms and revealed her calf – red with infection, swollen and with a suppurating ulcer covering several square inches. The smell was dreadful.]

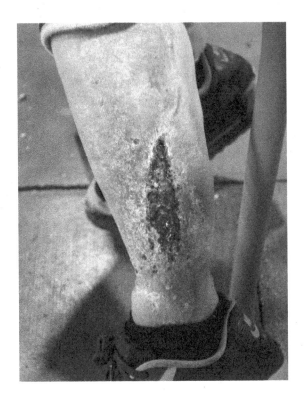

Holy shit! Jesus Christ, Kerry.

A lot of people will look at that and think it's down to drugs and it's not – it was the lorry.

You should be in a fucking hospital, woman. You walk on that leg? I'm horrified. Jesus. Who is looking after that leg?

Me. I have been to the hospital and they put me on five different lots of antibiotics, and all that happens is that it breaks down like that about every two or three months and they dress it again. The skin ruptures and it ulcerates, and they dress it again.

[Kerry was trying not to cry.] **Do you try and stay away from your feelings?**

I really do put them away – they really get in the way. How am I meant to carry on, live like this, sleep rough and let my emotions bother me – it just doesn't work. I would be an emotional wreck.

What do you think about the future?

I think ahead more or less just to the next day. Where the bloody hell I'm going to sleep that night and who the bloody hell is going to come and try and trouble me . . . am I going to land up fighting . . .

But you wouldn't stand a chance with a leg like that?

Oh, I can fight! My dad started me boxing when I was five. Thank you, Dad!

Have you ever been attacked or assaulted living on the street?

I wouldn't say 'attacked' – but 'started on' – yeah, people wanting to have a go – homeless people, passers-by, drunks. The only way I can deal with that is stand up and knock them out! Done that plenty of times!

Is it always men that bother you, or do women get aggressive?

Oh, women can be right bitches. Men are easier to handle than women.

Are you talking about other homeless women?

No, just normal women, women coming out of pubs and stuff. Oh, I don't know, they start, 'Oh, look at the state of you, can't you wash your clothes?' and stuff like that, you know . . . it belittles you, it really does. So, am I going to let it get to me or am I going to show you who the fuck you're talking to? Then I land up decking them, ha ha!

How do manage to keep your clothes clean?

You call these clean?

Well, your cuffs are grubby, but the rest of you looks pretty clean.

I've had this on for the past month. I hate it. I like to get changed every day. At the moment I am going commando! Fuck it, bollocks to the knickers! If I can't change them every day, then I might as well not wear them!

Where do you wash yourself?

Basically, public toilets. The one right behind you! And if you don't mind, I am going to go there in a minute!

[We walked to the public toilets alongside a car park. I let her have a pee in peace and then she told me to come into the disabled cubicle she was using.]

I wash up, wash up my face and all that, occasionally I will stick my head under the tap to like put some water through my hair.

[On the way out of the toilets, heading back to the cafe, I noticed quite how bad Kerry's limp was becoming.]

That looks excruciatingly painful.

Yeah, it doesn't tickle!

How do you keep a sense of humour with all this?

If I didn't keep a sense of humour, I'd be down in the gutter.

Have you ever been sexually assaulted?

[long silence] Been raped. [another long silence]

I'm sorry. Is it too painful to talk about?

Like everything else, it's just another one of those things that happen.

No, it's not just another one of those things.

But in a way, yeah, it is.

Can you tell me what happened? If you don't want to talk about it at all, fine, I'll move on.

Ah, well. [Talking slowly and haltingly.] I was talking to a couple of guys and that and they said, 'Where do you live? We'll come back to yours,' and I said, 'I'm homeless.' They were, 'Oh, we're on the street too – where are you sleeping?' and I said, 'Tonight, do you know what, I haven't got a clue.' And they said, 'We've got somewhere to sleep, we'll take you there.' Stupid bollocks – I wasn't really sure about it, but I thought they are men and – here's the joke – I thought, 'At least I'll be safe!'

Did it happen inside or outside?

Outside [in tiny voice]. Outside.

[Kerry was becoming too distressed. It felt wrong to continue, so I turned off the recorder and left her alone for a bit while I went and got us more coffee. When I came back, she looked suddenly terribly tired.]

And what about sleep?

I tend not to sleep much when I'm out. I don't like sleeping because you're always worried about what is going to happen – am I going to have a replay of the past? The rapes seriously affected me.

How long would you typically beg, before you got up and moved?

Two, two and a half hours.

How much could you do in that time?

Well, yesterday I got forty quid.

So, you get a bit of money together and then what do you do?

Go and meet someone else and score some crack. But yesterday I was sat there till about five o'clock and there was a bloke who works with abandoned dogs – and I spent about three quarters of an hour chatting to him – we were just having a conversation, a chat. Ah, that was so brilliant, so invigorating, so *normal* . . . just to actually have an adult conversation and not about homeless issues.

Do you miss the sense of being part of 'normal' life?

Yeah. Miss it big time, sometimes, I really do, but there is nothing I can really do about it. I grab the moments, like I had yesterday, when I can grab them, but they really don't happen very often. What I would really like is my own place again, my boy living with me and just being a mum.

Do you think it's going to happen?

No [almost a whisper].

Why?

[crying . . . there was no answer]

Who can you talk to about your feelings?

I avoid doing it. Completely. Just recently, I've made a new friend, a girl, and she is great, but we are still in the early stages of friendship so . . . one of my biggest problems is that I trust too easily.

Why is that a problem?

People take kindness for weakness. And then they walk all over you, so . . .

Describe yourself?

Ha! [a long pause] I call myself a joker. Never a dull moment when you've got me about! You never frown – always smiling, always laughing!

[I point to her plastic carrier bag.] **And this bag contains your life?**

Well, at the moment, yeah.

What's in your bag?

My books. I can't wait to read that. And a diary. And my sugar, because of my diabetes. And that's for my crack pipe. [Picking up a wooden chop-stick.] It's for pushing the gauze up and down and cleaning the pipe.

Kerry's prized possessions

What do you like best about yourself?

It used to be my hair . . . it was really long and really curly. It goes cork-screw, but I shaved it off to piss an ex-boyfriend off!

Tell me about the flower, there with your stuff.

It was left in my bag from yesterday and when I beg I put it behind my ear.

So this is your 'begging outfit'? It's cool!

Stop! You're making me laugh.

[A friend of Kerry's walked past our table, looking to repay £1.50 that she had borrowed from her. The two then decided to head down towards King's Cross to a place where homeless women can get a shower. Kerry limped away, roaring with laughter.]

Income Oddities

I had noticed early on that the women I was meeting consistently made much less money from begging than did the men. I couldn't for the life of me think why that was. I would have thought that people were, in fact, socially conditioned to be *more* sympathetic to women, but it seems not.

Perhaps the truth is that the sight of homeless women is simply too much of a social shame to even acknowledge, so people give less often.

Kerry mentioned that she'd made £40 the day before I met her and afterwards I regretted not asking her if that was atypical: it did seem like a lot. Charisse had had to beg for about three days to get half that, the £20-odd she needed for a night shelter at the weekend, whereas the men I talked to could typically make ten times that amount over the same period.

Beth and Jade said they slept in the day because it was safer, so it may be that women earn less from begging because they are too scared to try and sleep at night, thus losing prime begging time during the day.

Jade also commented that people – men, I suppose – want something *from* women in return for their coins. That would be sex.

And then there are the working homeless. Some, like Brad and Patrick, make money selling the *Big Issue*. Others, like Benji (who worked when he could doing agency jobs on building sites) or Martins (who was due to start a cleaning job even though he had no home to go to at the end of the day) don't make much at all. I also met a full-time van driver called Dave who lived in a tube station. (He's the man pictured brushing his teeth on page 3; he let me take his picture but he didn't want to talk about his life.)

I suspect that unless a person finds some sort of employment very soon after becoming homeless, the likelihood of that happening decreases rapidly with each passing month on the street. As these months start to take their toll, the mental and physical ability to beg successfully, let alone find a job, just slips further out of reach. Especially, it seems, for women, who become less able to attract money from passing strangers, as their physical appearance deteriorates.

Lewis

Lewis was sweet-mannered but simply too crippled by fatigue to talk at any length, although he was happy for his photograph to be taken. A lot of homeless people are too tired to talk – a sincere statement of fact. Exhausted bodies, exhausted minds and no energy to organise meaningful self-expression.

Lewis was almost apologetic when he told me that he was also too depressed to explain his life. All I discovered was that his wife had died, he had mental health problems, and that the week before, as he slept, someone had cut the strings on his bag and robbed him.

He asked for a coffee and as there was a Caffè Nero a few feet away, I obliged. As I was leaving he said this:

'There's no point to anything, no point talking . . . no one would care anyway. But ta for the coffee.'

John Leslie Picken

If John Leslie Picken had been Neil Armstrong and I'd been asking him what it was like to be the first man to walk on the moon, he would have said, 'All right, I s'pose.' I marvelled at his economy with language and his quiet resilience. To begin with I really did wonder if he was playing me, giving obtuse, monosyllabic answers to get rid of me. He wasn't.

John had been homeless for seven years. He'd lost his job as a security officer through drinking. Here are some snippets from our (extremely) brief conversation.

How did you cope with suddenly being homeless?

I just got on with it. It's fine. Somewhere to eat, somewhere to sleep, it's fine. You have to bear with it . . . through alcohol. It helps you relax and then eventually you can drop to sleep.

What's your mood like, most of the time? How do you feel inside?

I don't feel too bad, really. Probably worse things in life, know what I mean?

And did you ever go inside [prison]?

Yeah, quite a few times.

And what's it like not being free?

I don't mind.

You seem to cope with anything?

Yeah.

How far ahead do you think?

Next day. Take every day as it comes.

Where do you think you will be in one year's time?

Hopefully off the street and back into work. I've got a job lined up, the only problem, holding me up, is accommodation. As soon as I've got somewhere to live, I've got a job.

What do you find the hardest thing about this lifestyle?

I don't find it hard at all, honestly, I don't.

Is this for real?

It doesn't faze me at all.

Why?

I could be fighting in Afghanistan, losing me legs or me arms . . . there's a lot more people worse off than me. You've got to think, yeah, you've got people fleeing war-torn countries and everything – they're a lot worse off than me.

What are your prized possessions?

Me.

Yourself?

Yeah.

Do you have mementos, from the past?

No.

So, what do you keep with you?

A sleeping bag.

That's it?

Yeah.

You couldn't travel any lighter if you were a bird.

No.

Do you ever complain?

Not really.

What's your personality like?

Oh, I've got a real personality! I love me football, and I love the cars, especially going up Mayfair, Park Lane, in the car parks at the hotels. There's one in there, a six-wheel Mercedes, and it's plated gold and that's £25 million, on its own!

Night Frights

London at night used to be my backdrop for a fun evening out. Going to the theatre, to see a band or to eat in a restaurant: London belonged to me and the friends I was with. There was an obliviousness that accompanied us; the stage was somehow set only for me and mine – I never saw other people except as a part of my story.

That all changed on this trip and, notwithstanding the fact that I was quite edgy, ready for any threat, I found this new way of being in my city vaguely thrilling.

Dressed inconspicuously, with only my camera, fags and an emergency taxi fare home should I need it, I wandered invisibly, weaving through the multitudes and feeling the solitude of the melancholy backstreets. My eyes were generally cast downward as I scanned the doorways and the nooks and crannies of major tourist attractions, looking for the people that perhaps previously I'd not noticed. The National Portrait Gallery, the theatres, the churches and the English National Opera were not just venues for entertainment – they harboured the outcast and the lonely.

I was amazed at how some of the homeless were brave enough to bury themselves completely, with their heads and, more to the point, eyes and ears, hidden from potential predators, in a sleeping bag. Others were wide awake, hoping to make money from the casually and amiably drunk, who were looser with their spare change than usual.

There were also many drunk, loud and, I hoped, superficially belligerent young revellers about, jeering, leering and presumably having a good time. I was uneasy enough about coming face-to-face with them as a pedestrian, but they would have seemed a great deal more threatening had

I been sitting on the pavement. I saw a lot of fights, one bloodied face and plenty of screeching laughter, screaming and threats.

I never took the recorder out at night as there was little point – too much noise and too much tension. But I learned a lot simply by sitting down at street level and chatting as the night unfolded. Being invisible was becoming familiar (and not entirely unpleasant). I had never seen so many knees and generally kept my arm braced in front of me to stop people stumbling into me. My temper became slightly frayed.

The city is lit beautifully at night, ablaze with pretty lights and cheerful colours, but there's also a mournful cast to it all: crumpled people, sitting with their heads down and arms wrapped round bent knees, looking as though they've been lit by lanterns.

In the poorly lit alleys and side streets, particularly around the south side of the Strand, behind the Savoy Hotel and around Embankment, I tended to startle anyone I found. I often asked why they chose these hidden, dark spots and they said it was to get away from noise and light to try and get some sleep.

I would have been terrified. No one would have heard me scream.

Kieron Watkinson

Kieron and I had crossed paths before, but then he had been trying to come off Spice and was visibly suffering, so I'd left him alone. At daybreak one morning, however, he was in one of his favoured spots, and seemed quite altered: looking fresher and halfway to being well. He was clear he didn't want to talk about his kids nor much about his previous criminal life, but he did want to give me insights into the rest of his world.

He was thirty years old.

This is not a time to be talking, is it? Six o'clock in the bloody morning. Just before I turned on the recorder you were telling me about Spice.

The government have allowed it to be sold, yeah, because they say it's herbal incense – but we are not meant to be smoking it. That's the way the government is getting away with it, yeah, by saying it's 'not for human consumption'.

I saw you a couple of weeks ago, smoking it, and now you look quite different – a well, handsome man . . .

I stopped Spice. I would wake up in the morning and first thing, I'd be sick.

What made you decide to try and stop Spice?

My health – my breathing. I couldn't breathe properly. I can't run any more.

How would you describe your character?

Quite bubbly, outgoing – like a laugh. And I love dangerous sports.

What is it with guys and dangerous sports? What's wrong with knitting?

I just like to chuck myself out of a plane with a parachute on – it's an adrenaline rush.

Sitting here, with no power, how does that make you feel?

It makes me feel angry – but it's just the way the government want us. Yeah . . . the government don't work for us. They lie. The government lie to get in power and the government lie to keep power. They've got the money and the power to end homelessness, but they don't want to. Westminster are saying 'Cutbacks! Cutbacks!' . . . Wait on – no?! Three pay rises a year? Fuck that. The English people have fucked themselves by voting for the Conservatives.

What does it make you feel when people misjudge you?

Makes me angry. Yeah, they've not even tried to come and find what my soul is about. They've just gone, 'Oh, fuck it – he's homeless, he's a scumbag.' No – come and find out what I'm about and then judge me [pointing skyward] . . . He's the only man that's going to judge me. I'm no better than you and you're no better than me.

How do you deal with all this stuff, in your head?

I don't. I don't. I could explode at any minute. Don't worry, not with someone like you, yeah! You're safe, 'cos you're a woman.

Your future? Do you think it is achievable?

It can be . . . yeah, it can be.

Do you think you have the determination?

I have, yeah.

What do you survive on?

Charitable donations off the public.

And how much can you make in a week?

A good week? £300, £400. A bad week, £100. But I put money into my kids' bank accounts, so don't think I'm just taking money and . . .

Do you ever spend money to get a night in a hostel?

I can, yeah, but when you get over there it depends on whether they've got a room free or not. No Second Night Out – that's just a place to send you back home – it's shit.

['Back home' is a reference to councils trying to return homeless people to the place where they came from in the first instance: where they have what councils call 'a connection'. Ironically, this connection is often the very thing that the person has tried to escape from in the first place.]

They tried to send me back and I said, 'Listen, you're not sending me back nowhere, right?' Basically, it's a reconnection type place – they try and reconnect you to where you are from . . . but as I said when I came down here, I said, 'I've come down here for a reason, yeah? So why are you trying to send me back there?' The police were speaking to the support workers and that saying, 'You can't send him back here – there's gang trouble, you'll end up having the boy murdered.'

What is it like, never being able to close a door?

It's good. I can get up in the morning and I can just fuck off – I can just fuck off to another town.

What about friendships? If you fucked off, you'd lose them.

They come and go. In my way of life, I've never had friends – it's always been associates. After my best friend got shot, I always thought that if I made friends, my friends would get hurt.

What about loneliness?

Don't bother me. With all these people out here?

Yeah, but you don't know any of them.

I know, but I can still say good morning to them and smile at them. I actually had a woman come up to me this week and say, 'What do you want for Christmas, Kieron?'

What did you say?

'A nice fleecy tracksuit!' When that happens, I think yeah, there's good people out there!

So, you would say you've adapted?

Yep. If all the power went tomorrow – all the electrics went tomorrow? I'd survive! See all these people here? They'd crumble. And that's the one thing I know I can laugh about – because I *know* I've survived.

What do you think you need, to survive?

Air in my lungs, a good sleeping bag and a good pair of feet. And that's it. That gets me through. A good smile as well.

If you could wish for something, what would it be?

I'd wish for homelessness to end. It offends me.

Mark Wilson

Mark Wilson was thirty-five, came from Middlesbrough and had epilepsy.

He'd fallen out with his mum when he was fourteen. Since then they haven't spoken and he's been homeless, or on the edge of it. His first couple of years were spent living in a van outside a taxi office, surviving only because he could sleep the odd night at his nan's and his brother would bring him food from time to time. Back then, he was too young to qualify for a B&B. It was unclear whether he even went to school.

He was eighteen when he first came to London, and ended up with a serious cocaine problem – 'It can be so stressful, living on the street. I'm supposed to take medication for the epilepsy, but I'm totally out of it. I've got no medication, I've got nothing. My doctor's in Great Chapel Street, but I've got to wait till Monday.'

It was now dawn on Saturday.

I saw Mark many times and he was usually stoned and always looked really unwell. I wondered if he saw himself getting out of this life and once asked him where he thought he might be in six months. He said flatly, 'I'm going to still be down here.' I could think of nothing to say in response.

Masquerading

I prefer not to shop at Tesco – I believe they've damaged small (and not so small) local shops and I don't like the way they do business. It's a sort of credo of mine.

A credo that went out of the window during the work for this book. The more run-down and fatigued I became the more I found myself in the Tesco Metro at the bottom of my road in Highbury. The truth was that I could no longer be bothered to hike up to the Holloway Road and shop more ethically. It did make me wonder how much of your sense of self evaporates with exhaustion. Being perky and principled is a lot easier than being knackered and principled.

Anyway, at the end of a long day toiling around the West End, I was in Tesco, a few steps from home. All I wanted to buy was maple syrup and some crumpets. I didn't have any cash but I did have a debit card and was twitchy because I'd forgotten to transfer more money into the account and wasn't entirely sure I'd have enough left on it to pay for my shopping. (Remember when I said I didn't always manage my life well?)

A strange thing started happening as I was queuing to pay. And it wasn't nice.

It's a small shop and there were a lot of people in the queue but only one till was open. All the people in front of me seemed to have vast amounts of shopping and were taking forever to get through at the check-out – and the guy at the till was very slow.

I was growing irritable and impatient, dreading the idea that I would be embarrassed in front of everybody if my card was refused for a purchase that would come in at less than a tenner. I knew how ragged and unkempt I looked and was genuinely worried people would think I'd nicked the card. It would be mortifying, and if it *was* going to happen I wanted to hurry up and get it over with. When I was next but one in line, the guy in front dumped his basket on the floor to go in search of something he'd forgotten. Actually, it was several somethings, and he was gone for ages.

Then it happened.

I was aware that I was shifting from foot to foot, muttering audibly and aggressively to myself, saying things like, 'Oh, for Christ's sake, sort your shit out', and 'If you can't remember what you need to buy, write a sodding list!'

My mask had slipped. I wasn't behaving properly in public. I was sufficiently tired and fractious – me, after a mere few weeks – that I wasn't able to control my smouldering irritation. And that was all it was – irritation. What might I have been like had the surrounding events been more tense, more febrile than a long queue in a shop and had I been living on a pavement for the last six months?

I could see more clearly how the homeless lose their 'masks' – they have so much more reason to than I had ever understood. They are permanently exposed and raw with nothing and nowhere to hide behind at all.

Shame and embarrassment make you prickly, sharp even. The homeless have so few opportunities to show their beauty. Their outward expression of themselves belies the great hurt they carry on the inside. Perhaps the coarseness, the bad language and the posturing lie beneath all our veneers but most of us have a greater ability to keep a lid on it all.

Darren O'Shea

'I didn't learn anything useful in the army . . . being able to shoot someone from half a mile away doesn't help you get a job'

A random act, committed against him when he was just a toddler, altered the course of Darren's life.

At eighteen, he joined the army and was sent to Kosovo. The horrors he witnessed there damaged him permanently. When he came back from his tour, a few years later, he got married, started a family and raised his children. Outwardly, Darren had an unexceptional life. But his hidden story revealed something quite different.

He'd made a colossal attempt to rejoin ordinary domestic society – to go round the supermarket, change the plug on the kettle and do all those little things that glue our lives together – but it was precarious. He tried to conceal his mental deterioration and deal with it all on his own but, in the end, the pain was simply too much and things began to go very wrong.

And then, about two years ago, after yet another arbitrary event, his life fell into too many pieces and he couldn't put it back together again.

When I met Darren for the first time he had been reading, sitting on the pavement near the entrance to the Lyric Theatre. He shared this space with his friend, Matt, and they looked out for each other, travelled together and gave each other emotional support. (Matt's story is next.)

Darren was understated and articulate and, I think, a very complex man. I felt his gentleness and fury in equal measure when I spoke with him. Darren and Matt – who came as sort of banded pack – were enormously comforting, easy and fun to be with.

Sometimes, as when I took his portrait, we could sit for an hour together and not speak at all.

Darren O'Shea

The worst of all this? You've got no routine, you've got no structure. The days just roll one into the other and if it wasn't for the fact that we pick up the *Metro* and the *Evening Standard* each day, we probably wouldn't even know what the date was, let alone the day.

And people looking down at you. Throwing things at you. You're asleep and then you wake up and someone's pissing on you. Or people will go past in a car and think it's funny to throw a pound coin at you, as hard as they can, hoping they're going to hit you.

Most people, you can see it on their face – 'You must have put yourself in that situation, so it's your fault that you're there' – but if you bothered to find out, you'd realise it happened over the course of eight days when I was lying in a hospital bed and I had no control over *any* of it.

[Outrage in his voice at this point.] No. It wasn't my fault. It makes me angry.

You want to get up and kick their heads in, but you're the one who will get in trouble, not them. So, even when people go past and swear at you, you just have to say, 'Oh, thank you very much. Have a nice day.' You just have to ignore it. That's why I sit here and read books, so most of it just goes over my head. In one ear and out the other. But on the other side of it, you get people who really *do* care . . . so . . . it does balance out, a bit. Not as much as you'd like it to, but . . .

You just learn to live with the frustration. You have to or you go nuts. A lot of people, they *do* go nuts. They have mental breakdowns, they get sectioned for six months and then get kicked back out again. And because they just can't see a way out of the cycle they're in, next thing is they're in the middle of the High Street, tears running down their face, screaming at

God, you know, screaming at their dead mothers and going completely doolally. Then a couple of months' rest back in hospital and then they say, 'All right, off you go. Take this medication.' [laughs despairingly]

I was in the papers, the *Mirror*, when I was a baby. Over Christmas, back in the late seventies, I was kidnapped. By the babysitter, for two weeks. [an awful, hollow laugh and a very long silence] I was found in a pram outside a pub [very long silence]. My mum had a nervous breakdown. They pumped her so full of drugs and whatever that when they found me and brought me to her she said, 'That's not my baby.'

Toddler kidnap hunt

A TODDLER was missing last night with a girl he calls "auntie." Police hunting the pair said: "We think he has been abducted. We are very worried for the boy." Eighteen-month-old Darren O'Shea was last seen near his home in Peckham, South London on Monday with a friend of his mother.

So that was it – straight into foster care. I was under social services until I was twenty-one, so I didn't have a lot to do with my real family. I was fostered out to a very middle-class family but they had two kids and I was their whipping boy. I went back to my family briefly, back in Peckham, but I didn't fit in . . . and I wasn't going to change how I spoke just to fit in. They automatically thought I was looking down my nose at them. My mum recovered, she did . . . she's gone on to have more kids and whatever, but . . . [very long silence].

I went to a very, very good secondary school but I never took my GCSEs. I got kicked out! I was just too rebellious by then, so, you know . . . I left school and worked in my mate's barber shop, then lived in Benidorm for a year. I went back to Peckham for about a month. Walked in the Job Centre and thought, 'Fuck it, I'm joining the army and getting away again.'

Up to two years ago, everything was normal, with the missus, at home with the kids. My wife's a mental health nurse, so she was doing twelve-hour shifts and I was a house-husband. She went to uni and I looked after the kids. Then we split up and I moved out, rented a room but was still seeing the kids every day, 'cos I was still looking after them.

Then I went into hospital for eight days because I have some serious problems with my lungs. My tenancy agreement, for the room I was renting, ran out when I was in hospital. When I came out? No room, and all my stuff had been chucked in a skip in the front garden by the landlord. It had rained all week. I had 500 books – all gone. Some of them were worth some money, as well – some first edition hardbacks. I had every single Harry Potter in the hardback first edition and they were worth quite a few quid. I went through them one day, just the cost of buying the books from a shop, and it was over £15,000. Lot of money to lose. And that was all there in case my kids wanted to go to uni.

I love reading fantasy, *Lord of the Rings*, that kind of stuff, and ancient Rome ones. Although it's a fictional story – all the battles and main events – it's all real history and that's the way I think of learning history.

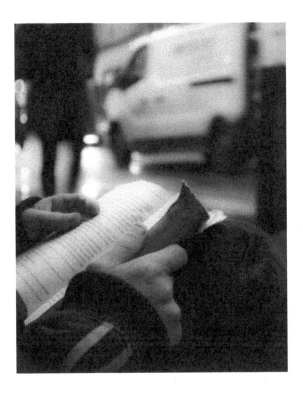

Anyway, I got hold of the landlord – he said, your tenancy agreement ran out, you weren't around to sign a new one. I hadn't made myself intentionally homeless, he said, so the council would help . . . and that's the biggest joke in the country, really. They didn't help. I wasn't priority. It was, 'Go and find somewhere to rent and we'll pay housing benefit, but finding the deposit is all down to you.' It's about £90 a week for a double room, so two weeks' rent in advance, that's £180, and another two weeks' deposit for that, so it's still £360. So, where do I get it from? I only get £250 a fortnight on the sick benefit.

If we want to use the night hostel it's £18 each a day, so that's why we sit here and try and raise £36. We haven't managed it yet but a lot of that is down to the drugs. It sounds great, but why should I hand over £18 to sleep in a big room with twenty other guys? The problems with my chest got worse because I *did* use a night shelter last winter. And that's why they thought I had TB. I'm better off sleeping outside. And if you want a hot shower and wash your clothes, that goes up to £28 . . . so I may as well be paying fucking rent, then! £28 a day for seven days is about £200 and rent for a *week* is only £90!

The charity workers come around at one, two o'clock in the morning saying, 'Oh, we've got room for you, we've got room for you.' I tell them to fuck off! 'It's hard enough to get to sleep as it is and you only want the fucking money – piss off and leave us alone. We were asleep. Come to us at eight o'clock in the evening!' They don't come any earlier, like at a sensible time, because they know you probably don't have the money from begging yet.

The £250 is because I'm signed off sick with bipolar and post-traumatic stress disorder, from being in the army. I go up, and then crash down. It took them over a decade to diagnose me with PTSD.

I joined up just before I was nineteen. I saw bad things. In Kosovo. I did, yeah. Uncovering mass graves [in a blunt, affectless voice]. I didn't mind being shot at – that was easy, the easy bit – but because it was the middle of winter and everything was frozen – all the bodies, they hadn't started decomposing so all the expressions on their faces were exactly the same as the second they died. It was just before I came out, so I was turning twenty-two.

No one should see it. Doesn't matter your age. For somebody to be confronted with that, it's going to mess you up, no matter what. I was in the Royal Green Jackets – a rifleman. [He abruptly stopped talking and became withdrawn somehow, as if he'd forgotten I was there. He was in another place.]

When I came back, I'd done my three years. That's what I signed up for and I was going to come out for a year and then go back, but then I met the kids' mum and she got pregnant. Then it got to a stage where [all this haltingly] well, you come out and you drink – I didn't even get into drugs until I was twenty-eight, and that was just smoking a simple joint. I had insomnia for ten years which didn't help! You start seeing things with sleep deprivation.

I wouldn't have got accepted back in the army – I was too nuts by then. Not violent against other people, but violent as in against brick walls, and very psychotic. You just lose all sense of reason – there's nothing in your mind that says, 'Right, that's a step too far.'

I did think I was going to get away from the army relatively unscathed but . . . that was it. I never regret joining. Surrounded by your mates, twenty-four–seven, you don't really want for anything. Apart from self-discipline, I didn't learn anything useful in the army. There are no skills that I learned that translate into civilian life – being able to shoot someone from half a mile away doesn't help you get a job.

That was my job. I was a professional soldier – that was the trade I learned. I didn't learn how to build engines or anything like that. My job was to learn how to be a better soldier, a better fighter. That was it. *None* of that translates into another job.

My wife wasn't able to help [emphatic]. She got *in* to mental health because of me. She wouldn't *dare* turn around to a patient, or a client, as they are called now, 'Oh, pull your socks up,' but she said it to me because I was her partner. I didn't get any help because no one knew there was anything *majorly* wrong until I tried to blow my house up, with just me in it. I'd had a row with her and she'd left. And she had a fixation with calling the police, and I decided I wasn't going to have the police in *my* house. I had headphones on, listening to music and it was all wired up to the doorbell . . . so the police would have come, gone *ding dong* and then *boom*.

Obviously I got put on remand, in prison [laughs an empty laugh] and they said, 'Oh right, OK, we're guessing there's something really wrong with you, then.' And then psychiatrists, 'Oh, you should have been on this medication ten years ago and you probably wouldn't be in this situation now' . . . but, ten years of not knowing what's wrong with you? The damage is done. [Darren's wife found a new partner. He'd not seen his kids since he'd lost his home and had come to London to see if he could find his mum.]

I miss seeing the kids. I went from seeing them every day to not seeing them at all. It was difficult but I was a good dad! So, you know, she always came home to a clean flat and I did all the cooking – none of this takeaway shit – I'd do all the shopping, buy the ingredients and cook from scratch and we always sat down at the kitchen table and ate.

Anyway, I was born down the road in Peckham, so after we split up and I lost the room I rented, I thought, well, I'll jump on Facebook, find my mum's address and I'll go there . . . but she hadn't used it in so long it's no longer active.

Being homeless is scary, because you just imagine the worst. You don't want to sleep on your own and obviously you don't sleep properly because you have to be half awake, no matter what.

With the drugs, I just started out smoking heroin in roll-ups and it's, 'Oh, this will warm you up . . .' and it does – you do it and you are lovely and warm. For a couple of hours. If you've got any aches and pains, you know, they go for a couple of hours and then you make the same mistake as everyone else . . . 'I'll be able to control this' – next thing you know it's, 'Oh my God. Why do I feel like this?' You're going through withdrawal – you need some more. The alternative is to go down and see this doctor and get put on methadone, but you ask any heroin addict – that's even worse to come off of than the heroin. It's worse than taking the gear. The only reason why people go on the methadone is that you can still do the gear on top of it.

But I'm also honest – I don't want to give up doing the drugs at the minute, but I've only been doing it for a little while, so . . . someone like Matt, he's been doing it for so many years that he *does* want to stop. To me, it's still a bit of a novelty and it breaks up my day. After a hit, I just feel 'normal.' If I *don't* take it, it just builds up and up – first of all you get stomach pains and you feel like you need to go to the toilet but at the same time you can get constipated. You get hot and cold sweats, restless, agitated, you can't sit still, you can't lay down, can't concentrate. I mean, ideally, you do it and you have your next hit before all that starts up. But that doesn't work in practice.

That's everything, there . . . [pointing to his stuff] the clothes on my back, a double duvet, a sleeping bag and a couple of pillows. There's no point in personal things, no point. Things go missing so quickly that you just have the basics. When you're asleep, you can't leave a cup or a hat out, because if there's any money in it someone – and it will be another home-less person – will steal off you. That's the sickening thing about it – the people that will rob you are the people that are in *exactly* the same posi-tion as you.

This is a ridiculous thing – we get arrested for begging, go to court, get a *massive* fine and then we stand in court and say, 'Excuse me, Your Hon-our, I've to go off and beg now, to pay this fine . . . and then I'm going to get caught begging and you're going to fine me on top of the fine for trying to pay the first fine – so fuck you, send me to prison.' I'll have six weeks in the nice and warm, a bed, three meals a day, telly, kettle . . . you know, everything I want and I won't be in the cold. But if you say, 'I want to go to prison,' they won't send you.

If you read my sign the only thing I ask for is hot chocolate. Everything else is just a statement of fact – ex-British army, homeless, penniless. I'm *not* asking for a damned thing. Their argument is that you're putting your-self in a position where you *can*. My argument is – well, people can just read the sign and then if they choose to give something, that's entirely down to them. I don't ask and I don't have a cup out. You're not allowed to have a cup out, 'cos that *is* begging. I just sit there and read my book. If someone comes up and gives me a tenner – 'Thank you very much, have a nice day.' I've never begged before in my life before I came here. It's hor-rible. It's just something I never imagined myself having to do. I feel low, cheap [wry laugh]. I didn't go back home, near my wife and my kids, because it would have been sod's law – the first time I sat down, my kids would have come past. That would have killed me.

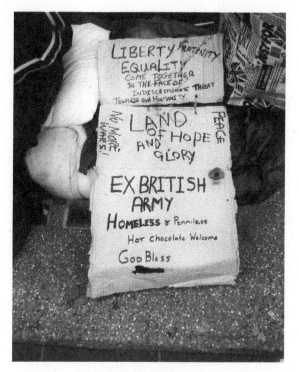

A controversial message

All this affects your health, of course it does. Pollution, for a start. You're at 'exhaust level' – over the centre of London it's *brown*. And then you think, 'Bloody hell! I'm breathing that in. Constantly.' And the cold – I've got a pair of shorts on now, tracksuit bottoms and a pair of jeans. Then I'm sitting on the double duvet, wrapped up. You have to stand up and walk around, stretch and move every so often. Coldest winter in fifty years apparently, this year . . . we'll make more money! That's about the only plus out of it! Last night was a horror – a bit windy! When you're trying to smoke a pipe under the cover, hah hah!

Sometimes I do think about the future, a couple of weeks ahead, but I haven't got an exit strategy [soft voice]. My plan was to go to Peckham, but I can't find my mum or that family. So, it's all a bit stuck. I'll see out Christmas as obviously it'll be good for money, especially if it's snowy, and then just see what happens in January. [long silence] That's about as far as you can plan ahead. [We sat, not speaking, for a long while. I was afraid to talk in case he cried. I didn't want to embarrass him.]

Funnily enough, the kids' mum has said it has made me nicer – more understanding. I don't know. I suppose 'cos you see what it's like right at the bottom but the world's never changed. It's never *ever* changed. Read books about ancient Rome, and it's no different to how it is here. No difference whatsoever. The ones that have money will always have money. The ones in the middle, they'll either make money or they won't and the ones at the bottom will always be at the bottom.

Do you think you are always going to be at the bottom?

I don't know. I hope not.

Matt

'I don't take heroin to get high, I take heroin to be well.
Not to die – there you go – not to die'

A tall, handsome, well-built man, Matt could have been one of those gallant heroes in a Jane Austen novel. Probably in his thirties, he was attentive, courteous and charming. A little shy and very sweet. I liked him very much indeed; he was a treasure of a man. Matt might be a missed chance for us all and could give much over the years of his life.

He may yet.

Matt

First thing, tell me about the mouse you were just talking about!
[before I had turned on the recorder]

I woke up about five o'clock this morning and I could feel something on my neck – it was a little mouse and it was really cute. I tried to get him to come back in my hood but he just stayed behind my pillow. I was going, 'Darren, wake up! Look! My little pet mouse!' Once before, on the street, I had a magpie, from a baby. He'd fallen down from the nest and the mum, she just buzzed around and checked on her other chicks and then left him – or her – and I thought I either put it out of its misery or I try and – and I think since I've had my daughter, my opinion of nature and nurture has changed completely – so, it sounds really gross, but I chewed up worms! And fed it like a mum would but I didn't realise you had to swallow it and then regurgitate! I didn't do that!

Did it survive?

Yep! I had him for seven months, yeah.

How come he didn't fly away?

He flew away a couple of times but he came back, because I was feeding him and they go to wherever they're feeding. I remember in my mum's back garden, my dad used to wait for this blackbird to come down and whistle and then he'd go out and feed it – I had the same connection with this magpie. Mad isn't it!

What was your life like before?

I was quite a poorly baby – I had my tonsils, my appendix and my gall bladder all taken out but then I grew into this big, huge person that I am now! I loved my childhood. I remember when we moved from London I got quite miserable.

Who brought you up?

My mum and dad and my grandma and my aunty. [a long silence] This is hard – I remember we hadn't been on holiday for ages because my grandma was really poorly, but my mum and my grandma had had a discussion that she would go to a care home and we could go away for a week . . . while we were on holiday my grandma died. And that quite devastated me. I'd come home from school and she was always there. So I asked my aunty Joey – my grandma's sister – to be my nan. And then she died. And then we moved away to Newbury. I didn't really settle in. Hated it. Then I left school and went to college.

Did you get any qualifications?

No. I left school with no qualifications and I then got taken out of the exams to go to Africa.

Tell me about Africa?

With my mum, dad, my brother and my aunty, I went on a three-month trip to Africa but I stayed on a bit longer there. I was sixteen. My aunty and uncle had moved over there because of his job at Zimoco, Mercedes in Zimbabwe. What a beautiful place – to see that wildlife up close and in real life changes your perceptions of zoos and that. I absolutely loved it and I didn't want to come home . . . but I did in the end. I stayed there six months. I came back and went to college, trained as a chef, whizzed past the practical – the theory I really struggled with – but I got distinctions after two years and went on to do little jobs and that in catering for about fifteen years off and on.

During these years, when you were working, what was your life?

I stayed at mum and dad's, at my girlfriend's and lived in at pubs and hotels where I worked. I built a . . . a regular life, yeah . . . me, the missus, kids, job. A life. Yeah, I had a life. It was just . . . you know when you don't feel you belong? I've never felt that I belonged anywhere.

What happened?

I got so depressed that whatever help the doctors tried to give me didn't seem to work. But . . . the drugs on the street, they did.

When did the depression start setting in?

Nine, ten years old? Didn't come on so severe until later on in life. I didn't want to work, I didn't want to talk to people, I didn't want to show interest in anything . . . I just didn't want to exist.

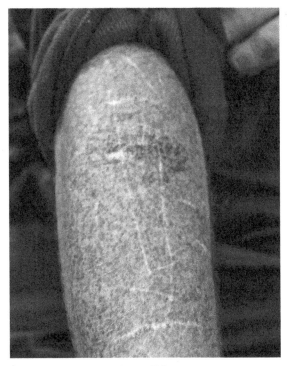

Scars from self-harming

I guess this was affecting your family life?

Yeah . . . [silence] . . . I . . . [silence] . . . just . . . you know people say they feel black and they just want to close their eyes and just stay in that dark room and don't want to see anyone – that's how I felt every day. But you have to get yourself up and you have to face the world – especially when you've got kids, you know – there are things you have to do.

How old were they then?

My daughter was a baby, like two or three, and my mum and my dad, they were great, they had my daughter every time I needed them to.

And your partner, the mum of the little girl? Was she supportive?

No! Not really, no. I think because I had tried medications with the doctors and that didn't work and I then chose to try something else – street drugs – that's when my life spiralled out of control with my family side of things.

And what did you try first, to try to fix your head?

I tried speed, pot and Es and then went round my friend's house and he was there, with heroin. He was quite a bad depressive and he seemed really fine on it so I said, 'Give us a bit,' and he was like, 'No, no Matt, you don't want this' – but I said I was old enough to make my own decisions. When I first tried it I was twenty-one and I was twenty-seven when I got addicted.

What did it make you feel, when you took it?

Unbelievable. The biggest blanket wrapped round me, I was so warm, everything felt right and the weight of the world had been taken off my shoulders. People say it's better than sex – I wouldn't say that, I wouldn't go that far, but it's like having the biggest hug in the world, and everything that can ever hurt you has just gone. But what you don't see, and what people don't understand, is that is the *first* feeling, and you never get that feeling again, but you are always chasing it. The first couple of times you feel that blanket, but by then you're addicted and you're sick. Now, when I do my heroin, it just makes me normal. It allows me to walk, talk and achieve things – it just stops me being ill.

What happens if you don't take it?

You feel very ill, very ill. You lose all your bodily functions – you end up pooing yourself, coming, being sick – not just food sick but ripping the whole of your stomach lining. I was like that on Sunday. I was very poorly on Sunday – such terrible pains while you're waiting to score. I don't take heroin to get high, I take heroin to be well. Not to die – there you go – not to die.

So, you had a perfectly ordinary life, you suffered from severe depression, you experimented with drugs – how did you end up losing everything?

I split up with the missus because of my drug use and went back to my mum's and lived in a caravan in her front garden before I became homeless. And then I just walked out one day. I'd had enough of living in a caravan and I ended up living in a hostel.

Why couldn't you live in the house with your mum?

Because me and my dad were constantly arguing, and it was better for me to stay in the caravan than me and my dad being in the same room.

Why were you arguing?

Because I was a great failure to him – that's how I feel – I let him down. I think he feels that I let him down. We were really close when I was little because I played rugby and he was my coach – he played for the adult team, but he coached us as well. I went to a proper school just for the rugby and I could have been quite good but when I gave it up, it upset him a bit that we didn't have that closeness any more, maybe.

And because of what the drugs do to you, you lie, you cheat – the number of times I lied to him to get money to buy the drugs. And then when they found out where the money went – it must have been destroying for them, you know? If my daughter ever came up to me and told me she was on heroin, I'd be absolutely devastated, so I can imagine what they must have been like when they found out.

After the caravan?

To a hostel in Newbury. It was full of alcoholics, full of drug addicts, so I knew I wouldn't be getting clean there. I just walked out of the hostel one day and ended up going to Swindon and then Bath.

Have people ever been aggressive towards you?

On the street I've had my head split open, my ribs broken – not by other homeless people but by normal people – I call them 'animals', really.

We are not seen by members of the public as members of society. We are seen as scum. People look at us like we are basically shit on their shoes – that's how I feel. And if you were to ask the majority of people that walk past what they saw, when they looked at us, they would say we are leeches on life.

How does that make you feel?

We've been called so many things, over the years, that that's how it makes me feel – that maybe I *am* that. Even though I know I am a human being. I don't get angry any more when people are abusing us or throwing bottles at us. It's pointless. Because we are the ones with no address, we are the ones that get blamed – even if we are the innocent party, we still get blamed – it must have been our fault somehow. When I had my head split open and my ribs broken, even though it was all on CCTV, I felt that it was my fault.

Who did that to you?

Two young guys. I was sat in the doorway. They threw me £2, asked me if I was all right and I said, yeah, I was fine. They came back four hours later and they both kicked me over and over in the body and head. They were off their head on whatever they were on and when I looked into their eyes, there was just nothing there. I even said, as a joke, 'Ding, ding, round four . . .' to try and make them stop, but I just curled up in a ball and . . . It took the ambulance four hours to come and by the time they got there, my friend had already mopped me up. I went in the ambulance but I refused to go to hospital, I don't really like them. I couldn't breathe properly for nearly a month, but my head healed quite well.

Where did you go to sleep, after that night?

Over the road, in another doorway for about three months, and then went back to Bath, but I was told that I had no local connection there and the council said I had to go back to London – I said I hadn't lived there for thirty years! But they said no, that's your local connection. And that's why I'm back on the streets of London.

What's the effect of all this on your head?

I know there is something better out there for us and I know that one day attitudes of people will change and we'll get somewhere – we'll actually get somewhere in life. Prison sounds a lot better than being on the street at the moment – the police can't understand that, but three hot meals a day?

Have you been in prison before?

Yes.

What for?

Breach of my DRO [drug rehabilitation order] – I was supposed to go to a group and I didn't bother going for three weeks so they sent me to prison for three weeks.

What was prison like?

Nice. Peaceful! I was locked up for twenty-three and a half hours a day. You've got time to think. I could have a shower. I could read books. I could watch TV. I could listen to the radio. I could have a cigarette in my cell with out anyone saying, 'Oh! You can't smoke in here.' It gave me time to be me.

Who are you?

Don't know! Shy! I love a laugh, I really love to have good laugh. I really find it hard to trust people – especially on the streets, so many people have stolen off me or we've fallen out over silly things. My pal at the moment, Darren, we're all right, but sometimes we get on each other's nerves. It's like a couple, twenty-four–seven. We've got to look out for each other. Where we stay, I feel it's quite safe because there's loads of traffic and loads of people. But . . . people that sleep down the alleyways and that? I wouldn't do it again. Anything happens – stabbings, people disappear.

Are you telling me this is what you are afraid of, or that this is what has actually happened?

I know in other areas people have disappeared and no one has ever seen them again. In Bath, last year at Christmas Eve, my best friend got murdered.

[I googled the details Matt gave me, and eventually found that a man called Tommy Downey had, indeed, been murdered.]

That was horrific because the day he got murdered I'd told him to 'f— off', and that I didn't want to see him again because he was drunk – and then to find out that he'd been murdered . . . I do wonder if that's going to happen to us on the street, but . . . then I look on the bright side – I could be doing this one day, sat in a cafe having a coffee and reading a book on my lunch break – that could be me in a couple of years' time. I do think there is a good chance that it will happen but at this precise moment in time, I don't think it will happen. Until they sort out the housing problem for homeless people – they need to start thinking that these guys need a bit of priority instead of giving people from other countries the chance to get a house first.

Who is it that you think you are now?

A homeless drug addict. That's all I am at the moment.

It's funny because, yes, those words are true, but I've been sitting with you guys for four or five hours and it's just not what I see.

Yeah, because you actually stopped and talked, whereas a lot of people walk past every day and not one person would be able to say, 'Yes, I noticed you.' They're too busy, headphones on and looking at their phones. We're not allowed to talk to people, not allowed to ask people for money and we're not allowed to engage with the public, so we rely on people who actually slow their lives down and stop . . . It's not all about the money, it's not all about getting a cup of tea or a hot chocolate out of people – just say hi to us . . . we're human, we'd say hello back. The times I've gone, 'Hello love, welcome to Matt's Shaftesbury Avenue!' and not one person has answered me, yeah! [laughs bitterly] . . . and then you get a little kid walk past and you go, 'Hello!' and then you see the parents grabbing their hand and pulling them off quickly, and you think, 'Hang on a minute! We're not animals.'

What does this do to you? Having this happen year after year after year?

You have to get tough. You have to get a thick skin, but it still hurts because we're all born naked and we're all supposed to be equal but then you grow up and you see that all the rich are getting richer and the poor are getting poorer. And in this day and age there shouldn't be this, on the streets, especially in this country – you should not have homelessness, you should not have people starving.

How far ahead do you think?

That day. Today. Just live for today.

Why don't you think further than that?

Because if you make plans, they just . . . [A choke in his voice and then a silence.]

What do you think will happen over the coming weeks, over winter and Christmas?

In 2008, I survived the snow. I was so chuffed. I was chuffed because I didn't die in the snow. I went to the Salvation Army, in Reading, and I could see there was space for me and I said, 'Look, I could sleep there, on the stairs,' but they said no because of 'health and safety'! So I went round the back of the hostel where there was a little bit of cover, where they kept the old fridges. I dragged them out, put my cardboard down and then laid like a tarpaulin sheet halfway up my body and got inside my sleeping bag. About four in the morning the outreach team were shouting my name – apparently for half an hour – they had a hot chocolate and bacon roll for me and they were just about to call the ambulance when I stuck my head out and said, 'What's going on?' And they told me they thought I was dead and when I looked at my tarpaulin it was all just covered in snow – but it had been like an insulator! And I thought if I can survive that, I can survive anything. That was the coldest I have ever been.

What do you wish for?

Somewhere to live. To get clean and have a job. So . . .

What kind of job would you like?

Pest controller – I'd like to be a pest controller.

But that means you'd have to kill mice . . .

No, no no . . . I'm going to *save* animals – they think I'm going to kill them but I'm going to save them! What did it was this – when I was in rehab in 2012, there was this massive wall with these bees on and I watched these guys come in and put this black bag over them . . .

And you weren't hallucinating in rehab? These were for real?

No, they came in, put a bag over them like they do with wasps, and sprayed some chemical. My uncle used to have hives at the back of his house and he used to spray this gas to slow the bees down, so you could get the honey out, and I knew it wasn't that spray. So from that moment I decided to be a pest controller. I want to save bees and certain other animals – but cockroaches, rats, no [makes a slicing throat sign]. I hope my little pet mouse comes back tonight – tiny little thing, he was.

That's it. That's my life.

And just remember – homelessness can happen to anyone. It doesn't matter your background, where you come from, what upbringing you had. Bad or good – it can happen to anyone.

Scratch 'n' Sniff

I was on Oxford Street and needed the loo, so I went into the big department store John Lewis. The moment I walked in, a sales assistant tried to spritz me with perfume, and when I said, 'Really, please don't,' she offered me one of those strips of card – that always remind me of the litmus paper in chemistry lessons at school – loaded with a hideous fragrant powder that you rub to release the smell. It got me thinking – what a shame I couldn't include a series of scratch 'n' sniff cards inside the book that you could you take out and use at appropriate moments while reading. Kind of bring things to life a bit for you, add another dimension.

The world really does smell different (as did I), the nearer you get to ground level. If it were a bottled perfume, I'd call it *l'aire du mausolée* – a noxious mix of rotting seaweed and dead furry things.

The homeless actually breathe different air from the rest of us. Darren pointed out that they live at 'exhaust level', and I was beginning to understand why I had this permanent headache and generally felt unwell – not to mention why most of the people I'd met looked so wan and grey.

A few minutes on Google told me that nearly *one tenth* of Londoners (I feel I need to say that again, *one tenth*) die an early death from pollution, and the most dangerous place of all is Oxford Street. I wondered how many of those dead people had been homeless. Then I looked up nitrogen dioxide (NO_2, the culprit) and got the gist of it all very quickly. The stuff is deadly. The list of symptoms and illnesses it causes was basically the same list of physical and mental complaints I'd been hearing from the homeless over the last few weeks. NO_2 was even mentioned in the same sentence as 'paranoid schizophrenia'.

So it wasn't a surprise to find that there are laws that say governments mustn't let the level of NO2 exceed an agreed (already stupidly high) limit for more than eighteen hours in any given year.

What *was* a surprise was to learn that in London, that limit was exceeded in 2015 and 2016 within the first few *days* of each January.

Probably no bad thing you didn't get the free scratch 'n' sniff card.

Rebecca

*'Sometimes I don't sleep for two or three days, and
then I'll just go to like a coma, or something . . . I won't
even know that I'm there, if that makes sense'*

Becki, as she said I could call her, was sitting outside a high street bank, looking tired and worn. She was twenty-six. She spent most nights a few yards away in the doorway of a charity shop, on a busy road. She made very little money from begging, sometimes as little as £5 a day, and was visibly struggling. She was chatty but stuttered a bit and sometimes fell over her words. She was very dirty and embarrassed by her looks.

After we had been talking for a while, Becki revealed the detailed story of how she had recently been raped. It had happened at night, in an open green space nearby. She had been sleeping on a bench when she was attacked. She gave me permission to include the whole story in her chronicle, but I have decided not to. On reflection I felt that a lot of the details she gave were so clear that they might (to someone, somewhere) suggest who the rapist was. This awful event is not discussed in Becki's story.

Rebecca

I am afraid of dying. I'm afraid of dying out here. Waking up dead – it happens – people say, 'Oh, that's just another tramp.' I'd rather not die at all, but I'd rather die where people know about me . . . but if I died on the street . . . [voice cracking]

To be honest with you, I ain't got a life. I used to do prostitution, but I've got out of that now. I spoke to my brother a couple of months ago and he said when I was prostituting myself I'd become angry and lose track of everything and I just wouldn't listen to people. When I'm not selling myself to men, I'm a different person. I know that begging ain't the right thing to do, but neither is selling yourself to men. I did it when I was sixteen, when I left care. To support myself. Obviously it's hard now, because I make a lot less, but I won't go back to that – no, I won't go back to that life.

I've been in and out of care since I was two years old and I've been homeless on and off for seven years. My mum passed away last Christmas. She had problems – nine kids, so it was hard for her. Very, very hard. We all went into care. She had mental health problems herself and she was going through a hard stage. She was like me, she was in care as well, and I think maybe she got herself trapped.

That's what I want to say, I don't want to become pregnant with babies that I can't really afford to give a life to. My dad was an alcoholic and he died. It all . . . yeah, we should have been given more help. All of us should.

In care, I was never given the opportunity to . . . I don't know how to describe it to you . . . what's the word? . . . they never gave me no 'after care'. It's like getting released from prison but you've kind of got nowhere to go. If you put me in my own flat that's not going to help me, because I can't maintain my own flat, because I've never lived on my own, and it'll end up like . . . and I've got mental health issues as well, I mean, waking up is a task.

This is a lonely life. Often, I'm out here, got no one. I have been with an ex-boyfriend, on the street, but sometimes that can be harder, because they can push you into drugs, they can push you into alcohol and into places where it is just too far to be [prostitution]. My exes were like, 'Come and take drugs . . . come and do this . . .' And whenever I had money it was going on drugs, but now I feel better in myself. I've got people I know, through begging, but I wouldn't call them mates. I mix with other beggars, that's about it. I've got no family, no network. I don't know where my brother is now and my other sisters, I don't speak to them.

At one point I used to take drugs 'cos of it, but it didn't help. I've been a lot better since I've been clean. When I was drinking and taking drugs, it was more or less *that* – I wasn't eating, I wasn't doing things, I didn't sleep, you know. It was just a whole load of issues but now I'm a lot better in myself.

I feed myself through begging – sometimes I only make £10, sometimes £5. Nothing more. Sometimes a passer-by might say, 'Do you want a McDonald's meal?' or if I've got a bit of money, I'll get it myself.

Generally, I wake up in the charity shop doorway or the park – anywhere I can find that's safe. Sometimes I don't sleep for two or three days, and then I'll just go to like a coma, or something, and I'll be out of it for like a day or a day and a half or whatever . . . I won't even know that I'm there, if that makes sense. I've been at the point where I've been so tired, where I'm like, 'I need to sleep, I need to sleep', and I'm crazy . . .

I have been to prison. Petty things. Criminal damage, swearing at a police officer, but then I thought, 'No, you know what? I'm not going to lower myself to that standard, because all I'll end up with is another record on my sheet.' I just decided that I've got to somehow fight through this.

I feel that society has let me down, I feel that more should be done. I feel that a lot of people who potentially do not need to go to jail end up in prison for the sake of a roof over their head. I don't feel that's right. Many, many occasions, I've been to jail, for the sake of getting a roof. I could catch up on sleep, eat, got three meals a day. Yeah, it was good in terms of that, but obviously, in terms of 'freedom' it wasn't that good.

I've lived in all kinds of places . . . semi-independent places which is supposed to help you but it doesn't – all kinds of places really, yeah. But I couldn't really manage. First of all, like, budgeting – they don't teach you how to budget your money, they don't teach you skills on how to cook, on how to do anything. You're just stuck alone basically and it's just horrible . . . they don't realise what problems you face in society. Just you're another number, another 'person in care' pushed out on the street.

I've got an emotional personality disorder – when I was younger I got sexually abused, in foster care. It's pretty hard, I mean . . . images in my head of my childhood. I wake up and I'm haunted by these images but I know that . . . I know that I've got to deal with these issues through other ways – I've got to somehow, like, get other pictures, because I don't want to be another statistic on the street. I don't want to be another statistic who dies on the street. No way. No way. I want to change that.

Yeah, I know, I look a bit [self-conscious about her clothes and appearance] . . . in terms of like . . . sometimes I *can* wash each day. There's a public toilet round the corner, but you can't wash your clothes there and sometimes I give up, but other times I go to homeless places and I can change my clothes, it depends . . . or sometimes there is stuff outside the charity shop, where people have left donations and I take them . . . I mean, I know it ain't right . . .

This is all I've got, this blanket. It's all I've got.

Have you ever been attacked on the street?
This is hard and especially for women, I'm not being rude, but women don't get appreciated as much as men do. I'm not trying to be sexist – homeless are homeless – but women don't get acknowledged as being homeless as much as men. As a homeless woman on the street, it ain't taken so much into account. We're just dirt.

Right now, all I think about, it's just getting a roof over my head, that's how I want it to be, but . . . I've got an outreach worker and they're trying to get me into somewhere, hopefully, near King's Cross, but they're saying that the borough is pretty much full up, so . . . I definitely want to get off the street. Having somewhere to live, being in a better place, being more stable in myself, definitely.

People in the street probably just see another homeless person when they look at me. And that's what I expect them to think. And that's it. I am not a horrible person. I suppose I've been a bit misled and misunderstood and maybe gone down the wrong path which I shouldn't have, but I've not done anything *bad*.

I can talk to people, the fact that I can communicate, have conversations – I like chatting. Since I've been homeless, yeah, some people have been nice but a lot of people walk by and give you dirty looks. Most people in society are probably struggling just as much as I am. If you're nasty to every single person who walks by, then you become an evil person . . . but if you think, you know what, these people must have been through something too, then . . .

I'd like to work in a project where I can help people like me, 'cos that's what I've always wanted to do, it would be brilliant. A lot of people wouldn't choose it, but I definitely would. I hear people saying about these projects for the homeless and it would be nice if I could do something. It's about maybe getting something done.

When my mum died, I found out when I was out here and that was the saddest day of my life and I nearly did something stupid. And this police officer I knew, he was the only compassionate person that came and he knew my mum had just died and he goes, 'Right, you can do two things here – you can do something stupid, which I know you are about to do, or you can sort yourself and say you are better than that.' And I took his advice and I didn't do anything stupid that day. I was thinking about jumping in front of a bus or something mad, because it just pushed me to breaking point and . . . I'm glad I didn't do it that day, I really am.

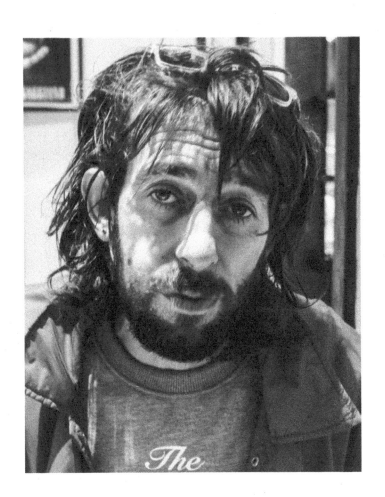

Tim Wright

'The worst thing is not trusting people and the loneliness'

Blimey, what a whirlwind Tim was. He was sitting outside a bank, surrounded by odds and ends – clothing, books, toys and even a boating life-belt, which rather struck a chord. He collected bits of junk and then sold it to the passing public. Some kind-hearted railway worker had let him padlock his wares overnight in a bit of spare land opposite where he begged, near the tube station, so they'd be safe and he could get to them each morning.

He seemed manic, had masses to say and had lived, for the most part, a dreadful life.

At first I wasn't even sure I ought to include him in the book. This was in part because we went off on a drug deal jaunt together and I didn't want to get him in trouble (he insisted it was OK for me to include it), but also because I wasn't sure if he was full of braggadocio or if he was for real.

Initially, we talked at his 'spot', where he was clearly a feature on the local commuters' landscape, shouting cheery things at them as they made their way to work. We moved from there to a cafe around the corner and slowly I began to see his 'cheeky chappy' facade fall away, revealing someone much calmer and more considered.

From there I went with him to a rendezvous with his drug dealer and lastly, we ended up in a room in a hostel that belonged to a mate of his so he could smoke his crack and finish his story.

Tim Wright

My mum got raped and that was how I came into the world.

I grew up in the countryside and I had a horrible childhood. I've got a stepsister who's my mum and my stepdad's *real* daughter and she got everything – I never got anything, because I weren't the real son.

This scar here is where my stepdad put one hand on my bollocks and one on my shoulder and chucked me onto the bed. I weed on the mattress and there was blood in it. I was eight years old.

My mum and stepdad left me when I was fourteen. They didn't leave me with a penny – they just got up and moved to Wisbech. You know when you buy another house but you've still got the old house, yeah? I don't know how they did it – a bridging loan or whatever – but I was left sleeping in the garage of the old house for three or four months. My stepdad came back to the house one day and saw all my duvets and that in the garage. He chucked them all out. He was an arsehole all my life – he'd whack me over the hands with a spoon at dinner and always give me the fat off the pork – no meat. And I never got a Christmas present.

At that point I was still at school but stopped going then. Social services weren't really bothered, you know what I mean? I had to live in a bus shelter for a week after the garage thing.

So, from being a country bumpkin, I went and moved to Norwich and worked my way up the ladder [of crime] and ended up being one of the top boys there. I was bringing drugs up to Norwich from London as a runner so I was getting £300 a trip and sometimes I'd get seven trips a week. It was a lot of money, you know what I mean?

I always had a beautiful girl on my arm. People used to come to me to sell whatever it was they wanted to sell – I was like a wheeler-dealer sort of thing. But I used to enjoy that life. But the thing is, if I had kept on going down that route, I'd have ended up in jail – I would have done – carrying 5,000 ecstasy tablets in a box in the back of the car or three and a half kilos of weed or nine eggs of cocaine? Yeah, yeah, it was good – until I got stabbed.

All this, being on the street, it started with that, back in 1990. I got stabbed in the heart.

[I have paraphrased the story as it was extremely gory and very graphic and I didn't feel that the details were needed to convey Tim's suffering. The story he told me was that a man turned up at the house that Tim was sharing, looking for someone who also lived there. He refused to believe that Tim didn't know this person's whereabouts, and ended up stabbing him . . .]

The knife went in me right up to the hilt . . . eight inches.

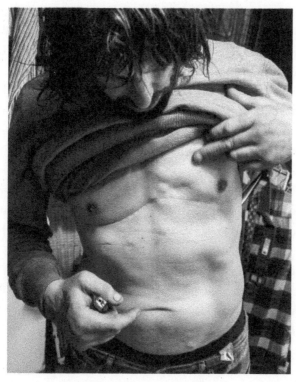

The scars from the stabbing and the surgery

They did an emergency operation in the ambulance and thirteen days later, I opened my eyes and my girlfriend's mother was holding one hand and my girlfriend was holding the other! I looked down and saw all these staples going across here!

After, I couldn't go and live with my girlfriend because her mum bred cats and I'm allergic to them, so I went and lived with an ex-girlfriend – that led to me splitting me up with my girlfriend at the time.

I didn't have a mum and dad I could turn to and say, 'Could I have three grand to pay my rent arrears and car insurance' . . . I'd got behind with the rent when I was in hospital and the landlord changed the locks – later I found all my stuff outside.

[We moved to a cafe around the corner because the workers at the bank were beginning to arrive.]

I never imagined in a million years I'd be homeless! I was a gangster! Seriously, I had gold rings on every finger and a big chunky gold chain! I was like top boy in Norwich – that's why I couldn't let my mates see me like that. I had to sell my gold. I felt ashamed.

After I left my ex-girlfriend's place, I lived in the car for three, four weeks in the middle of the winter. It was freezing cold. The insurance had run out and so I kept getting tickets on the car, so I had to get rid of it. I didn't want all my friends seeing me, from having everything to having nothing, so I packed a bag and moved to London.

I ended up sleeping on the street in the West End. That first night was tough. I was on my own down there – you couldn't trust anyone. I just begged. I didn't make a lot, you know, when I first started – probably £15, enough for the day. I was sleeping in an underground station at the time. I've slept on these steps [outside the bank] for the last seven years. The police have been nice to me – they know I am a kind person – I look after people's bikes [there was a bike stand next to us] and I walk all the elderlys' shopping home and that.

When the bank opens, I have to move – during the day I don't sit here.

Probably half of them [the people who are walking past us] I'd say hello to in the day – even if you're feeling really depressed in the morning, you still have to say hello to them. I've got a lot of people that like me, so I'm lucky.

Things are getting better now because I'm going into a hostel so I could get a flat at the end of all this . . . maybe two years down the line? The thing is, this hostel, it's not free, yeah? They charge £297 a week for a *room*. The government will pay that but if I *work* where the fuck am I going to find £300 a week? I had to give up my dog to my best friend – and that was one of the worst pains I've ever experienced . . . Freddy Barley is my baby – he's the best dog in the world! I still see him every day. My friend looks after him, I give her £30 a week – I don't get dole money so the only money I get is off the street.

[Tim explained that he had to meet his drug dealer shortly and suggested I went with him. We practically jogged up the busy main road as Tim, having been talking to me, was now very late. It was raining heavily and I gave Tim the recorder as it wasn't practical for me to hold it and try and keep it in front of his mouth while we were on the move. I made it clear I didn't want him to record anything of the actual drug deal itself. We had to keep stopping as Tim made a series of phone calls from different phone boxes to get the next instruction about where to go. I was knackered. Eventually, and unbeknownst to me at the time, we walked right past the dealer; suddenly Tim turned on his heel to follow him down a side alley, telling me firmly to stay put. When he came back for me, Tim said he'd had to pay a bit more for his drugs as the man was angry that he'd brought someone along who might be able to identify him – which of course I couldn't, as I'd barely noticed him before Tim did his U-turn.]

When you first come down here you don't know who to get the gear off . . . you get ripped off and you don't know if you're getting good stuff. I take it to just goof out. It's like putting a brick wall up. The pain is more mental than anything, though, you just want to tuck it all away . . . Ha! well, it did *that*, at first!

Now, without it I get sick, I mean banging sick. The worst sick that you could ever imagine. You feel if you don't take it, you will die, you don't get no pleasure out of it. Have you heard about *clucking*? Going cold turkey? I done a seven-hour cluck and I was screaming – I was that bad – I was piss-ing, shitting and wanking at the same time, yeah. I had a lady looking after me while I was doing it. It was willpower that got me through it. I was freezing cold but you can wring your clothes out, yeah, and my hair was dripping. And like I say I had the woman in front of me and that's embarrassing.

[We had now arrived at a depressing-looking hostel where a friend of Tim's had a room that Tim could use to take his drugs. The rest of our conversa-tion was in this room.]

Because I smoke crack and then have to sit on my pitch, I can't let all my regulars see me fucked out of my head, so I've learned how to be sensible on it, how to cope with it [showing me his syringes, which are used for injecting heroin].

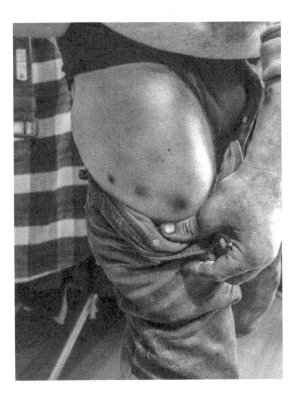

These are 1 ml, these are, from the chemist down the road. I don't go into a vein, I 'skin-pop', and that means you put it into a muscle and it takes twenty minutes to work.

[Now puffing away from the little tin] With alcohol, it takes a while to get a nice feeling but with this you get a nice feeling straight away, as you smoke it. See, now I feel nice, like a nice buzz. [Tim very courteously offered me some crack. I politely declined.]

No, I'm too scared. I have a really fast heartbeat and I'd be afraid that my heart would stop or something.

I admire you for that, though – I've always been easily led into situations where, you know, I've hooked up with the wrong people. I'm still fucked up. I can't keep appointments. I was supposed to get my methadone prescription two days ago and I haven't been because it's so easy to get distracted – I'm not even bothered that I don't make it, do you know what I mean? And I suffer from depression and I'm on Prozac and it's the same thing – I never take the tablets regularly so they don't work properly because I forget . . . [rolling my eyes] I know, I know, I should take them.

[Eventually, I decided I ought to leave as the pall of crack fog was starting to become worryingly thick. I felt fine . . . but still. Tim – what a prince – offered me two rather splendid gifts as I was clambering over the piles of clothes and general junk to get to the door of the cluttered room. He handed me a pair of jewel-encrusted peep-toe shoes with six-inch suede heels. I howled with laughter – 'Are you serious!? I mean, LOOK AT ME! I look like a bloody chimney sweep.' A little offended but not wholly deterred, Tim came back with a second, equally bizarre parting gift: a steam iron. I refused on the grounds it was too heavy, but I could at least see where he was coming from.]

The worst thing is not trusting people and the loneliness. I don't really want friends that are homeless because you can't trust them.

[And with those parting words, we kissed goodbye and I made my way back on to the street.]

Patrick O'Neil

'I feel like a great stress has been lifted off me –
I am lot happier now, a lot happier'

Patrick was the third and last person to give me a false name.

I'd met him some weeks earlier when he was waking up with his mate, Brad, in a side street near Covent Garden. Then, he had told me to come back when he was in a better mood and he would think about participating in the book.

This time we caught up in a cafe, where I'd spotted him giving some money to a young homeless couple so they could get some breakfast. He was sitting at a little table with his big brown dog (who also seemed to want to remain anonymous, and hid under the table) at his feet. Patrick had a ghastly consumptive cough.

Perhaps in his forties, he was a self-possessed man and I enjoyed talking with him – he was quick-witted and eloquent, and saw his situation as positive, to some extent. He was confident about his future.

He chose the name Patrick because it had belonged to his father.

Patrick O'Neil

I had a pub in Folkestone and it started to get quieter and quieter. The brewery doubled the weekly rent, the pub was starting to go down, and trade was slacking off. They put the price of the barrels up so I was starting to get into difficulties paying bills and things and I just went into administration. My flat was above the pub, so the whole thing went together.

It all took place over a period of about two weeks. The administrators came and I wasn't allowed to be in the building. I had to leave and I wasn't allowed to get my stuff for about two weeks. That was it.

There's no help out there. I was self-employed and went to sign on but they said, no, you can't for three months.

I still stay in contact with some of my friends and they just think I'm staying in a hostel. And my family, I phone them exactly the same, three or four times a week. None of them know. Because it's a blip, purely a blip. I don't see it as a long-term thing and my logic is that I don't tell them *everything* I do – you're selective about what you tell your parents anyway, right?

I don't really want my friends and family to know. I don't want to worry them and it's a stigma . . . I am very, very conscious of the stigma attached to homelessness . . . a can of beer and a dog on a piece of string, you know what I mean? [Coincidentally, at this exact moment, Patrick's friend returned from walking Patrick's dog.]

He's all right, he's healthy. I got him down the Blue Cross, you know, the charity for dogs – he's in fine shape. I've had him two and a half years. He was never negotiable when I lost the pub. It does create problems for me – he's not very good around other dogs – a bit barky. I just feel I made a commitment to him, you know? I've signed up to him, that's it [coughs violently]. He's bloody useless, he is! We had a break-in at the pub one night, and he slept through the alarm! But I don't feel any less safe or more safe with him . . . actually, *less* safe, because people steal dogs. People tried to steal him one night. Because if you beg with a dog, you get more money. Now I sleep with him inside, to the wall. He'd go off with anybody, he's that sort of dog. All you have to say is 'walk' or 'chicken' and off he goes! [After another alarming bout of coughing, which left Patrick looking quite ill, I asked if he thought he was well enough to make it through the upcoming winter.]

I don't mind the cold. I grew up in Ireland on top of a bloody mountain and *that's* cold – with no central heating. I can look after myself, I've always been able to do that. I'm very positive. I know one day I'm going to be all right. I'm educated – I've got a degree, believe it or not, in French and Italian – I'm not stupid. Now there's not much in the way of pubs, but I'm putting my CV out.

I never set my expectations high, I always assume the worst. I'm not a pessimist but a realist. Since being on the streets, I've got a lot more faith in human nature. There are so many kind people out there, it's unreal. And London, I thought people wouldn't care but there are so many good people out there, there really, really is. You're sitting there and people give you a coffee, something to eat, clothes and money. At four o'clock every morning, my little Chinese lady comes around and gives me two boiled eggs and a sandwich! She does it out of her own pocket, you know what I mean? It's restored my faith in human nature, honestly, a helluva lot.

See that shop over there? [an outdoor clothing shop] I was looking at this jacket two nights ago and it was £50 and the manager said, 'Look, I'll knock 50% off for you.' He said he's got blankets for us for the winter as well. What he does is, he goes and unpicks the stitching a bit and makes out it was damaged. If you go into any Pret A Manger the staff have been told to give any homeless a free filter coffee. The biggest insult to me was that one day I was sitting outside with my bag and my dog and the girl came out with a coffee and said, 'There you go, don't worry about paying for it.' You know you're living rough when Pret A Manger give you free coffee!

It's hard, on the street, because *everything* you do is in public. You're getting up in the morning and there are people walking past you. It's very public. At the start I was very, very embarrassed. If I saw someone coming I'd pop back under the sleeping bag – I know how I would have felt if I was the person walking by. I can remember how I used to feel – 'Oh, look at him . . . just get up and get a job, get a flat – there's loads of help out there,' you know?

I don't even go down to the food handouts any more because . . . just you know . . . the people that go down there . . . they're all on drugs, you know, the stereotypical homeless person – unwashed. I'm not being a snob here, I swear to God, but I just don't want to turn into that type of person. And I think, subconsciously, that being *around* that type of person would make me *into* that type of person.

I stay in a hotel [like his friend, Brad Lemon, he uses those 'rent by the hour' hotels] about three nights a week – I pay for it out of the money I make from selling the *Big Issue*. I can make £70 or £80 a day, doing that – it's because I'm quite good with people.

I stay away from violence and that side of it. I'm very choosy about who I mix with. I choose my circle of friends very, very carefully. I only give people one chance. Drugs I stay away from, people who use drugs I stay away from and also people who don't go out and *try* – I don't tolerate them either.

It's quite hard, with the *Big Issue*, because you are on your feet for six hours and you are having to be very public. It's strange though – why would you want to sit all day outside McDonald's with a dog and a cup and be seen but not want to be seen selling? At least you are trying to do something positive for yourself, get yourself out of . . . it's a business, you have to buy the newspapers and then you sell them at a profit. You're doing something constructive. You're not lying in a doorway, begging and taking drugs. I've never asked for anything – I've either been given it or gone out and got it.

I would say I was a very lively, positive, very people-orientated person – always have been a people person. I'd say I was strong-willed, a little bit argumentative. Yeah, happy-go-lucky, I've always been upbeat and positive. In other people I like to see openness, kindness, being trustworthy, honest, balanced and in control. I don't like selfishness, self-centredness or people that are quick to judge others – bigotry as well. I admire Margaret Thatcher – I'm not talking about her politics, I'm talking about her character – her go-get, her persistence – a woman in the sixties and seventies trying to break into politics to become one of the most recognised politicians in the world.

Politicians, now, pander too much to public opinion and the UKIP train of thought, you know, that 'all foreigners are shit, get them out and everybody is a scrounger'. I think the Tories, going after the UKIP vote, have become even more hardline.

I think there could be a lot more social support for people who legitimately need it, like me and Brad who, through no fault of our own, have ended up here. Purely through a series of events – we never *chose* to be homeless. I didn't choose *this* . . . *this* . . . chose *me*. It was the only option I had, I had no other options. I know loads of guys out there, like me, but you don't see them, they don't come out – they keep themselves very much to themselves.

I do miss TV. And being able to go to the toilet when you want to, making a cup of coffee when you want and cooking your own food – I used to cook a lot and I miss it. And it's expensive here, buying food, I eat a hot meal every day. I pay for it myself because I work, for the *Big Issue*, and I do quite well on it.

I don't look any different than I did when I had the pub – I'm actually looking better because I'm not so stressed. I feel like a great stress has been lifted off me – I am a lot happier now, *a lot* happier. You know, I'd rather be where I am now – as a person – than where I was six months ago. I'm happier, I've got no stress, I don't have to worry. Worry, worry, worry – all that has gone. To me – and I know it sounds weird – but to me it's a good swap, for my own emotional well-being. I've been neglecting myself and now I've been to the doctor for a check-up and an ECG. I've now got tablets for my blood pressure – before, everything was centred on the pub and not me. So, I'm in a better emotional and physical state than I was. This is the best I've been in years! You won't believe this, but I'm sleeping better – I swear to God, I'm sleeping better! I can have eight hours unbroken sleep now, honestly.

You are the *only* homeless person that I've spoken to who has had eight hours unbroken sleep.

Well, I have – I went to bed at eight o'clock last night and woke up at ten to four. But I put earplugs in, you see! So I don't hear the outside noise.

To be honest, I've been on the street longer than I thought I would be or wanted to be. At the end of August I thought, you know, by the end of September it would . . . that was my plan but it is taking a little bit longer. The plan is to get a deposit – either get another pub or get accommodation – but I need to get a roof over my head first and the job can follow. I need to get indoors.

Pets to Petty Snobberies

Animals are important to the homeless because the relationship is a warm, unconditional one and gives them something to love in an otherwise rather loveless world. Darryl said he'd take a dog over a room at the Savoy Hotel for six months. Patrick loved and took great care of his big brown labrador and the girl in the photograph was besotted with her ferret and shared her food with it. There is a basic human need to care for something other than oneself.

All of them assumed levels of responsibility that a lot of homeowners don't want to take on – they have to buy pet food, make sure there is water at hand, get up with tired and aching legs to take the animal for walks and clean up its mess.

It seems that the public give more money, and more often, to those begging with a dog than to those without. We can all speculate as to why that is.

Consequently, some people, like Paul, who I met on Tottenham Court Road, 'borrow' a dog to increase the amount of money they can make begging. It works – as soon as I saw his beautiful husky, I went straight up and asked if I could stroke him. A natural enough response. Having done that, how could I walk away without giving him some spare change?

It's odd – the general public give more to those with dogs, yet they sometimes take a disparaging view of the people who have them, perhaps feeling that they've somehow been hoodwinked. But how is it any different from borrowing a mate's posh suit, or a girlfriend's expensive handbag for a job interview? Isn't it just a version of putting your best foot forward?

Treacle

The public at large, the non-homeless public, seem to be riddled with prejudices and snobberies. They regard begging with a dog that's *not yours* as rather like taking liberties with your CV: a form of cheating.

But, make no mistake – the homeless are snobbish and intolerant just as often.

Patrick and many, many others thought begging was immoral, but he drank. Scott wouldn't touch drink and thought druggies were scum, but he begged for money. Darryl took drugs but refused to take the social benefit he was entitled to, and Charisse would beg but disapproved of drink *and* drugs.

And this really did surprise me at first. I mean, how could the downtrodden even *entertain* ideas of chauvinism, bigotry or narrow-mindedness within their own ranks? How could they not all be of one mind about *everything*? The answer is that all people have at least some petty snobbery hidden (or not) away somewhere, and the homeless are just that – people.

There is no archetypal homeowner, is there? So why would there be an archetypal homeless person? There's Michael, on p.236, who looks like a central-casting tramp, and others who you wouldn't know were homeless if you bumped into them at the local library or in a queue at the cinema.

It's the sleeping bags and cardboard that are the massive giveaway.

Donna King

'I think I'm just exhausted with it. With my whole life.
It's just too much, now. Just everything. Every little thing'

When I was a young child, I had a small, very soft cloth doll called Raggedy Ann. Donna reminded me of her. No hard edges, nothing brittle, gossamer breath.

We had agreed to talk, having bumped into each other several times beforehand. On previous occasions she had either been too unwell and lacking the energy to talk or was waiting for her boyfriend, Peter, to come back from scoring her drugs. I went searching for her, and having been so long on the streets by now, I was able to recognise her stuff, in a heap, on the pavement near the McDonald's at Piccadilly Circus.

I took her into the downstairs part of a Costa Coffee where she was very ill at ease to begin with. It was ridiculously cold out and I insisted we went indoors.

Donna was all but extinguished with exhaustion. Utterly wiped out. She looked as if she would fold up like a soft towel. She spoke so slowly that I barely had to press the pause button on the recorder when I transcribed our conversation.

She was twenty-one years old but looked about fourteen. Donna expected little from life and life responded in kind.

Donna King

Do you want to tell me about your childhood?

I had a normal childhood, really. My mum and my stepdad and three older sisters. I don't think it was that bad, really. It was just 'normal' – it wasn't good and it wasn't bad.

And what do your sisters do?

One of them's in university, the other one has got her son and boyfriend and she's settled down, and the other one's got like a proper manager's job and she's married and got a family.

And did you get on with your stepdad?

Until I was twelve. And then it just went downhill – I went a bit off the rails, I went a bit, you know, 'fuck it' sort of attitude. I used to run away from home a lot as well.

Did you? If someone had asked you, 'Why are you running away?', what would you have said?

'Cos of my stepdad. He was just a dickhead. After he realised I could speak my own mind and he couldn't control me anymore . . . he just . . .

What was your mum's feeling, do you think?

She was always on his side – always chose him over us. Even when he hit us – we'd go to the police and my mum wouldn't say anything.

He hit you sufficiently badly that you would have to go to the police?

Yes. He's punched me in my head and pulled my hair.

When you were little?

No, when I was about thirteen or fourteen.

Donna – that *is* little. What did the police say?

They said it must have been my own fault.

And what was the situation like at home, after they left?

Not very good. He would just basically laugh in my face – that's when I started doing drugs, heroin and crack, and drinking heavily. I think it was to block everything out.

And do you still enjoy it?

No.

What happens if you *don't* take it?

I get all . . . I feel really sick, my stomach feels like you've got constant cramp and I'm always like sniffing. You just feel horrible. I started drinking at twelve, but not heavily. I started drinking heavily – cider – at fifteen when I was doing the drugs. And even when I got off the drugs I was still drinking. Then, when I was sixteen, I got with my ex-boyfriend – he was nineteen. He was a bad drinker. We were alcoholics.

You say you drank to block things out – what was the pain?

Truthfully, 'cos of the way my mum always used to choose my stepdad over us, it just made me feel like . . . she doesn't really care. I felt like I was worth nothing. That's the thing . . . and that's how my stepdad used to *purposely* make me feel, like I was just . . . [silence].

Did you finish school?

No. 'Cos I was skipping school *a lot* from when I was twelve, so when I was fourteen, I dropped out.

Social services didn't hunt you down and drag you back?

Yes, they put me into a sort of 'naughty people's school' called Haybrook. You didn't have to wear a school uniform or anything like that. It was like a chilled down school.

Were there any subjects you liked? Anything you were good at?

English, drama . . .

Really? So you didn't want to continue with the drama and the English?

I did, but it was just, at the time, I thought . . . I just thought that I could never do anything with my life.

Why did you believe that?

I don't know.

Do you still believe that?

Kind of . . . I don't know . . . I've talked to a lot of people and, like, everyone has tried to tell me that I could have done *so* much with my life . . . even up until now . . . but . . . [long silence]

So you dropped out of school – where were you living?

In a hostel.

[We stopped recording and chatted for a minute about her sugar intake. Donna was putting eight sugar sachets in her coffee and said:]

It's still not enough! My mum hates it because diabetes runs in the family. I used to just *eat* sugar – I used to get these and just pour them in my mouth.

So how come you're not the size of a house?! You're a tiny wee thing.

When I was young, I was always small, skinny – up until I was seventeen, and then I put on loads of weight. I got up to a size sixteen. Since I got with Peter, so about two years ago, I started losing weight.

Did you lose it deliberately?

I just started on the drugs again and I was back on the street.

What made you go back on drugs?

I just thought I'd just have a little smoke 'cos I always said to myself I would *never* get back on heroin . . . and then it got to, 'Oh, I'll just go and buy a bag – I've got enough money', and then I'd want more, you know what I mean? And then before you know it, you're addicted to it. There's nothing you can do about it – you're stuck.

So, why did you leave your hometown? And when?

Only about three weeks ago. I decided to come because Peter was coming. I want to go back, actually.

What's stopping you?

I can't get there! I haven't got enough money! I keep spending it on drugs.

How much do you have to spend a day on drugs?

At least sixty, seventy pounds a day.

A day . . . ?

And that's just on the gear, really . . . and with the crack as well . . .

How do you get the money? Be honest.

Begging. Begging.

But you can't beg a hundred quid a day?

I can – because I look young and innocent. To be honest, I don't think I look like I'm on drugs. But I *hate* it. I *want* to get off it. I want to be able to have money, you know what I mean? For myself – not spending it all on drugs. I am twenty-one years old, you know what I mean?

What do you want to spend money on?

Clothes, make-up – get my hair sorted! You know, *girlie* stuff!! Girls like to be able to take care of themselves.

What does it feel like, not being able to buy a mascara or a nice shampoo?

At the moment? I feel dirty. Not good, not at all. Disgusted with myself, really.

You shouldn't feel disgusted with yourself. You are only twenty-one and you have a long life ahead . . .

Yeah . . . that's what everyone says, that I have time to sort it out.

What do you want, for your life ahead?

A lot of people have asked me this question – 'where do you see yourself in five years?' I'd like to have my own place with Peter, both of us clean, kids, marriage – a proper life. And the only people that can make that happen is ourselves.

Do you think you have the strength to do it?

Well, to be honest, I never thought I'd have the strength to give up drinking but I did, two months ago.

What does that tell you about yourself, that you could quit the drink?

It tells me that I could give up the gear. See, the thing is *me* – I've always been like it – I need help in my life. I need a push. I'm the sort of person – 'Oh, I'll do it tomorrow, do it tomorrow' – and it just never happens!

What's the worst of this life that you're leading at the moment?

[very long silence] Everything – trying to find somewhere to sleep at nighttime, walking around just trying to find a little place where it's safe and there's not too many people walking around, and somewhere dry.

How long can it take you to find somewhere to sleep?

Hours. But most of the time I don't sleep – I'm too scared. I sleep about three or four hours every few days. Most of the time, when you see me, I'm like this – falling asleep. Absolutely just *tired*. Just no energy.

What do you own?

Between me and Peter we've got three sleeping bags, one pillow, two rucksacks . . . a hairbrush – not that it looks like I brushed my hair!

You've got lovely thick wavy hair – you're lucky. With hair like that, you can always make it look nice.

What else? Toothbrush. Toothpaste.

And do you buy these things or do you have to steal them?

People give them. My hairbrush, I bought myself.

Do you have any mementos, precious things from your life?

No. I've never been able to keep anything. Anything that I had before kept getting stolen.

Who steals from you?

Other people on the street, believe it or not. And, actually, there are some people who are *not* on the street, who steal from homeless people. Which I think is wrong, you know. We are *homeless* – we've already got *nothing*, do you know what I mean?

What effect has all of this life had on your physical health?

Oh, a lot! A couple of months ago I was in hospital with pneumonia. For a couple of weeks I literally had *no* energy at all. I was walking *so* slowly. Peter was always, like, 'Come on, love, come on,' but everywhere I'd sit down, I'd fall asleep and I was coughing up shit. It's bad enough being on the street as it is, but being *ill* on the street – it's just horrible. And then for three days I couldn't move. Peter knew something was wrong so he called the ambulance – I had a really bad temperature and was *freezing* cold but sweating and they took me straight to the hospital. They ended up saying it was pneumonia. But they still only kept me in for three days.

Three days?

Yeah, three or four days and I ended up with a whole load of antibiotics, and that was it. Because I'm homeless – because we are just 'taking up the beds'. I was better than what I was before, obviously, but I still felt like shit. Still do, now. Always. I don't even know if it's completely gone or not, to be honest with you. But I think that's because of the drugs as well, plus I don't eat. Sometimes I can eat nothing in three or four days. Sometimes half a sandwich. A lot of the time, I just don't feel like it. I'm always depressed but I show that I'm not.

Why do you hide it?

I always have. Even before I was on the street – even when my life was *shit*, absolutely shit – I always put a smile on my face, always. I don't like to see other people depressed, I try and make them happy so I show that *I'm* happy. And now ... like ... I can't be bothered.

What's caused that, do you think?

I don't know. I think I'm just exhausted with it. With my whole life. It's just too much, now. Just everything. *Every* little thing. Like, when I'm sitting on the street – *not* begging – the way people look at me.

How do they look at you?

Like I'm a piece of shit on the floor, basically. It makes me feel that I *am* a piece of shit on the floor. It's horrible. Like, I've always thought about it in this way – *any* person in this room could end up on the street. Could end up in my position. But they don't see it that way. Everyone's the same, we're all human. We all have feelings. Everyone's got their own problems.

Do you like who you are?

[very long silence] ... I don't know ... yeah, kind of. I think I am a very honest and open person, I always have been. And I've always put other people first and that has, a lot of the time, been my downfall, but that's just who I am, so ...

Was there stuff when you were younger that you really loved?

Drama. I've always been a sort of dramatic person [It was hard for me to believe, given how lifeless Donna was while we were talking.] ... when I was young, I used to always say to my mum, 'I'm going to famous! I'm going to be on TV.'

What appeals to you about acting?

Everything ... I like being on stage ... well, half and half ... because I am actually quite a shy person but then, the thing is, when I've done plays, in school, when I'm on the stage it's completely different . . . because it's what you like to do.

Can you remember any of the productions you were in, at school?

Bugsy Malone, but I was only one of the little parts. I liked standing up in front of people [giggles]. It was fun and behind the stage, everyone was obviously messing around and joking. It is, it's fun.

Have you ever been in love?

In love? Yeah . . .

Are you in love now?

Yeah [giggles]. My ex, the one I told you about, I was with him since I was, what, fifteen, sixteen – till I was nineteen. About four or five years, yeah, on and off. He was a bit . . . we were both alcoholics at the time and that was why it ended up not working out. But I still get those butterflies in my stomach . . . I'd liked him since I was twelve but I broke up with him to get with Peter.

Is it very difficult to sustain a relationship on the street?

To be honest . . . I feel more safe with him, but it's *not* the reason why I'm with him, at all. It is hard – we argue a lot. I think it's because we're together twenty-four–seven and he's a very jealous person, and because we are always stressed all the time, we are always trying to get money, always try-ing to sort everything out. I've broken up with him a few times! But I always go back to him because . . . there is love there, do you know what I mean?

Is there anything else you want to say, or that you think I should know?

I don't know – I find it very difficult to think!

Do you find it *more* difficult to think straight, these days?

Yeah, I do. It's hard to think. But I was saying to Peter that I do think it is a very good idea that you are doing this book because maybe it will get more people to understand and realise what it is like on the streets. Because everyone just *judges* us, straight away . . . I've had so many people come up to me, 'Oh you crack-head, you smack-head' – but do you know what? I know people who are on the streets who don't even smoke a cigarette, that don't do drugs, that don't drink.

If someone was reading the book, and you could speak to them directly, what would you say?

Don't judge homeless people – it's *not fair*.

Getting the First Punch In

A book like this might attract all sorts of criticism.

There may be those who believe I've been naive, have made colossal errors of judgement and shouldn't have commented on issues where I have no expertise or training. Social workers, GPs, psychiatrists, police and charity workers will know and will have spent far more time with the people in this book than I ever have. They may have knowledge of the people I met that I don't.

This book didn't set out to define or 'profile' the homeless, but to give thirty people who live on the streets, thirty individual human beings, a place to speak for themselves, about whatever they wanted to, freely and without fear or prejudice. A space for them to share the world they inhabit as *they* see it, as *they* pass through it. This idea of sharing is central to the book. They very much wanted you to hear their voices – unfiltered, as it were – so you might understand something of their realities, their truths and their sense of the world.

They are all flawed and damaged but their stories are just that – *their stories*. Their lives as they wish to tell them. Some are longer than others and none offers a complete picture but all have been told as the teller wanted.

So, other queries or thoughts you may have . . .

There may have been times when you wanted to shout, 'Why didn't you ask her . . . ?' or, 'Why didn't you pursue that point, that was interesting and you let it go?' I know how frustrating that can be. Sometimes I simply forgot what my original line of thought *was*, and sometimes questions didn't occur to me until too late.

And I wasn't, for the most part, trying to *challenge* people's views, so if someone said, 'I have no money but I'm free, I can go where I want,' I wouldn't say, 'But you're not really free then, are you, because you can't actually afford to go anywhere,' because that might have made them feel stupid or belittled. And sometimes, just a look on someone's face might have been enough to make me back off from pursuing a particular idea.

Did I spend a year living on Shaftesbury Avenue? No. If I had, I would have ended up writing a book that was much more about *me* and not the homeless. I can't pretend I'm homeless. It's not a costume to be put on and taken off on a whim. Either you are homeless or you aren't. Spending a few nights on the street, with a full stomach and in a new sleeping bag wouldn't have served any purpose.

This book canvasses real issues that affect real people living in the most disgusting conditions, outdoors, riddled with mental illness, fear and disease.

The Beginning of the End

The day came when I had to stop.

I had to stop getting up and going out and listening to these stories from this strange 'other' world. I had to leave this peculiar life I had been living, because it didn't belong to me and because I had to move on, get the stories told and share what I had been given.

During the weeks I'd been in London, a part of me had grown almost dependent on spending time with strangers, listening and learning. And I'd grown to like feeling adrift and invisible. No one had any expectations of me at all. I came and went unseen.

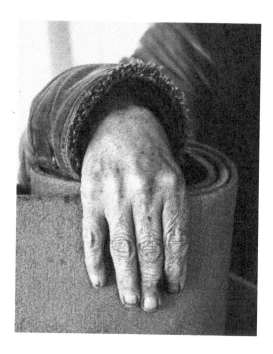

The giving up, the inevitable decline, the simply not being able to swim hard enough for long enough against the tide, is heartbreaking when you come face-to-face with it. If I went back next year or the year after, would those optimistic people like Brad and Charisse still be living on the street? How many would still be alive?

I can see clearly how the homeless can totally lose their minds. There's nowhere to go. Doors are always slamming shut. And when a door does open, it's never wide enough to really get *in*. Someone's got their foot against it, on the other side. That's just the way it is. At least for them.

But not for me. I went home.

Acknowledgements

Acknowledgements, which I am rather fond of reading myself, are generally rather retrospective. These ones aren't.

Those people that made the book possible, the homeless heroes who gave you these stories and insights, are already named in the list of contents at the front of the book, and all those amazing folk who dug deep to help get the first edition funded are named in the subscriber list. The rest of us were just doing our jobs. Well, Katy Guest went rather above and beyond, but then she's a legend.

But it's you – the reader – who I especially want to acknowledge.

Sadly, I don't know your name but perhaps that's not important. What is, though, is that you are someone who has soul, humanity and enough interest and compassion to have bought and read this book. Thank you from the bottom of my heart.

Supporters

Unbound is a new kind of publishing house. Our books are funded directly by readers. This was a very popular idea during the late eighteenth and early nineteenth centuries. Now we have revived it for the internet age. It allows authors to write the books they really want to write and readers to support the books they would most like to see published.

The names listed below are of readers who have pledged their support and made this book happen. If you'd like to join them, visit www.unbound.com.

SUPER FRIENDS
Paul Lindo
Annabel Portsmouth
Serafina Village

SUPPORTERS
Dora Adamik
Anna Adlam
Felicity Alberici
Gisella Alberici
Simon Alberici
Ayse Alibeyoglu
David R Allen
Eli Allison
Lulu Allison
Ruth Alsancak
Karen Altabev
Holly Anderson
Lindsey Appleby
Fiona Ashcroft
John Ashton
Afroze Asif
Karen Attwood
Madeleine Ayling
Karen Badenoch
Steve Bagshaw
Arron Baker
Mike Baker

Lucy Bannister
David Barker
Liz Barron
Anne Shannon Baxter
James Beck
Sally Beckwith
Philippa Bellhouse
Dean Bennett
Victoria Bennett
Chris Bertram
Jack Bertram
Antonia Bertschinger
Helen Bilton
Pippa Blackford
Kaitey Blair
Rebecca Louise Blake
Patricia Boyer
Richard W H Bray
Andy Brereton
Jenny Brocklebank
Andrew Brooks
Tracy Brown
Sara Bukumunhe

Tanvir Bush
Darren Butler
Alex C
Anthony Carrick
Dermot Carroll
Marian Carty
Peter Casely-Hayford
Elaine Chambers
Kam Chana
Emmanuelle Michele
   Henriette Charriere
Paul Child
Kenny Choi
Ei-Cheng Chui
Felicity Cloake
Melvin Coleman
Gordon Conroy
Liam Cooke
Christina Cordes
Brooke Courtenay
Tamsen Courtenay
John Crawford
Fiona and Edna
   Cunningham-Reid
   and Loebinger
Tony Davey
Deborah Davies
Melissa Davies
Linda Davis
Julie Day
Toby Day
Manon de Moor
Dominic Deeson
Louise and Geoff
   Delaye-Hand
Vanessa Dennett
Catherine Devlin
Breda Dick
Catherine Donald
Mark Donoghue
Dooby Dooby
Donna Dowdall

Francis Downes
Jessica Duchen
Bob Duffield
Bill Dunlop
Bob Elder
Mark Eltringham
Jennie Ensor
Ilana Estreich
Valerie Evans
Rupert Farley
Imran Farooq
Finbarr Farragher
Lynn Ferguson
Melrose Fernandes
Claire Ferraro
Linda Ferreri
Gary & Charlotte Fielder
Caroline Fletcher
Rose Forman
Sharon Foster-King
Anthony Fritz
Peter G
Trish Gant
Amro Gebreel
Luke Gething
Ryan Gibberd
Julie Gibbon
Miranda Gold
Susannah Grant
Juliette Green
Victoria Green
Paul S Greenfield
Rebecca Greer
Judith Griffith
Alice Griffiths
John Griffiths
Jon Grunewald
Katy Guest
Daniel Hahn
Tanya Haldipur
Sarah Hall
David Halliwell

Peter Hardcastle
Bekky Harrison
Sally Harrop
Sam Hatfield
Maximilian Hawker
Jake Hayman
Moira Haynes
Steve Haywood
Monica Henriquez
Marianne Heredge
Francesca Herrera
Helen Hewitt
Emma Hilton
Sally Hilton
Julie Hirst
Ellie Hoare
Kirsten Holliman
Antonia Honeywell
Alan Hooper
Michael Houlihan
Jennifer House
Eva and Billy Hulme
Rivka Isaacson
C Jacob
Kate Lockwood Jefford
Kerensa Jennings
Peter Jones
Sue Jones
Zhivko Juzevski
Elena Kaufman
Michael Kavanagh
Keith, Joanna & Cameron
Paul Kern
Tessa Kerr
Abda Khan
Rachael Kiddey
Dan Kieran
Steve Kilham
Gavin Killip
Patrick Kincaid
Alistair King
Julia Kite

Amanda Knowles
Rebecca Krahenbuhl
Pierre L'Allier
Margaret Lally
Patricia Larkin
Rhian Last
Hyun Suk Lee
Ruth Lessells
LJ
Peter Logan
Fatima Lopez
Yvonne Lyon
Akif Malik
Gautam Malkani
Campbell and Judith
    Malone
Mark Mark
Susan Marling
Fiona 'Fee' Martin
Victoria Mather
William Matthews
Richard Mayston
Cat McCabe
Laura McCormack
Polly Fiona McDonald
Rob McDowall
John McGhie
June McGowan
Adrian McLachlan
Tim McLeod
Chris McMillan
Bairbre Meade
Dave Mendes da Costa
Rob Metcalfe
Jayne Miller
Peter Minns
John Mitchinson
Mark Mordey
Katy Murray
Rosie Murray
Carlo Navato
Maja Neske

Cassandra Ng
Ivy Ngeow
Phuong Nguyen
Kevin Offer
Kate Oprava
Bruno Ornelas
Kwaku Osei-Afrifa
Lev Parikian
Sheila Parry
Devina Patel
Anjala Patmore
Perdita Patterson
Joanne Pattinson
Timo Peach
Sarah Perry
Stephen Phelps
Margaret Pickering
Al Pitcher
Ian Plenderleith
Justin Pollard
Samantha Potter
Lorna Prescott
Anna Price
Jo Ralling
Cristian Ramis
Richard Rathbone
Samantha Ravenscroft
Jonny Rawlings
Milly Reilly
Cristiana Ricciuti
Jane Richardson
Patrick Riordan
Mike Robbins
Frances Robinson
Ian Robinson
David Roche
Philip Roddis
Danny Rosenbaum
Daniel Ross
Gerald Rowe
Jonathan Ruppin
George S

Nishaan Saccaram
Bob Saddington
Karen Saunders
Richard Scarborough
Lynsey Searle
Katya Selvestru
Samuele Serafini
Daniella Shaw-Gabay
Christopher Shevlin
Matthew Shillaber
Robert Simpkin
Brett Simpson
Amarjit Singh
Peter Slade
Gilly Smith
Peter Souter
Ally Spicer
Leo Spicer-Phelps
Sarah Spiller
Waney Squier
Graciela Staps
Tarcila Stein
Clare Stephens
Gavin Street
Ken Stringer
J. Stuart Williams
Ian Sullivan
Andy Sumpter
Russel Tarr
Angelo Tata
Claire Taylor
David Taylor
Helen Taylor
Viv Taylor
Nikki Thomson
Tony Thorne
Tomas Thurogood-Hyde
Douglas Tollemache
Jan Tomalin
Geoff Torry
Sabine Totemeyer
Angelique Tran Van Sang

Anthony Trevelyan
Jonathan Trigell
Mira Tudor
Margaret Tuite
Annalisa Valente
Victor van Amerongen
Mark van der Heijden
John Varley
Ellie Vennelle
Hedwig Verdonk
Helen Verity
Vishaal Virani
Mandy Waal

Damon L. Wakes
Ben Walker
Peter Walker
Julie Warren
Rebecca Watkins
Bryan A Watson
Chris Weller
Kevin West
Annie Whelan
Hannah Whelan
Sue Whitehouse
Andrew Whitman
Rosemarie Whitman

In memory of Diana
  Whitworth
Chloe Wilson
Linda Wilson
Anthony John Winter
Helena Wisden
Daniel Wood
Maureen Wood
Kevin Wooding
Fergus Worthy
Thomas Yellowley
Rachel Yule
翟彧 Zhai Yu Zöe